Criminal Enterprise

Criminal Enterprise

Individuals, organisations and criminal responsibility

Christopher Harding

WILLAN
PUBLISHING

Published by

Willan Publishing
Culmcott House
Mill Street, Uffculme
Cullompton, Devon
EX15 3AT, UK
Tel: +44(0)1884 840337
Fax: +44(0)1884 840251
e-mail: info@willanpublishing.co.uk
website: www.willanpublishing.co.uk

Published simultaneously in the USA and Canada by

Willan Publishing
c/o ISBS, 920 NE 58th Ave, Suite 300,
Portland, Oregon 97213-3786, USA
Tel: +001(0)503 287 3093
Fax: +001(0)503 280 8832
e-mail: info@isbs.com
website: www.isbs.com

First published 2007

Hardback
ISBN 978-1-84392-229-2

British Library Cataloguing-in-Publication Data

A catalogue record for this book is available from the British Library

Project managed by Deer Park Productions, Tavistock, Devon
Typeset by GCS, Leighton Buzzard, Bedfordshire, LU7 1EU
Printed and bound by T.J. International Ltd, Padstow, Cornwall

Contents

Preface

I would sit there late in the evening turning it over in my mind. Maybe Herbert Hart did have a point: human beings were cursed, as part of their natural condition, with a need to interpret each other's behaviour, and this was a crucial need. We cannot live without engaging in the 'moral' activity of judging each other, of finding some 'right' and 'wrong'. But it is not just a functional necessity for social survival. We also enjoy this activity, and do so to the extent of often loving villains more than saints. There is a widespread fascination with bad behaviour, and crime – as the graphic manifestation of bad behaviour – is one of the most enduring preoccupations of literature, drama, art, everyday gossip, media presentations, not to mention academic discourse. And I thought about, for instance, how I would be really high remembering that moment, towards the end of *Godfather 1*, when Michael Corleone calmly states: 'Today, I have settled all outstanding Family business' and proceeds with his impressive list of assassinations. So let's be honest and admit that we engage in the business of casting judgment on criminals, not only because we feel that it is morally necessary, but also because we are fascinated by the whole business. And that fact must colour the activity of casting judgment.

Contribution to a research seminar discussion, 2003

This project has its origins in a now long-standing interest in and reflection on the subject of criminal responsibility. From my earliest reading of Hart's essays, I was struck by the enduring puzzle presented by this topic, which poses some of the fundamental questions relating to human identity and the distinctive features of human nature. To determine the extent and the way in which we should be accountable for our actions is an essential part of the process of understanding ourselves and the whole history and development of humankind. But my more recent reflection took a particular turn. It is a commonplace observation that modern society is characterised by the number and sophistication of its organisations, so that human activity increasingly takes place within organisational structures and is subject to the influence of organisations. We are no longer, as human individuals, acting very often in splendid isolation. What bearing should this have on the issue of human responsibility? Are organisations in some way supplanting individuals as responsible actors? Does organisational activity moderate the normative role of its human components? These seemed to be relevant and important questions, but infrequently posed by jurists beyond a few topical contexts, such as the issue of responsibility for major industrial or transport 'disasters'. But also the individual–organisation question struck me as particularly interesting since it contains a great enigma. Organisations are necessarily composed of individuals, so do they possess any separate identity, and does it make sense to talk about individuals and organisations, rather than individuals outside organisations and individuals within organisations? This ontological debate is central to the whole subject, but is notoriously slippery in that neither philosophical nor sociological enquiry have provided any clear answers. This makes the subject all the more challenging but also fascinating for the lawyer and the criminologist.

My approach to the subject, as I started to work it out and present my pitch, encountered some frankly sceptical reactions. Nobody would doubt the significance of these questions, but my interdisciplinary ambition and my proposed focus did not convince some specialist epistemic groups. In particular, the idea that such a discussion could take business cartels, human rights violators, and Mafia and terrorist groups, and forge a convincing theory of responsibility from such a diverse and eclectic collection, encountered a fair amount of incredulity. I suspect that my idea that companies, governments and organised crime groups may sometimes have much in common offended against more purist analysis, as did my apparent selectivity ('So, why not also churches, trade unions, and all the other types of corporate person the world has seen?'). In fact, my choice was based partly on topicality, but also on an intuition that legally significant and revealing patterns would emerge across my chosen spectrum.

And I believe that, in the outcome, the gamble (if that is what it was) has proven justified.

Interested readers may particularly look forward to any conclusion from this study on the grand ontological question of whether organisations really do exist as separate entities. As I discuss at some length, that debate was lively over one hundred years ago, and remains so today. All I am prepared to say at this stage is, teasingly, that I think that it depends on what one is willing to believe. Much of what is being discussed in this subject is, after all, interpretation of social fact. But even if it is, in the end, a matter of interpretation, it is a hugely important business of interpretation, since so much policy and law depends on how it is made. There will probably always be those who steadfastly maintain that the company, the State, or whatever organisation, is a fiction, 'what the rules say it is', or no 'ding an sich'. Equally, there will probably always be those who steadfastly maintain that there is something real out there, other than the human parts, and more than the sum of those parts. I think that personally I am willing to see things the latter way, but I recognise that to do so is an act of interpretation, preference and 'view of the world'. But *my* preferred view is not the important point. Rather, what is important is to make some effort to understand why some prefer it one way, and some the other, and to recognise how and why this process of interpretation has led to inconsistency across the whole spectrum, and that is the issue which needs to be addressed and which this book seeks to address. My project therefore has been to explain different legal outcomes and to search for a consistent and coherent argument on the allocation of criminal responsibility in the context of individuals and organisations. I suggest a model for this purpose. It is for the reader to judge how convincing this suggested model may be.

I have tested some parts of the argument in this work in a number of ways. In particular, a draft of Chapter 7 was presented as a paper ('Human or Corporate?') at the Australia and New Zealand Society of Criminology Annual Conference in Wellington in February 2005, and a draft of Chapter 6 was presented at a meeting of the Law and Political Philosophy Discussion Group in Aberystwyth in November 2005 ('Revisiting H.L.A. Hart'). A version of what has become Chapter 8 has appeared as 'Human Action or State Action? Locating the Site of Supranational Criminality', in Roelof Haveman and Olaoluwa Olusanya (eds), *Sentencing and Sanctioning in Supranational Criminal Law* (Intersentia, 2006), and some of the material used in Chapter 9 was also used in 'The Offence of Belonging: Capturing Participation in Organised Crime', which appeared in 2005 *Criminal Law Review.* Some of the argument relating to the *Rainbow Warrior* incident has been used and developed further in 'Vingt Ans Après: Rainbow Warrior, Legal Ordering and Legal Complexity' in 2006 *Singapore Yearbook of International Law.* I have appreciated the critical comments of audiences and readers of this work. More specifically I should also express my appreciation of those friends and colleagues who have helped me in my search for 'critical edge' during this period and on these questions, and for that purpose would like to single out Mitch Robinson, Alun Gibbs, Uta Kohl, Naomi Salmon, Chin Lim, Mick John-Hopkins and Katerina Novotna. I am naturally also appreciative of the willingness of Willan Publishing to take on the project for publication. Finally, I am also grateful for the award of a period of 12 months' research leave from the University of Wales, Aberystwyth, during which time I was able to develop some of my ideas and carry out a good part of the research for this book.

A word on the layout of the book might be helpful at this point. Since this study draws upon some apparently disparate sources, and much of it is based on challenging metaphysical and conceptual discussion, I have sought to guide readers by providing for each main chapter a kind of abstract. These abstracts are intended not only to provide a summary of argument, but also to set the argument in context, with some reference to other research and literature, while also emphasising salient, novel and tricky points of argument. The abstracts may be read collectively as a kind of 'rough guide' to the work and I would recommend their perusal first of all to any potential readers who may be tempted but still unsure about taking on the whole book. The book is divided into parts. After an introduction to the subject and the main problem, Part I (Chapters 2 to 5) provides the theoretical basis of the discussion; Part II (Chapters 6 to 8) draws argument from three principal or paradigmatic sites of individual–organisation interactivity; and Part III (Chapters 9 and 10) extrapolates models of criminal responsibility, by focussing on the autonomous criminal organisation and the joint criminal enterprise, leaving my concluding remarks to a very brief endnote.

In the final stages of writing the book I was visiting Potsdam in Germany, and walked to Cecilienhof, that quirky reproduction of an English country house where the Potsdam Agreement was negotiated and signed in 1945 by Stalin, Churchill and Truman (to be exact, Truman replaced the deceased Roosevelt who had attended the earlier Yalta meeting, and during the Potsdam Conference Attlee later replaced Churchill who had during that time lost a general election). That most famous event in the building's history prompted a reflection on the theme of this book. How should we interpret the Potsdam Agreement? As the act of three human individuals – powerful political leaders, but nonetheless individual human actors? Or as the act of three of the most powerful victor governments at the close of a global conflict (Churchill had smugly described the meeting as that of a very exclusive club with an entrance fee of at least five million soldiers or their equivalent). Or as the act of a joint (criminal?) enterprise or political cartel, intent on dismembering Germany, sharing global power, and so producing that sad historical condition we look back upon as the 'Cold War'? These options of interpretation are the subject-matter of the following pages.

Aberystwyth, May 2007

Chapter 1

Introduction: searching for the responsible criminal actor

First of all, let us acknowledge the 'individual–organisation dilemma': the problem of how to evaluate the activity of organisations given that they are composed of individuals. Can organisations then be regarded as autonomous actors, capable of moral and legal agency? On the other hand, it should also be asked how an organisational context should be taken into account in assessing the conduct of human individuals acting within such a context. In addressing these fundamental questions, the study here adopts a method which combines a development of theory and the testing of argument in three main paradigmatic sites of human and organisational interactivity of contemporary significance. The main theoretical elements comprise organisations as a social phenomenon, the criteria of agency for purposes of assigning a normative (moral and legal) role, the legal routes between the identification of agency and the allocation of responsibility, and responsibility as a device within normative ordering. The choice of the three paradigmatic contexts (the business cartel, the delinquent governmental actor and the criminal organisation) may be explained and illustrated through three narratives of individual and organisational activity, in tales of delinquency perpetrated respectively by a transnational corporation, war criminals and a terrorist arm of government.

1 Individuals, organisations and criminal responsibility

In a contemporary world within which a range of organisational, non-human actors play a significant and sometimes dominating role, there are an increasing number of important and challenging questions relating to the evaluation of organisational and individual behaviour. Self-evidently such organisations are made up of human individuals and many of their dealings are with human as well as other organisational actors. But how should we understand the relationship between these organisations and individuals, and more specifically how should we attribute responsibility for the actions of these various organisational and human actors? To what extent is it meaningful and useful to hold States, intergovernmental organisations, companies, political factions, crime gangs or other non-human entities responsible for certain conduct, either instead of human individuals or in some way together with individuals? Is it possible to say that in some areas of activity organisations have replaced individuals as the real agents of action? Or, on the other hand, is it impossible to escape from a reduction of all organisational activity to its individual component parts? These are important questions because of the pervasive presence of several kinds of organisation in contemporary global society, and because this complexity of social structure inevitably affects ethical and legal processes through which we allocate responsibility for conduct viewed as problematical and causing harm to others. In short, who should we regard as the responsible moral, legal and (in relation to some kinds of conduct) criminal actors in contemporary society?

A few moments' reflection across a spectrum of activities will demonstrate the relevance and significance of these questions, even confining attention to the legal sphere rather than the broader ethical and political context. Who should be held responsible for severe human rights violations: governments and States, or individual politicians, soldiers or police officers? Who should be held responsible for the damage arising from industrial or transport disasters, or for the economic harm arising from financial delinquency, or for the long-term damage arising from environmental degradation – companies, or the individuals working for those companies? Who should be held responsible for the suffering caused by the activities of terrorist organisations, organised crime groups or extreme political or religious factions – those organisations or their individual members? In each of these examples, the kind of conduct and the resulting level of harm are usually considered to justify the extreme legal response embodied in the use of criminal responsibility and its associated sanctions. In this way, issues of agency – of identifying the relevant actor – and of criminal responsibility are brought together. The task is that of searching for and identifying the responsible criminal actor, and as such it is a task of philosophical enquiry and broader jurisprudence as well as of criminal law and criminal justice.

These are not wholly new questions and it has already been practically necessary to provide some legal solutions in relation to such issues of responsibility. A study of this kind is necessarily therefore to some extent a critical evaluation of what has been done so far in the way of allocating legal responsibility. But it may be argued that much of the legal development to date in this area has a piecemeal character, based on responses to the dilemma of agency and responsibility in particular contexts. In this way, we have arrived at a certain idea of, for instance, the war criminal in one context, corporate liability for 'disasters' in another context, or company fines and personal prison sentences for price fixing in yet another context. Are these approaches and solutions consistent, in the light of the fact that they are all ways of dealing with the relation between individual and organisational responsibility? Should we be looking for and expecting consistency in this respect, and is it feasible to discuss matters in terms of a general theory of individual and organisational responsibility? A primary objective of this study is to consider a range of such situations which raise these questions in a sharp and paradigmatic form so as to test the value of a general theory, regarding what it may offer in terms of both an understanding of delinquent and criminal behaviour and of practical solutions in the distribution of legal responsibility.

Although the focus of this discussion is the issue of legal and more specifically criminal responsibility, it will be necessary in disciplinary terms to cast the net more widely than legal or even jurisprudential discussion. At the root of these questions lies the fundamental issue of our understanding of human behaviour and how society works. It is necessary to ask why and how human beings have increasingly arranged their lives around organisational structures, and then consider the impact of these structures on individual human autonomy and behaviour. These underlying questions and their discussion are inevitably first of all philosophical, and then sociological. The philosophical problem is one of identity and ontology, probing the existence and co-existence of human and non-human actors. The sociological aspect is more empirical – what do we know and understand about the functioning of different types of organisation, of the role of individuals within such organisations, and of the impact of organisations on human life? But both types of enquiry are necessarily prior to any specifically juristic analysis of legal responsibility, criminal law and criminal sanctions.

There are three major questions that form the backbone of the ensuing discussion and it may be helpful to summarise these questions here so as to provide a first signpost for the way ahead:

- May an organisation meaningfully be regarded as an independent actor for purposes of allocating moral and legal responsibility, and more particularly criminal liability? This is the question of *the ontology of organisations*.

- Assuming that the answer to the first question is positive, where and how should the line be drawn between organisational and individual responsibility, generally or in particular contexts; and in a society in which complex organisations dominate many areas of life, how much remains of individual human responsibility? This is the question of *the allocation of responsibility*.

- In what ways should the criminal liability of individuals, when acting within an organisational context, be affected by their role within such organisations? This is the question of *organisational impact*.

2 Mapping out the discussion

One of the challenges in writing this kind of work resides in the need to integrate theory with more empirical observation. Moreover, some of the theory is complex and is drawn from a number of sources and different disciplines – not only law and jurisprudence, but also philosophy and social science. There is also a danger with this kind of subject, once it becomes familiar, of slipping into the language of shorthand abstractions and to talk frequently about, for example, agency and actors, corporations and non-human entities, personality and identity, responsibility and accountability, while having in mind more explicitly and materially companies and chief executive officers, presidents and generals, or terrorists and assassins. Consideration for the reader eventually suggested that the argument would be more accessible if fact were put before theory, even though the theoretical structure is crucial to the subject. The discussion therefore opens, in the later part of this chapter, with a more descriptive and empirical account of the contemporary terrain of individual and organisational actors, before proceeding to a critical exploration of the theoretical framework and then a more detailed examination of selected paradigmatic cases. But in taking this approach, it is probably still helpful to provide the reader here at the outset with some continuing idea of the main argument which is being tested in the book, and some sense of the theoretical basis of that argument.

3 Main lines of theory

(a) Stating the problem: the role of the individual and the organisation in contemporary life

This opening part of the discussion is intended to provide a picture of contemporary society whose activities involve organisations as much as individuals. In some respects this is to report on what is well-known. We can quickly identify significant organisational forms in most walks of life. Governance and public affairs are conducted through well-established types of organisation, from the State in a key position, and then moving upwards (for instance, intergovernmental organisations (IGOs)) or downwards (for instance, government departments or units of local government). Commercial and economic life is dominated by the organisational form often referred to as the company or the firm. Civil society is increasingly expressing itself through a range of non-governmental organisations (NGOs) carrying out a variety of representative roles. The educational and cultural world is structured around a spectrum of institutions, including the like of universities, research institutions and those managing collections or sites of cultural significance. Also the realm of more shadowy delinquent and criminal activity has a significant organised dimension, manifested in terrorist and organised crime groups and delinquent political and military factions.

But this area of general knowledge requires some explanation as well as description. Chapter 2 explores the significance of the range of organisational actors in contemporary life and considers the role of individuals within such organisational structures. One of the main puzzles within the subject arises from a certain identity of human individuals and their organisations, since the latter are of course formed by and constituted through the membership of human individuals. This overlapping of identities – after all, we are talking about *organisations of humans* even if theoretically we may like to characterise such entities as *non-human actors* – requires some exploration. Much of the later theoretical argument addresses this phenomenon of interaction between human person and organisational structure, and should be informed therefore by some prior idea of how this occurs in practice. A particular aspect of this interaction of the human and the organisational which merits close attention is the impact of organisational culture on individuals acting within organisations. To what extent does an organisational role take over the 'original' human identity and is there any evidence to support the idea that the individual as a member of an organisation is a different kind of actor from the human individual in a more general and basic sense – does the organisation 'snatch the body' of its human components?

Moreover, the complexity and perhaps to some extent messiness and flaky edges of the world of organisations needs to be presented in a usable form for purposes of the later discussion. To this end, Chapter 2 also suggests a typology of main forms, so that the reader can bear in mind some kind of mental atlas of the subject-matter. Any such typology should not seek to be hard-and-fast or a final word, since the subject is both evolving and uncertain in its more precise boundaries. Some types of organisation are based upon a tight legal construction and definition – for example many of the corporate forms. The definition of others – especially for example terrorist groups and organised crime – is a matter of seemingly endless debate. Then again, governmental polities, such as the State and its components, may have their own clear and formally determined constitutional foundations, yet be the subject of varying interpretation in theoretical discourse (for instance, in relation to the concept of the sovereign State, which may be deconstructed in international relations (IR) writing into 'States' and 'Quasi-States'). But for the sake of clear exposition some working typology should prove helpful.

(b) The theory of agency and responsibility

In theoretical terms, this subject is set against an ironic outcome: that, as Bovens expresses the matter,[1] in Western society which prizes so much the value of individual autonomy organisations have come to play such a major role in social and political life. This fact provides a major source of tension within theoretical debate. Within Western moral philosophy and jurisprudence there is a strong sense of the role of the human individual in the social and ethical sphere: that the individual is the primary agent in terms of

---

1 Mark Bovens, *The Quest for Responsibility: Accountability and Citizenship in Complex Organisations* (Cambridge University Press, 1998), p. 9.

being a social, ethical and consequently a legal actor. This view of the world has an ontological basis, in the argument that human actors are demonstrably 'real', whereas organisations are constructed from human action and act only through human agency. Any State, company, foundation, intergovernmental body, terrorist group or political faction is established through human decision and action, is necessarily comprised of human members and operates through the activity of those human members. In the words of a leading British judge, referring to the identity of a company, there is no *ding an sich* – the corporate person does not exist as such.[2] It is no more than a construction, whose ability to 'act' is determined by human beings, and dependent on the actions of human beings, through a legally (and humanly) defined process. Such 'ontological individualism' leads to a 'methodological individualism', according to which social action should be explained and understood in terms of the activities of human agents. The outcome of this approach is to reduce the role of the organisational actor to a technical legal matter – a question of what legal rules determine regarding the capacity of an organisation to carry out certain defined tasks.

Yet at the same time we tend to claim, as a matter of social observation, that organisations are significant, even dominating actors who effectively determine a good deal of how the world works. A discussion of globalisation, for instance, refers to the activity of governments, intergovernmental institutions or transnational companies, rather than human individuals. Economists may see corporate commercial actors – 'firms' – as rational independent agents, and construct economic models or engage in game theory predictions based on the activities of such persons rather than individual human actors. And in one particular context, that of international law and relations, we have gone so far as to treat the State – undoubtedly a classic form of organisational actor – as the primary person within the system. IR theorists and international lawyers imbue States anthropomorphically with human capacities for reasoning and behaviour and demote the individual human person to a 'derivative' status or personality, dependent upon the whim of State decision-making. Thus, we look at the world around us, we see organisations in action and we say that they count for a good deal, and we invest them with an identity which is in many respects analogous to our own human identity. But then, in certain contexts,

---

2 Lord Hoffmann in the Privy Council, in *Meridian Global Funds Management Asia Ltd v. Securities Commission* (1995) 2 AC 500, at pp. 506–7.

especially when engaging in the argument of moral philosophy and legal responsibility, we hesitate in attributing real agency to these organisational entities.

This contradiction, which results in an ontological and methodological conundrum, provides a theoretical underpinning to the discussion in this book. It supplies a leading question: is it possible and meaningful to talk about organisations as moral agents and independent, legally responsible actors? It is a debate which in particular informs the discussion in Chapter 3, as a second main area of theoretical argument, and which leads to the theory of legal and criminal responsibility.

Chapter 3 addresses the basic question of agency. What is required to be recognised as a moral agent, a legal person and thus an appropriate bearer of criminal responsibility? Starting with the individualists' comfortable attribution of agency and responsibility to human actors, the possibility of extending this agency to organisations is considered. While it may be difficult to escape from a resort to the human actor as the primary *model* for agency and responsibility, it is necessary to take the discussion further with an open mind, contemplating the possibility of analogous or different forms of agency, and testing that possibility through the formulation of convincing and workable criteria of a separate identity for non-human actors. Such criteria are likely to include elements of structure, independent capacity for action, role and representation, and may be drawn from theorising in a number of different disciplines.[3]

Chapters 4 and 5 then proceed to a more specific examination of the theory of criminal responsibility, and how that may be mapped onto a model of non-human agency. It is necessary here also to explore the process of allocating responsibility as between actors and how criminal responsibility may relate to other forms of legal responsibility. To

---

3 The interdisciplinary character of this theory-building is important, and provides a kind of 'triangulation', or testing and corroboration of argument. It is interesting to note how sociology, moral philosophy, law and international relations have grappled with similar theoretical and conceptual questions, working along parallel lines, but without necessarily cross-referring very much to each other. Other disciplines may also be relevant – for instance, those working in the field of information technology have recently begun to address issues of identity and agency in cyberspace; see, for instance, Emily M. Weitzenboeck (2001) 'Electronic Agents and the Formation of Contracts', *International Journal of Law and Information Technology*, 9: 204.

discuss criminal responsibility in isolation would limit the usefulness of the discussion since in the reality of legal ordering different categories of legal process and liability co-exist together and interact with each other. The question of allocating responsibility is thus not only one of possible distribution as between actors but also of distribution of process and heads of responsibility. For example, we might well (and do at present) distribute responsibility for genocidal action between States and governments (for committing a violation of human rights) and individual perpetrators (as committing crimes against humanity) and deal with the first as a matter of State responsibility under international law and the second as a matter of criminal liability under national law. Or to use another example, antitrust violations may be held to be the responsibility of both corporate actors and of individual company executives, and may be prosecuted as criminal offences or subject to civil claims for compensation. The purpose here is to explore and identify the theoretical structure for these choices in terms of allocating responsibility and to consider specifically the role of criminal responsibility within such a theoretical structure.

(c) Paradigmatic cases of interaction of individual and organisational responsibility

The contextual and more specific part of this study comprises a series of case studies, which probe the issue of organisational agency and responsibility, and its relation with individual responsibility. Each study explores the subject within a significant contemporary context, each one of which is also illustrative of the problems arising from the allocation, or possible allocation of responsibility, as between individual and organisational actors.

Corporate actors. Chapter 6 considers the role of a paradigmatic corporate actor[4] – the firm or company as a commercial actor – in

---

4 The term 'corporate actor' will be used here to refer to legally constituted organisational actors, set up for a specific purpose. The company, and analogous business actors, come to mind immediately as a typical form. But the term could equally well encompass such organisations as foundations, charitable organisations, educational establishments (such as universities), religious organisations, trade unions and various representative organisations. The term will also be confined in this discussion to non-State organisations, although care needs to be taken in using the dichotomy of 'public' and 'private'.

the specific context of illegal business conspiracy. The company is an established legal actor which has often been attributed with a rational decision-making capacity. Nonetheless, in legal theory the nature of the company's agency and the basis for its legal liability, and in some cases criminal responsibility, has been a matter of controversy. The subject of business conspiracy in the context of antitrust or competition regulation provides a particularly rich example of problems of identity and responsibility as between different actors. By focussing on the operation of business cartels, it is possible to explore the interaction between three levels or types of agency: individual executives working for companies, the companies which engage in illegal collusion, and the cartel as a collective arrangement for the achievement of that collusion. In different ways all three may be the subject of legal process (for instance, the cartel may be the subject of legal investigation, and the companies and their employees may be the subject of liability and sanctions) and as such all three may be seen as possessing some kind of legal agency. There are existing significant issues of corporate and individual criminal responsibility in this area in a number of jurisdictions, which also allow for an analysis of the interaction between organisational and individual behaviour in a business context.

Organisations of governance. Chapter 7 explores the role of a different kind of organisational actor in a different context, that of public governance. In some respects, this is an enquiry into the accountability of the State in its various organisational manifestations. This may be viewed by some readers as a 'public law' dimension of the subject, since the conventional approach to many issues involving governmental bodies and institutions is in terms of the relationship between the individual citizen and the State as a public authority. However, one of the purposes of this discussion will be to deconstruct any monolithic idea of the 'State' and 'public authority', and therefore 'organisations of governance' will be used as a term which may avoid some of these established connotations.

The State represents a special and significant case in the context of this discussion of organisational and individual responsibility. In one sense, it is a well-established paradigm of a constructed non-human actor, itself inevitably and in a very complex way constituted of individual human components. Yet, as already noted, in a particular political and legal context – that of international relations and international law – it appears as the *primary* type of actor, whose own actions construct and determine the character of the system within which it operates.[5] This is graphically the case in relation to the 'modern' or 'Westphalian' model of international law, within which the State is viewed as the 'primary' type of person, while human individuals possess a derivative and subsidiary identity and personality. Thus the assumptions of individualism are turned upon their head, or at least the State is substituted for the human individual as the 'core individual' actor within the system. However, in the contemporary international context this State-centric view is increasingly open to challenge, as a range of non-State actors take on an increasingly significant role at both a national and international level. Such developments suggest that it would be a useful and indeed necessary exercise to deconstruct the idea of the State, so as to identify and analyse the role of other appropriate responsible actors within the broad realm of governance, in addition to the monolithic State and the individual. Some such actors may be carved from the existing concept of the State, both upwards (for example, intergovernmental organisations) and downwards (for instance, components of State governance, in particular the government as distinct from the State as such), or may extend to competing entities of governance, such as factions, regimes and insurgent groups, or even civil society NGOs. Such an exercise would also serve to probe ideas of autonomy and representation as guiding criteria of identity and personality for purposes of responsible agency.

A topical focus for this kind of discussion is provided by the issue of delinquent behaviour on the part of governmental actors, of the kind where accountability has traditionally been achieved through the legal concept of violation of human rights. To an increasing extent, an alternative legal accountability has been realised through the attribution of criminal responsibility on the part of individual perpetrators acting within the framework of governance, and seen as committing war crimes and crimes against humanity. This possibility of re-allocating responsibility to individual actors is significant in itself, raising problems concerning the relationship between such individuals and official structures. At the same time, it also provides the trigger for considering the possible allocation of responsibility to

---

5 This may be more definitely the case as a matter of international law than international relations. IR theory hosts the 'agent-structure' debate, which analyses critically the role of the State in the construction of the system of international relations, while the theory and practice of international law remains for the most part comfortable with the idea of the State as a governing force within the system.

11

other governmental actors, distinct from both the State as a whole and from human individuals.

Delinquent organisations. A major challenge for contemporary society arises from the activities of powerful but delinquent organisational actors which operate alongside and sometimes in competition with 'legitimate' non-human actors such as the corporation and institutions of governance. At the present time such delinquent organisational actors manifest themselves in particular in the form of terrorist and organised crime groupings, which naturally lack formal and legal incorporation but nonetheless operate effectively and powerfully as organisational entities. Informally, the organised crime grouping may be seen as a delinquent parody of the legitimate corporation, while the terrorist organisation may be seen as a delinquent parody of legitimate government. The delinquent characterisation of this kind of organisation complicates their formal recognition, since there are natural political and ethical reservations concerning any process of formal accreditation, which may be interpreted as validating their existence and identity. Yet they are significant actors in a material sense and are important objects of legal control, particularly through the process of criminal law. In this way, such delinquent organisations provide another but distinctive paradigm of organisational actor, producing some different problems of identity and responsibility.

But there are also more familiar questions relating to the allocation of responsibility as between individual members of such groups and the organisations as such, raising again the fundamental question: may such a delinquent organisational actor meaningfully be regarded in itself as a responsible actor? If so, what kind of legal process and sanctions may be appropriately used? This kind of discussion also touches upon a slippery aspect of identity – the possible transition between delinquent and legitimate versions of the same actor (for instance, a terrorist organisation converted into a recognised government; or a former head of state into a war criminal; or both conversely). How should such possibilities be taken into account in a system of criminal responsibility? The present and continuing legal attempts to control and regulate such organisations and the individual membership and participation in the activities of these organisations provides a focus for this part of the discussion.

(d) Linking the individual and the organisation: the concept of the criminal enterprise

The final two main chapters then return to the construction of a theoretical model by drawing some lessons from the contextual study and utilising the theoretical framework supplied in the first part of the book. It is the role of these chapters to revisit the three principal questions identified above – the ontology of organisations, the allocation of responsibility, and organisational impact. Chapter 9 deals especially with that first issue of ontology by summarising the conditions according to which it may be possible to talk feasibly about a genuinely distinct organisational agency and responsibility. The discussion there also addresses part of the question of allocation of responsibility as between individuals and organisations in that it aids the determination of the dividing line between those two domains of responsibility. Chapter 10 finally takes up some issues relating to individual responsibility within organisational contexts, following on from that second question of allocation of responsibility but also considering the problem of how organisational context may have a bearing on the nature of any individual responsibility. Drawing upon the evidence of recent legal and political developments in the context of regulating business cartels, war crimes and severe human rights violations, and organised criminality, the model of the common criminal enterprise or design is analysed as a device for the construction of a distinctive form of individual responsibility, deriving its essential character from participation in a collective activity.

4 Back to some fact: illustrative narratives of the subject

In order to ensure a clear appreciation of the direction of argument, the theoretical structure for that argument, and the contemporary ethical and legal significance of both, the remaining part of this chapter will sketch out some illustrative situations in which the above-mentioned issues of agency and responsibility have been prominent. The approach taken here will provide first a straightforward short narrative description of each situation and then juxtapose a 'legal narrative' of the same, which will then be used to bring out some key questions concerning agency and responsibility.

(a) The transnational corporation's tale: the prosecution of Infineon

In early December 2004 four executives of Infineon Technologies AG, a German company, and its American subsidiary, Infineon Technologies North America Corporation, agreed to plead guilty under US criminal law to participating in an international conspiracy to fix prices in the dynamic random access memory (DRAM) market. Each of the executives (three German nationals and one US national) agreed to pay a $250,000 criminal fine and serve prison terms ranging between four and six months for participating in the conspiracy. At an earlier date, in October 2004, Infineon AG, the company, had pleaded guilty to a charge of participating in the same conspiracy and had been sentenced to pay a fine of $160 million. The convictions, fines and prison terms are all provided for under Section One of the Sherman Act 1990.[6]

This was a classic case of business conspiracy, more exactly of antitrust violation under American law, involving an international price fixing cartel (three other companies were being investigated by the American Department of Justice in relation to the same price fixing agreement).[7] The offending parties being dealt with in the Infineon case included a number of corporate actors – the German parent company and its American subsidiary – and a number of individuals working for those companies. These persons – corporate and human – were treated under American law as conspiring together to fix prices. More specifically, the individuals, representing their respective companies, had met with individual executives of the other companies involved in the cartel, and taken part in discussions in the US and elsewhere, in order to talk about the prices for selling DRAM, agreeing to charge certain prices, issuing price quotations, exchanging information on sales so as to monitor and enforce the operation of their agreement, and making arrangements with subordinate employees. The whole activity, described as a conspiracy or a cartel, possessed an identifiable

---

6 US Department of Justice Press Release, December 2004. Proceedings in the US District Court, Northern District of California (San Francisco), *US v. Infineon Technologies AG*. For later developments in the prosecution of this cartel, concerning the action taken against other participating companies, see Department of Justice Press Release of 13 October 2005 (www.usdoj.gov).

7 Including the Korean company Samsung and its US subsidiary. The $300 million fine imposed on Samsung was the second largest criminal antitrust fine in US history. See Department of Justice press Release of 13 October 2005, note 6 above.

operational infrastructure for planning and implementation of the main price fixing agreement, which extended over a period of time and was carried out in a number of places.

The above is a straightforward factual account of the price fixing activity and its prosecution. Translating the narrative into a legal account of agency and responsibility renders the matter more complicated and raises a number of questions. In terms of legal agency, the conspiracy was seen as a coming together of two different types of actor, corporate and individual, in relation to the same activity of discussion, planning and implementation of the agreement. But, although prosecuted in relation to the same conspiracy or agreement, these different kinds of actor – who possessed in the material world an overlapping identity, since in one sense the executives *were* the companies – were dealt with separately, and were subject to distinct orders and sanctions. The subject-matter of the investigation leading to the prosecution was the cartel, arguably an entity in itself – certainly a kind of organisation, possessing an identifiable structure, mission, and internal ordering – in short, a kind of informal corporate personality, similar in some respects to a crime organisation. But the cartel, although the *object* of legal proceedings, was not formally dealt with as a legal person regarding the outcome of the proceedings.

It can be seen already that the legal narrative, comprising legal persons and legal procedures, is both different from and more complex than the first factual narrative. This exercise in narration should quickly serve to indicate the distinct ontologies of the material world and the legal domain. Within the latter we need to make an imaginative leap and visualise not just a group of company executives sitting around a table but, simultaneously, a meeting of corporate persons. Unfortunately we are most likely to visualise the latter in the same way, which becomes problematical when the law tells us that the companies were conspiring alongside and with their executives. So, we are forced to imagine a kind of parallel universe which then fuses with the normal world of familiar human actors, although not so as to replace their identity but to duplicate it.

We shall return to this example, and to the whole issue of this kind of business conspiracy in Chapter 6. But sufficient may have been said to provoke some challenging questions of agency and responsibility. How exactly have the companies and their employees conspired with each other? Is it ethically and legally justifiable to take action against both and impose sanctions against both in relation to what appears to be a single body of conduct? There is, underlying these questions, a fundamental question of responsibility: in such a situation, who is the responsible actor – the company or the individual acting for the company? Alternatively, is it possible to divide responsibility – for instance, to hold the company responsible for promoting an anti-competitive culture, and the executives responsible for specific anti-competitive actions?

Such questions cannot be easily or quickly answered. But it is evident that one legal system at least has entered some deep and murky water in using its system of criminal law in this way. In other words, in attempting to regulate this type of conduct, the interplay of individual and organisational activity has thrown up some challenging problems regarding both identity and the allocation of criminal responsibility.

(b) The war criminal's tale: membership of a criminal organisation

When the International Military Tribunal was established at Nuremberg at the end of the Second World War, it was provided in Article 10 of the Tribunal's Statute that the Tribunal could declare certain groups or organisations criminal, following which individuals could be put on trial for having been members of such criminal organisations. The rationale for establishing this offence of membership is set down in an American memorandum[8] of 1944: 'It will never be possible to catch and convict every Axis war criminal, or even any great number of them, under the old concepts and procedures', the latter referring to the doctrine of individual criminal responsibility for specific criminal acts. Thus 'proof of membership, without more, would establish guilt of participation in the mentioned conspiracy' to engage in acts which would be regarded as war crimes or crimes against humanity.[9] Subsequently, the Tribunal declared[10] a number of Nazi organisations criminal under Article 10 of the Statute: the Leadership Corps of the Nazi Party, the Gestapo and the SD, and the SS. However, at the same time the Tribunal ruled that a 'criminal organisation' was equivalent to a 'criminal conspiracy':

---

8 Memorandum of Colonel Bernays (a lawyer in the US War Department), 15 September 1944, in B.F. Smith, *The American Road to Nuremberg – The Documentary Record, 1944–45* (Hoover Institution Press, 1982), p. 35.

9 *Ibid.*, p. 36.

10 *Göring and others,* IMT, judgment of 1 October 1946, *Trial of the Major War Criminals before the International Military Tribunal, Nuremberg,* vol. 1, 171–341.

.... the essence of both is cooperation for criminal purposes. There must be a group bound together and organized for a common purpose. The group must be formed or used in connection with the commission of crimes denounced by the Charter.[11]

Thus criminal membership of the organisation should not extend to

persons who had no knowledge of the criminal purposes or acts of the organization and those who were drafted by the State for membership, unless they were personally implicated in the commission of acts declared criminal by Article 6 of the Charter as members of the organization.[12]

This commitment to the principle of responsibility on the basis of individual action rather than membership of a group was evident in later trials, such as that involving officials of the I.G. Farben industrial enterprises. The Tribunal in that case stated that:

responsibility does not automatically attach to an act ... merely by virtue of a defendant's membership of the *Vorstand* [administration board]. Conversely, one may not utilize the corporate structure to achieve an immunity from criminal responsibility for illegal acts which he directs, counsels, aids, orders or abets. But the evidence must establish action ... with knowledge of the essential elements of the crime.[13]

This is an account of an attempt to establish criminal responsibility on the basis of proven membership of an organisation rather than evidence of direct involvement in specific criminal acts. Although apparently approved at a legislative level in the Statute of the Nuremberg Tribunal, judicial interpretation of the provision quickly retreated from this idea of a presumptive responsibility and re-established the conventional individualistic basis of responsibility so deeply engrained in Western jurisprudence.

Retelling the narrative in terms of agency reveals again an interplay of individual and organisational actors, out of which the individual

---

11 *Ibid.*, p. 255.
12 *Ibid.*
13 *Krauch and others*, US Military Tribunal sitting at Nuremberg, judgment of 29 July 1948, in *Trials of War Criminals before the Nuremberg Military Tribunals* (TWC) (US Govt Printing Office, 1950), VIII, 1081.

agency was eventually accorded precedence. Questions come to mind regarding the character of the Nazi criminal organisations. These bodies had a clear formal identity as institutions of governance and it would seem that the legal process of establishing the Nuremberg Tribunal had in Article 10 of the Tribunal's Charter clearly provided for a recognition of the moral agency and criminal responsibility of any organisations so designated by the Tribunal. However, what appears less clear was the consequence for the organisation of being designated criminal – did this amount to a kind of conviction, and what sanctions might follow? In the second place, the relative position of these organisations and their individual members appears uncertain in terms of agency as distinct from legal outcome, since the fact of membership seemed to fuse the identity of individual and organisation in terms of responsibility – the member was part of the organisation. The Tribunal's later reversion to the idea of conspiracy served effectively to relocate the agency from the organisation to the individual members by identifying the arrangement as an *aggregation* of individual actors with a common purpose. On the other hand, the Tribunal's actual definition of conspiracy, quoted above, continues to give the conspiracy of individuals a clear and structured organisational identity. In this kind of analysis, matters become very murky.

On the other hand, in the Farben trial, when individualism had undoubtedly recaptured the commanding ground, a clear distinction was drawn between the individual agency of the company's officials and that of the corporation itself. The corporation was not seen as a criminal actor. The Tribunal stated that 'corporations act through individuals' and that Farben 'could not be subjected to criminal penalties in these proceedings'.[14] Nor should the individuals seek to transfer their responsibility to the company. This is therefore a clearer delineation of individual and organisational agency, which also effectively denies any morally or legally relevant impact of corporate membership on the behaviour of the individuals.

(c) The Rainbow Warrior *tale: states and non-governmental organisations*

In 1986 the *Rainbow Warrior,* a vessel belonging to the non-governmental environmental organisation Greenpeace, was blown up in Auckland Harbour in New Zealand by French secret service agents just as it was about to leave to protest against French nuclear testing in the Pacific Ocean. The French agents were subsequently tried and convicted of

---

14 *Ibid.,* p. 1153.

criminal offences under New Zealand law and each was sentenced to 10 years' imprisonment. New Zealand had also complained about the French violation of its sovereignty and following negotiations the two governments referred all legal issues between them arising from the incident to the UN Secretary-General for arbitration. The arbitral award was to be 'equitable and principled' and the Secretary-General, without giving reasons, ruled that France should formally apologise to New Zealand for the violation of its sovereignty and pay 7 million US dollars to New Zealand as compensation for damage suffered. New Zealand was also required under the ruling to transfer the convicted agents to French custody, and France would then be required to keep them in a French military facility on an isolated island outside Europe for a period of three years. France also entered into a compromise with the Stichting Greenpeace Council (acting for itself, organisations associated with Greenpeace and the owners and operators of the vessel), under which it was agreed to negotiate a settlement providing compensation for Greenpeace. In the event of a failure to reach agreement on this matter, it would be referred to named arbitrators, whose function would be to decide appropriate compensation.

This is an account of an international incident, involving the perpetration of a 'terrorist' act which was illegal under international law and national criminal law and was committed by the agents of one State on the territory of another; and of how the incident was resolved, legally and politically, through the criminal prosecution and conviction of the agents who carried out the blowing up of the vessel, and the settlements arrived at between France on the one hand and New Zealand and the Greenpeace organisation on the other hand. The factual narrative is not complicated. A legal narrative, and analysis in terms of agency and responsibility, is much more complex.[15]

In the first place, it may be possible to identify three distinct jurisdictional narratives, involving different actors and different types of responsibility. There is first of all the 'human' narrative, within which the French agents were prosecuted by the State of New Zealand, using New Zealand criminal law (so that the State is acting internally within its own legal order). Secondly, there is the

---

15 For a fuller discussion of the legal complexities arising from this narrative, see Christopher Harding (2006), 'Vingt Ans Après: Rainbow Warrior, Legal Ordering, and Legal Complexity', *Singapore Yearbook of International Law*, 10.

'international' narrative of two States acting under international law to resolve the breach of New Zealand's sovereignty. This is the same act in a factual sense, but the actors are different (States in their external or international role), the offending conduct is defined differently, and the whole matter is dealt with under a different system of rules, resulting in the application of different sanctions. Thirdly, there is the narrative involving Greenpeace and France. Although at first sight this appears to involve some kind of legal process, it is difficult to locate these dealings within any established legal order, since it appears to be a matter of neither national nor international law, nor may the legal personality of the actors be confidently identified. Thus, these three legal narratives in themselves complicate the first more factual account.

But there are further more difficult resulting questions of agency and responsibility. For instance, we may ask whether the States concerned may be regarded as the same kind of actor in each of the legal narratives. New Zealand appears as a prosecuting and penal authority in one account, and as a government on the international stage in the second account. France appears as a government on the international stage in one account, and virtually as a State terrorist organisation in the third account. Then we may compare the kinds of responsibility invoked in each narrative, and the resulting sanctions: conviction and imprisonment of human beings, compensation on the basis of State responsibility under international law, and compensation paid to an NGO under an indeterminate system of rules. Does this in any way convert a State into a criminal terrorist organisation? Or, finally, we may reflect on the way in which the international legal settlement affected the operation of 'internal' criminal responsibility and penal sanctions – what does this say about the role of national criminal law and its system of responsibility in the wider context of international law and relations?

In one dimension, these events raise once more the question of overlapping identities (of the individual and the organisation, the agent and the State), and of the responsibility of each, while acting in one sense as the same, for the act in question. But the example also shows how identities, legal or otherwise, may alter and shift as between jurisdictions and different orders; but also how resolutions within different orders may affect each other, so modifying for instance findings of criminal responsibility and penal accountability.

(d) The significance of organisations

It is possible to view each of the three situations discussed above as accounts of human action: that of human actors engaged in business, in governance, in political activities and in terrorism. But legal, ethical and political analyses emphasise the organisational presence within these events and suggest that we cannot understand the events themselves without recasting much of the human activity into organisational form. To make sense of what was happening, we need to see the matter in terms of the actions of companies, States, governments, State agencies and NGOs. The interests and dynamic of these organisational actors significantly shaped the events in question. Moreover, it can be seen in each case how legitimate organisational actors, such as companies and States, may spawn delinquent organisational forms: companies may form cartels, and States may evolve criminal structures, such as the Nazi organisations criminalised at Nuremberg or the 'terrorist arm' of the French government. It is difficult therefore to avoid this organisational dimension of criminal behaviour, and a consideration of its relevance to questions of responsibility.

5 The enigma of the responsible actor

The above discussion is intended to demonstrate the central line of enquiry being pursued in this book – to penetrate the enigma of the individual and the organisation in the context of moral agency and criminal responsibility. There is a single main puzzle: how to unravel the role of the individual and that of the organisation made up of individuals. This puzzle gives rise to two fundamental and interlinked questions. First, how should we evaluate the behaviour of an individual acting as part of an organisation? More specifically, to what extent should we say that, for purposes of moral and criminal responsibility, an organisation has captured the autonomy of its individual members or 'snatched their bodies'? Secondly, there is the issue of organisational synergy – to what extent is it possible to identify a distinct and autonomous organisational actor which is more than the sum of its individual parts? To the extent that this is possible, there is then a functional and ethical basis for shifting responsibility from individuals to the organisation. Both questions point in the direction of organisational responsibility, either in place of or alongside that of individuals.

But it should be recognised at the outset that organisational identity is by no means a novel concept in the wider field of law or social science and that individualist reservations have held sway principally in relation to the more specific question of moral responsibility and criminal liability. This contributes to the enigma of the subject. For example, the State, as a form of organisation, has been accorded a clear identity as a political and legal actor and indeed, as already noted, is viewed as a primary and original actor in the theory of modern international law. For international lawyers, there is no problem in talking about State responsibility for a range of illegal actions, the most extreme of which might be seen as analogous to criminal conduct in a national legal context.[16] At the same time, lawyers have readily accepted the legal personality of a range of corporate actors, which has entailed the recognition of a number of rights and obligations on their part. In this context, there has been a conscious drawing of a line between criminal and non-criminal liability, sometimes on the ground that corporate persons lack some quality of sentience, or susceptibility to certain kinds of sanctions, as a disqualification for criminal identity. Yet, we may ask: if a company may breach a contract, or cause extreme personal damage, and then conversely claim entitlement to human rights protection, why should it not so readily be a subject for criminal responsibility?

The discussion is therefore as much one of criminal responsibility, and the nature of that concept. The underlying question is whether there is something especially distinctive about this kind of responsibility, so as to justifiably reserve its application to the conventional human actor. In an 'age of organisations', is it still sensible to draw that distinction?

---

16 See the discussion of the International Law Commission's *Articles on State Responsibility* in Chapter 8 below.

Part I

Theory: the individual–organisation dilemma

Introductory note

The chapters in this first main section of the book lay down the theoretical groundwork for the discussion. How should we go about the task of defining and distinguishing individuals and organisations and how should we seek to understand the actions of these two entities, for purposes of evaluating such actions and then allocating responsibility? In this section, we need to move from the ontological (in what sense do either individuals or organisations exist?) to the normative (on what basis may we and do we interpret and pass judgment on their actions?). In order to answer such questions it is necessary to draw upon a number of intellectual disciplines and a range of existing writing and research: the sociology of organisations; the philosophy of collective action; and the jurisprudence of identity, legal personality, agency and responsibility. It will be seen that these disciplines, albeit from their own perspectives, sometimes address the same questions and produce parallel argument. That they do not always meet each other is perhaps not surprising, but can be instructive. So, we can see that the sociologists, the moral philosophers, the jurists and the lawyers have all, using their own methods and vocabulary, grappled with the grand ontological issue: does the organisation, as a collectivity, exist separately from its individual human members – is it a human aggregate, or is it an autonomous non-human-yet-human actor and agent? Not surprisingly, in each discipline we find opposing schools of thought and an unresolved question.[1] It is

---

1 It is also instructive that, as a disciplinary group, lawyers and criminologists have confined their attention mainly to one context – the *company* as a

important to appreciate and grasp hold of this underlying theoretical uncertainty.

The purpose of this section, therefore, is to help the reader to navigate these tricky theoretical waters. The plan is to guide the reader successively through the social and the philosophical to the normative. First, we need to consider what we know and understand about the world of organisations and how we may describe and categorise these phenomena. Then, there is the question of their identity and how it may be interpreted – may we ascribe to organisations, as we do to individuals, the capacity for autonomous, reflective action, so as to see them as *agents* inhabiting a normative domain, and thus candidates for the allocation of accountability, perhaps in the form of criminal responsibility? If so, how more precisely may we construct this legal responsibility – what are the legal routes to this outcome and what forms may be taken by such responsibility?

The key stages in this discussion are therefore: organisations and individuals as social phenomena, the possibility of organisational agency, and the legal routes by which responsibility may be based upon such agency. Or, to put the matter in very simple terms – this is the journey from social actor, to moral agent, and then to legally and criminally responsible person. It may be useful at this point finally to provide a checklist of what will be required for a satisfactory theory of criminal responsibility in relation to individuals and organisations:

- a definition of the organisation in contemporary society;

- identification of the criteria of agency, and in particular organisational agency, as a basis for the allocation of responsibility;

- tracing the legal routes to the allocation of responsibility (for example, individual *qua* individual, organisation *qua* organisation, individual as a collective actor (e.g. via joint criminal enterprise), State as a human rights violator); and

---

delinquent actor in particular circumstances, such as financial crime, and breach of standards resulting in industrial and public transport 'disasters'. This is revealed in some of the leading titles in this category of literature, such as *Corporations and Criminal Responsibility* (Celia Wells, Oxford University Press, 2nd edn, 2001), *Corporate Crime* (Gary Slapper and Steve Tombs, Longman, 1999), and *Corporations, Crime and Accountability* (Brent Fisse and John Braithwaite, Cambridge University Press, 1993), where 'corporate' clearly refers to companies.

- responsibility as a device for the location of moral and legal accountability within a normative structure, through an ordering of the Hartian elements of role and capacity, causal link, and liability.

The next four chapters will set out a theoretical structure by successively pursuing these four main elements of theory.

Chapter 2

The organisation in contemporary society

The sociology of organisations is clear enough regarding the significance of organisations in contemporary society, something which is put forward as self-evident in view of their number and their range of social, economic, political and cultural roles. But, although we may feel that we are able to recognise an organisation when we see one, are we able so easily to define these phenomena in generic terms, in order to distinguish organisations from both individual actors and other types of social grouping? The sociology of the subject appears less helpful in this respect, giving rise to opposing theories on the question whether organisational action can be distinguished from individual action, and to varying definitions and typologies. However, one key consistent element in the sociological literature is a very broad distinction which is drawn – often in somewhat different terms – between, on the one hand, looser, more random social structures and, on the other hand, more purposeful collectivities which possess formal and enduring structures. The latter type of collectivity – in Weber's language, the 'corporate group', or in the language of others, the 'formal' or 'large-scale' or 'complex organisation' – has a bounded, structured, and purposive character which serves well as the basis for the idea of an 'organisation'. It is proposed here to base discussion on a threefold categorisation of collectivities in the social domain: aggregates, which have an essentially random and happenstance composition (e.g. a crowd or an audience); social groups, which have a shared but loose feeling of being bound together (e.g. an ethnic group, or social class); and organisations, as groupings which are co-ordinated and structured in the pursuit of particular objectives. It is the latter type which will be referred to as an 'organisation' for purposes of the present work. Historically and at the present time there are many different examples of such organisations, but it is argued that a typology of this collective form may usefully be based on two major divisions: organisations of governance and representation, and organisations of enterprise.

I A self-evident significance?

It is now a commonplace observation among social scientists that the structure and working of contemporary society is dominated by the organisational form. Writing in the early 1960s Sheldon Wolin spoke of people living then in an 'age of organization',[1] and Robert Presthus referred to Western society as a characteristically 'organizational society'.[2] More recently Mark Bovens has referred to formal, large-scale organisations as being typical of the twentieth century, and having 'penetrated into almost all facets of daily life' so that 'their importance as social actors on a number of terrains is much greater than that of any single individual'.[3] Amitari Etzioni has argued that 'modern civilization depends largely on organizations as the most rational and efficient form of social grouping known'.[4] The need to take on board the contemporary social significance of organisations is stated in the following terms by Barry Hindess:

> Nobody would deny the importance in the modern world of actors other than human individuals – capitalist enterprises, churches, political parties, state agencies, trade unions etc … It is impossible to conceive of a complex modern society in which such actors did not play a major role. Any approach to the analysis of modern societies that admits only human individuals as effective actors must be regarded as seriously incomplete.[5]

Few, therefore, are likely to doubt the ubiquity of a range of organisational actors, in fields of activity such as public governance,

---

1   Sheldon S. Wolin, *Politics and Vision: Continuity and Innovation in Western Political Thought* (Allen and Unwin, 1961), p. 352.
2   Robert Presthus, *The Organizational Society* (Alfred A. Knopf, 1962).
3   Mark Bovens, *The Quest for Responsibility: Accountability and Citizenship in Complex Organisations* (Cambridge University Press, 1998), p. 10.
4   Amitari Etzioni, *Modern Organizations* (Prentice Hall, 1964), p. 1.
5   Barry Hindess, 'Classes, Collectivities and Corporate Actors', pp. 157–171 in Stewart R. Clegg (ed.), *Organization Theory and Class Analysis: New Approaches and New Issues* (Walter de Gruyter, 1990), at p. 157.

commerce and business, religion, education and culture, and this is widely accepted as an inevitable characteristic of a complex and sophisticated society. On the one hand, collective action is functionally necessary; and on the other hand, such action is a natural outcome of human endeavour and the nature of humans as interactive, sociable and ambitious creatures, reflecting 'a fundamental human propensity to form and join associations'.[6] In one sense, therefore, the significance of organisations and organisational action appears largely self-evident and the point does not require labouring. It is not difficult to list a number of organisational forms, corporate and otherwise, that participate in political, economic and social activity, and to indicate their political influence, share of economic markets and prevalence in social relations. Bovens, for instance, suggests[7] four indicators of the significance of organisations during the twentieth century: the increase in the number of corporate bodies;[8] an increase in the number of bureaucratic organisations;[9] an increase in the number of legal proceedings to which complex organisations are party;[10] and an increase in the attention given to such organisations in the media.[11] But, while Bovens' argument draws upon a range of sociological data and research from a number of countries, it may be argued that this data is primarily quantitative, and that his final two indicators reflect no more than the increase in numbers. Thus, while we are in no doubt as to the number of organisations of various kinds, and consequently the number of encounters between individuals and

---

6 Mancur Olson Jnr, *The Logic of Collective Action* (Harvard University Press, 1965), p. 17. See also, Gaetano Mosca, *The Ruling Class* (McGraw Hill, 1939), p. 163, referring to the human instinct for herding together; not to mention, more classically, Aristotle's assertion that man is by nature a political animal (*Politics*, i.2.9.1253a).

7 Bovens, note 3 above, p. 13 *et seq.*

8 Drawing upon for instance the work of James Coleman: *The Asymmetric Society* (Syracuse University Press, 1982); *The Foundation of Social Theory* (Harvard University Press, 1990). Coleman refers to a census of profit-making corporations in the US, and Bovens cites comparable Dutch statistical data.

9 Referring for instance to Bendix's analysis of the bureaucratisation of firms: Reinhard Bendix, *Work and Authority in Industry; Ideologies of management in the Course of Industrialization* (Harper and Row, 1963).

10 American and Dutch data, categorising the identity of litigants, and demonstrating a dramatic rise in the proportion of corporate litigants during the first half of the twentieth century.

11 Taking samples of media reporting in the US and in the Netherlands.

organisations, and between organisations themselves, something more qualitative still needs to be said about their social, political and economic roles. In particular, for purposes of the present discussion, we need to penetrate further the assertion that organisations have in some senses supplanted individuals as the main social actor in certain contexts.

Indeed, the natural human drive towards organised activity is productive of an ironic outcome which lies at the core of this study: that the human need to organise has resulted in a phenomenon that transcends individual human action, so leading ultimately to some tension between individual and organisational activity. But such an enquiry into the relationship between individual and organisational actors is complicated by an important characteristic of organisations, and something which will feature prominently in the ensuing discussion: *their human membership*. This fact of organisational existence supplies the basis for the classic individualist response to sociological claims regarding the significance of organisations: that whatever the number and size of organisations, in the final analysis they are no more than collections of individuals, so that it is still individual action that provides the key to understanding social life. The simple, and at first sight self-evident, assertion that organisations are inescapable and important, is thus based upon ontological shifting sands: on one interpretation, we might still be talking about human individuals as the basic units of social interaction. But, even taking on board this individualist argument, at the very least there is a *context* of organisational structure, which may be relevant for purposes of assessing and interpreting individual action, both within and without such a structure.

It will be necessary to revisit these ontological issues in the subsequent chapters. What may be helpful at this earlier stage, however, is first some descriptive mapping of organisational forms, and some discussion of what is known and understood about the ways in which these organisations act.

2 The organisation as a social phenomenon

To what more precisely are we referring when we use the term 'organisation' in the context of social action? It is worth noting at the very beginning that the term has only been used in this context relatively recently and that prior to the twentieth century people did not refer to social groupings as 'organisations'. As Starbuck comments:

The *Encyclopaedia Britannica* of 1910 used the term only in the context of biology; early organization theorists such as Michels (1911) and Weber (1910–14) did not speak of organizations but of bureaucracies; Fayol (1916) spoke of 'social bodies'; and Urwick (1933) spoke of 'governmental, ecclesiastical, military and business structures'.[12]

This is not to say that what we now commonly refer to as organisations did not exist before the twentieth century, but rather that there was little conceptualisation of what was involved in such social groupings. In so far as people reflected on what we might now describe as the 'problems of organisation' they did so with reference to specific groupings or structures without generalising the issue, and by discussing specific managerial matters largely in terms of personal hierarchical relationships.[13] This may provide us with an important perception – that, in earlier periods, individuals saw themselves as individuals working together within a structure of interpersonal relations, rather than as part of a distinct entity: 'their exact job assignments were secondary because their first responsibility was to do whatever their superiors asked of them'.[14]

The evolution of the modern organisation as a significant social player is nicely encapsulated in Starbuck's historical analysis of how this came about, using the following headings: organisations become topics of discussion – (1) education, specialisation and technology create the concept of the organisation; (2) education makes it possible for large organisations to proliferate and to work effectively; (3) growing populations and new technologies make large organisations efficient and increase the benefits of white-collar work; (4) the term 'organisation' evolves and splits into several concepts; (5) companies and corporations become immortal persons ('in one of the most implausible social constructions of the nineteenth and twentieth centuries, business and voluntary organisations changed from temporary special-purpose coalitions of specific owners into

---

12 William H. Starbuck, 'The Origins of Organization Theory', Chapter 5 in HaridimosTsoukas and Christian Knudsen, *The Oxford Handbook of Organization Theory* (Oxford University Press, 2003), p. 157.

13 Violina P. Rindova and William H. Starbuck, 'Distrust in Dependence: The Ancient Challenge of Superior-Subordinate Relations', in T.A.R. Clark (ed.), *Advancements in Organization Behaviour: Essays in Honour of Derek Pugh* (Ashgate, 1997).

14 *Ibid.*, at p. 147.

immortal legal persons having rights independently from their owners, members, or other stakeholders').[15] This account provides some understanding of the emergence of both the concept and the actuality of the modern organisation – the complex process involving both the activities of bodies and groupings and how these activities were increasingly self-consciously ordered to produce the idea of the organisation.

A key element in this process of the emergence of the organisation, which will reappear as a theme at a number of points in the later discussion, is the shift from self-conception as a *collection of individuals* to one as part of a *distinct entity*. This transition may be exemplified by a number of cases, a famous example being that from joint-stock companies and partnerships to incorporated companies having their own legal personality and distinct powers and obligations.[16] The organisation in the modern sense has its earlier form in the long-established concept of the corporation, as originally used in relation to the Roman Catholic Church,[17] monasteries, craft guilds, universities and municipalities. Indeed, 'corporation' is a revealing term, literally suggesting the taking of a corporeal form, something being given a body of its own. In this transition, the language and procedures of incorporation are also accompanied by a linguistic shift from plural (representing a number combining together as a collective) to singular,[18] when the collective is transformed into a single unit having its own distinct identity. The award of legal personality to what were formerly plural combinations but had become single entities, at first to churches, municipalities and State, and later to companies and international organisations, may in some ways be regarded as the

---

15 *Ibid.*, pp. 150–59. Starbuck's account is recommended as a particularly revealing overview of the complex subject of the emergence of the concept of the organisation and to what that term was being applied.

16 The classic exposition of this transformation is that presented by Adolf A. Berle and Gardiner C. Means, *The Modern Corporation and Private Property* (Macmillan, 1932). See also: Arthur W. Machen Jnr, 'Corporate Personality', (1911) *Harvard Law Review* 24: 253 and 347; Harold J. Laski (1916) 'The Personality of Associations', (1916) *Harvard Law Review* 29: 404; Naomi R. Lamoreaux (2000) 'Partnerships, Corporations and the Problem of Legal Personhood', UCLA and the National Bureau of Economic Research.

17 It should be remembered that the Catholic Church claimed a status as the *embodiment* of Jesus Christ.

18 See Laski, 'The Personality of Associations', note 16 above.

crowning point of this development. The psychological, ethical, and legal aspects of this development of collectives into single entities, and the implications for the question of responsibility, are explored in greater detail in the succeeding chapters below.

3 The sociology of organisations: no clear answer to the ontological question

What may be learnt, for purposes of the present discussion, from sociological enquiry into organisations and organisational forms? There is a wealth of research and literature, mainly under the headings of 'sociology of organisations' and 'organisational theory'. These two terms are sometimes used interchangeably, although the latter may be seen as having a somewhat wider remit, embracing non-sociological work in the field of management studies. But, whatever disciplinary descriptions may be used, it is doubtful whether sociological research and discussion has produced a commanding or overarching theory of organisations. Hall, for instance, has commented that:

> It is clear ... that the field of organizations does not have a theory, or even a set of theories, in the sense of a set of empirically verified propositions that are logically linked. We do have a number of perspectives or conceptualizations that are becoming increasingly crystallized and increasingly based on previous research ...'[19]

The sociology of the subject has thus comprised a number of approaches, based upon different emphases and points of focus, and these approaches sometimes appear to overlap, and sometimes to compete with each other. Earlier sociological enquiry fell into two main categories. First, there was that which was primarily concerned with the *structure* of organisations, examining the position and powers of organisational personnel, and their relation to organisational goals (for instance, the work of F.W. Taylor and Max Weber). This approach tended to see the organisation as a *closed* system, as a kind of instrument designed for the pursuit of clearly specified goals. The second focus of enquiry was concerned more with *social process within organisations*, especially for instance the interaction between

---

19 Richard H. Hall, *Organizations: Structure and Process* (Prentice Hall, 1972), p. 14.

informal relationships within the organisation and the pursuit of organisational goals (for example, the work of Chester Barnard and Philip Selznick).[20] Such a perspective characterises the organisation as an *open system*, viewing organisational goals as just one of several important needs to which an organisation is oriented – for instance, its survival may be seen as an equally significant need. Later research has embodied more diverse approaches,[21] entailing the construction of typologies, the investigation of organisations as social systems, and viewing organisations as structures of action. Moreover, various elements of organisational phenomena have become the focal point for different bodies of research – for instance 'management theory' being concerned with the productivity and efficiency of organisations, 'technology theory' examining the impact of technology as part of the organisational environment, whilst the role of power within organisations has provided yet another focal point for research.

Much of this research may be approached to inform the main line of enquiry being followed here: the relationship between individual human actors and organisations, and the reality of the organisation as an entity distinct from its human composition. Thus sociological definitions of the organisation may contribute to the resolution of ontological questions concerning the separate existence of organisations. Equally, questions and data regarding the role of individuals acting within organisational structures and for organisational purposes can be used to inform discussion of the respective social and ethical roles of individuals and organisations. But this large body of argument and empirical data appears to provide conflicting ammunition for the ontological and philosophical debate regarding the reality and respective roles of human and non-human actors. Sociologists are equally divided on this key question.

Weber's conclusions, for example, have reinforced the reductivist argument that ultimately all organisational action is individual action, in his assertion that the actions of corporate actors:

---

20 See for instance: Chester I. Barnard, *The Functions of the Executive*, (1938, Harvard University Press); Philip Selznick (1948) 'Foundations of the Theory of Organization', (1948) *American Sociological Review* 13: 25.

21 For an overview, see Stewart Clegg and David Dunkerley, *Organization, Class and Control* (1980).

must be treated as solely the resultants and modes of organization of the particular acts of individual persons, since these alone can be treated as agents in a course of subjectively understandable action.[22]

Later work which has expressed scepticism regarding a distinct organisational identity has centred around the 'interaction perspective', which accords a social primacy to the interactions of individuals making up an organisation: nothing in the organisation may be understood apart from the individuals involved. Thus, David Silverman has doubted the reification of organisations, preferring to analyse organisations as the outcome of the action of individuals addressing their own human problems and to question the sense in viewing organisations as institutions which pursue organisational goals.[23] Taking this approach, Peter Blau has analysed organisational action as a series of direct or indirect individual actions – for instance, providing descriptions of how officials receive material rewards from superiors within an organisation, or the approval of colleagues, for any conformity with organisational standards, which are themselves the result of individual contributions to decision-making within the organisation.[24] This kind of argument has also exploited a methodological puzzle, in that information about organisations is necessarily derived from individuals, so making it more difficult to conceptualise the organisation as such.

On the other hand, others have strongly contested the 'treatment of social actors as if they themselves are reducible to human individuals'.[25] In responding to phenomenological claims,[26] Hindess for example argues:

22 Max Weber, *Economy and Society* (University of California Press, 1978), p. 13.
23 David Silverman, *The Theory of Organizations* (Heinemann, 1970). For another leading statement of this kind of argument, see: Herbert A. Simon, (1964) 'On the Concept of Organizational Goal', *Administrative Science Quarterly* 9: 1.
24 Peter M. Blau, *Exchange and Power in Social Life* (Wiley and Sons, 1967), p. 329 *et seq.*
25 Hindess, note 5 above, at p. 159.
26 Phenomenological sociology is based on the argument that consciousness is the only phenomenon of which we can be certain: our experience of the world is constituted in and through consciousness. The main principles of this approach were laid out in Alfred Schutz's work, *Phenomenology of the Social World* (1932).

The decisions of corporate actors cannot be seen as the products of a unitary consciousness. Yes – but we should be wary of the presumption that human individuals are in contrast characterized by a unitary consciousness: that their decisions are not also the dispersed products of diverse and sometimes conflicting objectives, forms of calculation and means of action.[27]

Opponents of the interaction perspective have marshalled a number of arguments against the reduction of organisational action to individual behaviour. In the first place, it is asserted that individual interaction within organisational contexts frequently involves routine and learnt behaviour. This learning may have taken place through direct interactions, but the actual behaviour takes place without mental reference to the interaction process. In that sense, the consciousness is organisational. As Hall argues:

> Much behaviour in organizations is of this type. The organization trains, indoctrinates, and convinces its members to respond on the basis of the requirements of their position. This response becomes quite regularized and routinized and does not involve the interaction frame of reference.[28]

Secondly, it is pointed out that organisations endure over time and replace their human membership. In this sense, they are not dependent on particular individuals and establish a system of norms and expectations to be followed regardless of the identity of their personnel. Finally, the decision-making process within organisations has been understood as transcending and influencing the individual contributions to that process. At its lower levels, organisational decision-making may be seen as 'programmed', and at its higher levels as pervaded by organisational factors, such as tradition, precedent and the impact of power positions. In this way the genesis of the action may be said to lie in the organisation.

In this way, it will be seen that sociological theory and the interpretation of sociological data tend to shadow and supply analogies for the philosophical debate on the nature of human and organisational agency, which will be discussed further below in Chapter 3. Sociological research therefore easily confirms the human

---

27 *Ibid.*, p. 161.
28 Hall, *Organizations: Structure and Process*, note 19 above, at p. 11.

tendency to organise itself, but has provided no clear answer to questions regarding the nature of that organisation and in particular its autonomous operation beyond the role of its individual human constituents.[29]

4 Definition: organisations and social groups

But we may also look to the sociology of the subject for some means of identifying organisational action, so as to achieve a working definition and understanding of the phenomenon for purposes of further discussion. What may be seen as the characteristic features and roles of the organisation as a form of social activity? This question necessarily precedes any listing or typology, which is itself a useful precursor of discussion, in that we then have some idea factually of this social phenomenon.

There are a number of definitions which have been offered in sociological writing,[30] but Weber's classic exposition of the concept remains a useful starting point.[31] Weber draws a major distinction between 'corporate groups' and other forms of social organisation. Weber's concept of 'corporate group' corresponds in some respects with what other writers have variously referred to as 'formal', 'large-scale' or 'complex organisations'. A corporate group is described in Weber's words as a 'social relationship which is either closed or limits the admission of outsiders by rules ... so far as its order is enforced by the action of specific individuals whose regular function this is, of a chief or 'head' and usually also an administrative staff.'[32] The main elements of his definition would seem to comprise:

29 But it should not be assumed that all sociological writing falls squarely into one camp or another, insisting that individuals and organisations exist separately and exclusively of each other. Hall, for instance, carefully points out that there may be some scope for individual autonomy in organisational contexts, but that it is difficult to generalise about the proportion of individual behaviour which may or may not be overridden by organisational factors (Hall, *ibid.*, at p. 12). Indeed, this is a central point of argument for purposes of this work.
30 For an overview of definitional work, see the first chapter of Hall, *Organizations: Structure and Process,* note 19 above.
31 Max Weber, *The Theory of Social and Economic Organization,* transl. A.M. Henderson and Talcott Parsons (The Free Press, 1947), pp. 145–6.
32 *Ibid.*

(a) social relationships or individual interactions within closed or limited boundaries;
(b) order – a structuring of interactions imposed by the organisation itself;
(c) interactions which are 'associative' rather than 'communal'[33] (distinguishing the corporate group from other forms of social organisation, such as the family);
(d) the performance of continuous purposive activities of a specified kind (pursuit of goals).[34]

Weber's definition has been associated with the concept of an organisation as a closed system, since it emphasises in an abstract fashion the system rather than the actions of the individual members within the system.[35] Etzioni's definition replicates that of Weber to a large extent, distinguishing again between what many would refer to as formal and informal organisations:

> Organizations are social units (or human groupings) deliberately constructed and reconstructed to seek specific goals. Corporations, armies, schools, hospitals, churches, and prisons are included; tribes, classes, ethnic groups, and families are excluded.[36]

The main elements to be extracted from Etzioni's analysis would comprise:

(a) planned divisions of labour, power and responsibility for communication;
(b) power centres which control and review the efforts of the organisation;
(c) the substitution of personnel.

While the first two features cover ground similar to Weber's idea of an associative, goal-oriented ordering, the third characteristic of substitutability of individual personnel adds an important insight into the distinctive nature of at least certain kinds of organisation,

---

33 *Ibid.*, pp. 136–9.
34 *Ibid.*, pp. 151–2.
35 Contrast for instance the approach taken by Chester I. Barnard, *The Functions of the Executive,* note 20 above.
36 Amitai Etzioni, *Modern Organizations*, note 4 above, p. 3.

enabling the latter to transcend the identity of its human membership at any one time.

Such definitions, however, remain largely rooted in the formal and abstract aspects of organisational phenomena. An important perception gained from sociological research relates to the actual deviation between formal goals and other objectives which may be pursued within organisations, an aspect which may prove important in any discussion of the relation between organisational and individual action. As Hall has commented:

> A major consideration [is] the fact that while organizations are goal-seeking entities, many of their energies are deflected from goals as they react to internal and external pressures. The test of this perspective ... lies not in logic, but in empirical reality.[37]

This significant and almost systematic phenomenon of deflection from the pursuit of formal goals is explained by Blau in the following terms:

> ... Social interaction and activities within organizations never correspond perfectly to official prescriptions, if only because not all prescriptions are compatible, and these departures from the formal blueprint raise problems for empirical study. Paradoxically, therefore, although the defining characteristic of an organization is that a collectivity is formally organized, what makes it of scientific interest is that the developing social structure inevitably does not coincide completely with the pre-established forms.[38]

Furthermore, as Blau later points out,[39] such informal departures from official procedures should not be viewed as idiosyncratic but as socially organised and, as the work of Barnard had indicated,[40] are essential for the operation of organisations. Indeed, this aspect of organisational activity will prove relevant to later discussion of the relationship between organisations and their individual members. It would be useful therefore to add this element of goal deviation to a working concept of the organisation.

---

37 *Organizations: Structure and Process,* note 19 above, at p. 38.
38 Peter M. Blau, entry in *The International Encyclopaedia of the Social Sciences* (Crowell Collier and Macmillan, 1968), vol XI, at p. 298.
39 *Ibid.,* p. 301.
40 Barnard, *The Functions of the Executive,* note 20 above, at pp. 1115–123.

From these earlier efforts at definition, a working definition of organisation may be put forward for purposes of the present discussion. It would appear advisable, or even necessary, to follow most other writers on the subject and draw a cardinal distinction in the first place between what are sometimes described as 'formal' organisations on the one hand and looser forms of social grouping or organisation on the other hand. This distinction is based in the first place upon empirical observation of the way in which different social groupings actually operate. The difference being here referred to, between 'formal organisations' and 'social structures', or what have sometimes been termed 'enacted' and 'crescive institutions',[41] has been summarised by Blau in the following terms:

> The government of a society, or a football team ... are social structures deliberately established to achieve certain objectives, and the regularities observable in them reflect deliberate design ... Social systems produced by formally enacted procedures, rather than merely emergent forces, are organisations.[42]

On the other hand, Blau distinguishes 'social structures' as phenomena which 'may emerge as the aggregate result of the diverse actions of individuals, each pursuing his own ends' and from which 'an economic system or class structure develop, which reveal organized patterns of social conduct, although nobody has explicitly organized the endeavors of individuals'.[43] In this way spontaneously emergent groupings such as social classes, ethnic groups, nations (as distinct from States), kinship groups and (perhaps) families have frequently not been classified as organisations, since they lack this characteristic of pre-considered and purposeful design.

---

41 The term used by William Graham Sumner.

42 Blau, *Encyclopaedia,* note 38 above, at p. 298.

43 *Ibid.* This broad distinction may also be seen as corresponding in some respects to the categorisation formulated by Ferdinand Tonnies between *Gemeinschaft* and *Gesellschaft.* The former is used to refer to groups that form around essential will, in which membership is self-fulfilling (exemplified by the family or neighbourhood, as a kind of community). *Gesellschaft* on the other hand refers to groups in which membership is sustained by some instrumental goal or definite end. Ferdinand Tonnies, *Gemeinschaft und Gesellschaft,* first published in 1887, English translation by Charles P. Loomis, *Community and Society* (Michigan State University Press, 1957).

But this distinction is also theoretically supported by the ultimate purpose of this study, which is to judge the allocation of responsibility for action as between individuals and organisations. Briefly, for present purposes, any allocation of responsibility is meaningful only in relation to social groupings or organisations possessing a certain degree of cohesion and purposiveness. As should become clear in the subsequent discussion, there is a point within the spectrum of collective social action at which the looseness of association within a collectivity renders doubtful the identification of the collectivity as a single actor, and thus also any allocation of agency and responsibility to the group as distinct from its individual members. The exact location of the boundary or the point of distinction may be (and perhaps is inevitably) open to argument, but the need for the distinction is inescapable. For both practical and theoretical purposes most people will easily see the difference between a collection of passengers on a routine train journey and the personnel of a company. Thus, an important purpose of defining something as an organisation is to identify characteristics of cohesive structure and purpose which may lead to a sense of separate and single identity for a particular grouping of persons.

On that basis, the following working definition of an organisation may be put forward. An organisation may be viewed as a social grouping with the following features:

(a) it comprises a framework for social relations and interactions contained within defined boundaries;
(b) it embodies an ordered system of collective decision-making and implementation of such decisions;
(c) its activities are directed towards the achievement of particular goals, which include both formal organisational goals and other goals which are generated by the actual operation of the organisation;
(d) it is maintained through a system of positions associated with particular organisational roles rather than dependent on the participation of particular individual human actors.

The above, it is suggested, may be seen as essential characteristics of an organisation which may be a candidate for single identity and a responsibility-bearing role. It is less easy to select a convenient and concise label to describe this kind of organisation. A term such as 'corporate group', as used by Weber, may be misleading in that it could suggest the exclusion of legally unincorporated organisations (for instance partnerships, or trade unions), which would not be desirable. Terminology such as 'complex' or 'large-scale' organisations may again mislead, in that there are socially and legally significant collectivities which are neither complex nor large-scale. The term 'formal organisation' may be nearer the mark, but nonetheless suggests a legally constituted and publicly visible form, all too evident in examples such as the company or the State, but absent in the case of significant groups such as terrorist or criminal organisations. It is therefore proposed, in this work, to simply apply the term 'organisation' to the kind of cohesive social grouping defined above, and to refer to looser collectivities as either 'social groups' or 'aggregates'. These latter two terms also reflect different ranges along the spectrum of social cohesiveness, and along with the term 'organisation' will be used as a basis for a typology, as laid out in the following section.

5 Constructing a broad typology

A moment's reflection should demonstrate that social, political and economic life present a wide range of situations in which human individuals act collectively, in numbers of two or more, so raising the question whether taking action in a group can lead to that action as being viewed as that of the group rather than that of its constituent individual members. In many cases everyday language commonly ascribes such action to the group rather than to the individuals comprising the group – thus: 'the crowd roared in applause', 'the middle classes would not accept this policy'; 'the university established a new degree programme'; 'the firm marketed a new product'; 'the United Nations condemned the terrorist attacks'. Sometimes language is further used to identify the group actor more definitely as a single entity by describing it in metaphorical terms – thus: 'Brussels [for the European Union] or Whitehall [for the bureaucracy of the UK Government] or the Pentagon [for the US Federal Government] resisted these demands'. There is therefore clearly some established sense of the existence of collective action and collective identity; the more difficult question, however, concerns the extent to which that collective identity supplants the identity, agency and responsibility of the individual members of the group, effectively replacing the individuals as actors. In social and moral terms, our answers to that question tend to vary according to the nature and circumstances of the collectivity in question.

Let us pose three examples:

- a rioting mob attacks (attack?) and kills (kill?) the person attempting to quell the riot
- a tribe banishes (banish?) one of its members
- a company concludes (but here it makes little sense to say 'conclude') a contract.

In each case would we normally ascribe the relevant action to the group or to its members? If the latter is decided upon, it may then be necessary to enquire further into the role and responsibility of particular individuals within the group.

In the case of the rioting mob we may well be unlikely to find the relevant agency in the crowd as a whole. Many individual members of the mob may not have been directly involved in the physical perpetration of the killing and would object (with a real prospect of success) to being brought within the net of moral and legal responsibility.[44] The case of tribal banishment may appear to be more marginal and we might well find ourselves asking further questions and exploring the circumstances: how large was the tribe, how many members, what kind of process was used to carry out the expulsion, and what degree of involvement did the general membership of the tribe have in that process? The case of the company's contract, however, raises few doubts. We would almost certainly ascribe this action to the collective actor called the company (as would legal rules), rather than to an individual director, manager or employee of the company.

These three examples provide typical situations which might be used by social scientists to indicate meaningful differences along a scale of more or less cohesive and integrated collective action, such as may be indicated by vocabulary of the kind 'formal' and 'informal organisation'. In terms of social characteristics (which then inform moral and legal categorisation) three main types may usefully be identified along such a scale or spectrum of collective activity. These main types may be referred to respectively as 'aggregates', 'social

---

44 But this is not to argue that there ought to be no responsibility at all for some members of the mob. One possible argument is to assert some kind of accessory responsibility, but for individuals. Such complexity and sense of fragmented action is a reason for finding a single group responsibility. The matter is discussed further in Chapter 4.

groups' and 'organisations', and this scheme of discussion may be summarised in Table 2.1 below.

It will be argued here that the dividing line for purposes of establishing a distinct group identity, agency and responsibility should be drawn between the first two of the above and the third; that is to say, that only those groupings defined as 'organisations' should qualify for the ascription of such agency, as actors distinct from their individual membership. The basis for that conclusion lies in the observed social structure and role of the collectivities in question.

Let us further consider the character and role of these three main types of collectivity.

(a) The aggregate

This term is being used to refer to a *non-organised and for the most part randomly constructed* collectivity. Straightforward examples would include an audience, a crowd in a public place, or a group of travellers. In each case the individuals concerned have come together for a common purpose (to listen to a concert, to shop in a town centre, to travel to the same destination), but their coming together is in other respects random and accidental. They *happen* to have that same purpose at that particular time and in that particular place; but in other respects they may have nothing in common or not know each other. Their coming together is loose and happenstance and they are only temporarily bound by pursuit of an occasional goal. In social terms, as a group at a particular moment they have only a

Table 2.1 Main types of collectivity

Aggregate	Social group	Organisation
Random, happenstance composition	Shared feeling of unity or being bound together	Co-ordinated and structured in pursuit of particular objectives
Typical instances:	*Typical instances:*	*Typical instances:*
Audience Crowd	Ethnic group Social class Kinship group	Corporation State Club Delinquent gang [Family?]

small degree of cohesion and a minimal relationship to each other as individuals. It would be a different matter if the audience comprised solely members of a single musical club; or the crowd solely members of a particular consumer organisation; or the travellers solely members of a party travelling together for a particular purpose; or if the group was suddenly collectively taken hostage. But that would be to transform in a significant way the nature of the collectivity, taking away its random character and providing it with a much greater degree of social cohesion. A social reading of the random, happenstance collection of people described here as an aggregate would suggest little reason for replacing a number of individual independent agents with a single collective agent in evaluating the actions which occur in this collective context. Another way to put the matter would be that such a grouping possesses a minimal sense of community or collective structure for purposes of expressing a sense of community. This kind of grouping achieves expression most naturally through individual agency.

(b) The social group

In this category of collectivity there is, however, a clearly identifiable sense of community and of shared values or culture. Members of such a grouping have a great deal in common and relate to each other in a significant way, but their behaviour is not co-ordinated towards the achievement of specific goals. The term 'peer group' readily comes to mind as a sociological description of this kind of collectivity. As discussed above, these are groupings which possess strong common feeling and experience but which emerge through social action rather than being organised for a particular purpose. They have a crescive character. There are a number of clear examples: ethnic groups, nations, kinship groups, social classes, trades and occupations, epistemological communities (such as philosophers, or sociologists), and persons with a shared philosophical or belief orientation. Such groupings occupy a middle point on the spectrum, lacking the essential characteristics of organisation as defined above. But they may and frequently do provide a basis for organisation. Thus a nation may be organised into a State, a social class into a political party, a trade into a professional association, an occupation into a trade union, an epistemological community into a university faculty, a belief system into a church.

There may be some argument around borderline instances of social group and organisation, particularly in relation to tribes, kinship groups and families. Much depends upon the definition of organisation. While on the one hand a kinship group would seem to fit into the category of shared community lacking organisation, tribal groups on the other hand would often appear to possess clear and developed structures of governance which render them analogous to simple versions of States. Families are more difficult to locate. In one sense they may be regarded as a smaller scale, more closely bounded category of the kinship group. But families may also possess features of internal regulation, governance and representation which provide them with some sense of organised activity in the pursuit of particular goals.[45] Certainly, there are historical examples of formally arranged and tightly structured family units which may bear some comparison with corporate actors. This will be so in the case of families which possess a clear structure of authority (with a 'head of the family'), an allocation of roles as between members, and action constructed around family 'policies' and 'goals' (what might be referred to as a 'nuclear' family). The biological category of family may also shade into social, political and economic categories of 'clan' (as a political grouping), gang (a delinquent organisation, classically typified by Mafia 'families'), or family business (as a significant form of economic undertaking). Again, the important point to note is that family as a social group may well provide the basis for a number of kinds of organisation, although the latter may still retain in some way the label of 'family'.

Aggregates and social groups may appear very different in relation to their respective degrees of shared community, culture and values, but they have in common a relative absence of structure and goal-oriented activity, which then marks them off from the third category of 'organisation'. For purposes of the present discussion, both aggregates and social groups appear to be too sociologically diffuse to support an allocation of single agency, and consequently of responsibility for action taken into the context of such groupings.

---

45 For some leading studies of the social roles of the family, and transitions in such roles, see: Talcott Parsons and Robert Bales, *Family, Socialization and Interaction Process* (1955); William Goode, *The Family* (1964); Christopher Lasch, *Haven in a Heartless World* (1977); Michael Young and Peter Willmott, *The Symmetrical Family* (1973); C.C. Harris, *The Family and Industrial Society* (1983); Philippe Aries, *Centuries of Childhood* (1962).

(c) The organisation

This concept is based upon the working definition put forward in the preceding section and is very much coloured by the argument that the organisation is the kind of collectivity which may be meaningfully viewed as a single actor, in place or alongside the individuals who comprise, at least in part, that organisation. Within that definition there are of course numerous examples of such organisations.

A number of attempts have been made to construct sociological typologies of organisations. These efforts have been bedevilled not only by difficulties of classification, but also by lack of agreement concerning what may qualify as a unit of organisation in the first place. It may be recalled that some theorists, for instance Talcott Parsons and Etzioni, while excluding tribes, classes, ethnic groups and families from their definition of organisation, cited as examples: corporations, armies, schools, hospitals, churches and prisons. That list in itself may raise some quibbles. Does 'corporation' mean, in a rather loose but popular sense, the business firm or company, or does it mean, in a more technically precise sense, any formally incorporated body, and therefore various types of company, but also municipalities, universities and a number of other entities established by charter and some incorporating process? Some of the other entities listed there might be thought of as institutions rather than organisations: schools, hospitals and prisons are specific institutions within educational, health care and penal organisations. The term 'army' is ambiguous: on the one hand, it may represent an arm of State organisation, or on the other hand, as a private and mercenary version of an armed force, it might be more akin to a business organisation or criminal gang. The problems of typology are therefore quickly encountered and in particular questions arise concerning main categories, sub-categories and the difference between organisations and institutions.[46] A university is undoubtedly an organisation, and one of a corporate type. But within a university, faculties, schools and registries may also validly be characterised as organisations in themselves, competing

---

46 A current example of this terminological issue is the habit in international relations discourse of using the term 'institution' in place of 'organisation', so that both States and intergovernmental organisations such as the UN may be referred to as institutions, as for instance in Toni Erskine (ed.), *Can Institutions Have Responsibilities: Collective Moral Agency and International Relations* (Palgrave Macmillan, 2003).

with each other and possessing distinctive structures of authority, decision-making, goals and cultures. It is quickly evident that the construction of a typology of organisations is in itself a massive and contestable exercise. As Hall has commented: '... there is not a generally accepted typology of organizations ... in spite of the general agreement that a good typology is desperately needed.'[47]

6 The value of typology: what's in a name?

Taxonomies and labels, and the whole business of typology, is important, useful and inescapable. In Coppola's film *Godfather II*, the following exchange takes place in the Senate Hearing scene:

'Are you a member of the Corleone crime organisation?'
'I'm a member of the Corleone Family – we call it "family"'.

Having made that point about typologies of organisation, it is also important to recognise that typologies may serve different purposes, depending on the criteria which they adopt for purposes of classification. Since many definitions of organisation emphasise their role in the pursuit of certain goals, a classification according to main types of goal or function might appear useful. Talcott Parsons[48] proposed a fourfold main typology of this kind, listing:

(a) organisations oriented towards economic production (the business firm being the typical form within this category);
(b) organisations oriented towards political goals[49] (most typically government organisations, but also for instance banking institutions);

---

47 Hall, *Organizations: Structure and Process,* note 19 above, at p. 41. See also the discussion by J.E.T. Eldridge and A.D. Crombie, *A Sociology of Organisations* (Allen and Unwin, 1974), Chapter 3.

48 Talcott Parsons, *Structure and Process in Modern Societies* (The Free Press, 1960), pp. 45–46.

49 This category was adapted by Katz and Kahn as 'managerial or political organizations', which would then include not only the State and governmental sub-systems, but also trade unions, pressure groups, and special interest organisations: Daniel Katz and Robert L. Kahn, *The Social Psychology of Organizations* (Wiley, 1966).

(c) integrative organisations, concerned with the adjustment of conflicts (cited here are courts, political parties, interest groups and hospitals);

(d) pattern-maintenance organisations (and cited here are cultural, educational and 'expressive' organisations, including churches, schools and artistic and research institutions).[50]

The comparison with Katz and Kahn has been referenced immediately above to show how different writers may adjust such a classification. Thus political parties and interest groups may be seen variously as 'integrative' or 'managerial' in their role. A further problem arises from the fact that the role and function of organisations are not necessarily static over time, but may evolve and become more complex. So it may be argued that trade unions have evolved a significant welfare role as well as that of interest representation; or that governments have evolved a business role alongside of their main function of political management; or that universities in the twenty-first century are emerging as economic as much as educational and research enterprises.

Typological endeavours in this field are therefore fraught. But it may be argued that, for purposes of this discussion, it is the analysis and definition of the organisation as a general type of social entity that is crucial, rather than the construction of a detailed typology. The latter may serve as a background mapping of the scope of the discussion, but is not central to the argument. Nonetheless, as part of such a background mapping, it might still be said that a broad survey of organisational forms over time and space does suggest two main categories in terms of role. These two broad categories are not mutually exclusive, in that a particular type of organisation might perform, although usually to a differing extent, both these main kinds of role. These two primary roles, which organisations have been used to carry out, may be encapsulated in the concepts of (a) enterprise and (b) representation and governance.

(a) Organisations of enterprise

The kind of organisation being here referred to is probably the type that readily comes to mind for most people, as something which

---

50 Some of these entities are classified by Katz and Kahn (note 49 above) as 'maintenance organizations' (churches, schools, and health and welfare institutions) and some differently as 'adaptive organizations' (universities, research and artistic institutions).

has been established to achieve specific, aspirational and forward-looking goals. In a modern context of industrialised capitalist society, the business firm supplies a paradigm for this kind of organisation, and indeed the term 'enterprise' is sometimes used to describe such an entity.[51] Economic goals in relation to processes of manufacture, financing, supply of commodities and the making of profit are clearly identifiable and definable, rendering the business firm a leading example of contemporary organisation. The essential concept underlying this classification is the achievement of a specific, desirable objective which is in some sense *over and above* the level of activity associated with basic human existence – colloquially, it might be said, taking matters further, to another plane of activity, improving upon the business of brute survival. For this reason, the term 'aspirational' might well be employed in this context. These 'value-added' goals comprise generally such matters as an enhanced standard of living, economic profit and the generation of wealth, increasing knowledge and developing a feeling of personal fulfilment. In this way, business organisations (which may include organised crime groups), research and educational entities, and clubs and societies comprise the main part of the list of organisations under this heading.

(b) Organisations of governance and representation

On the other hand, this second main category of organisation serves a basic need of human society, as an essential component of social and political order, providing necessary units within structures of regulation, governance and the representation of varying interests within society. Governance in any society requires some kind of organisation, and more advanced societies require more numerous and more sophisticated kinds. There are obvious gradations of organisations of regulation and governance – principally, it might be argued: families, tribes, States (and departments of State), churches, and intergovernmental organisations. But the political process also requires means for the representation of interests, and this has resulted in the development of representational organisations –

---

51 In French, the term 'entreprise' can be used for firm, venture or undertaking. In European Community vocabulary (for instance in the EC Treaty) the term 'undertaking' is used to refer to firms and businesses, and in some earlier literature the terms 'enterprise' and 'undertaking' were used interchangeably: see, e.g. Berthold Goldman, *European Commercial Law* (Stevens, 1971), which has a section on the 'concept of the enterprise' (p. 165 *et seq.*).

political parties, interest groups, guilds, professional groupings, trade unions, and the like. The goals of such organisations are for the most part concerned with the maintenance of ordering and contributing to such ordering.

This discussion may therefore, in the end, be condensed into a truism: that all societies are concerned with the maintenance of order (governance) and with their own advance and development (enterprise), and so organisations will inevitably fall into those two main categories, or in some cases reflect a mixture of those two primary objectives. In terms of a substantive mapping of the organisational world, it may be helpful to bear in mind these two very fundamental objectives of organisational activity. This may be summed up in the non-exhaustive typology represented in Table 2.2 below.

Table 2.2 A main typology of organisations

Organisations of governance and representation	Organisations of enterprise
Families (at least, of the nuclear kind)	Companies (business firms)
	Foundations
Tribes	Financial institutions
States	Charities
State organs (departments, enforcement agencies, services)	Universities
	Research bodies
Municipalities	Monasteries and other religious foundations
Intergovernmental organisations	
Churches	Clubs and societies
Guilds	Media enterprises
Professional associations	Criminal groups or gangs
Trade unions	Artistic and cultural enterprises
Interest groups/civil society NGOs	
Political parties	
Factions	
Terrorist groups?	
Conspiracies?	

Chapter 3

Agency: the philosophy of the collective

We appear to have little difficulty in accepting that human individuals may act and be judged as individuals, or that individuals may act (perhaps in some ways differently) within organisations, but there is more controversy in the idea that individuals may lose their identity in the latter situation to the organisation, which then becomes the socially and morally relevant actor and agent in their place. The debate between adherents of individualism (organisations are reducible to their individual components) and those of holism (organisations may be regarded as distinct actors and agents) remains largely unresolved. The argument is developed here that a distinct organisational agency may be based upon an organisational or group rationality, which is of a different kind and character from that associated with individual human action, but derives from a structure of human interactions. Building upon that argument, it may be said that to qualify for a distinct identity and agency (in the sense of a capacity for moral and reflective action) organisations must satisfy criteria relating to both (a) structure and capacity for autonomous action and (b) the performance of a representative role. Such criteria correspond with elements of the definition of organisation set out in Chapter 2: a bounded, purposeful entity with an enduring structure, which is independent of the identity of particular individuals, though reliant on the participation of (anonymous) individuals. On this basis, organisations may be validly and convincingly regarded as distinct autonomous actors in the social domain and as distinct autonomous agents in the normative domain, and in that sense accountable and perhaps criminally responsible actors.

The aim of this chapter is to provide a convincing theoretical basis for considering some kind of organisational responsibility alongside that of human individuals. As noted already, the underlying dilemma within such a project is that organisations are set up, composed of, and operated through human individuals, and this fact reinforces the individualist claim that organisations cannot be, in any real sense, distinctive actors or responsible agents. The plan of discussion here will first of all investigate the idea of individual and organisational actors as moral and legal agents, or it may be said, as actors within certain normative 'domains', of which the moral and the legal are significant examples. The problem of how an organisational actor may be understood to have an identity as a moral or legal agent which is distinct from that of its individual human parts will then be probed with reference to the idea that *human interactions within an organisational structure* may be productive of a distinct organisational identity. Finally, it will be suggested that certain general criteria of organisational agency may be used to identify such agency in particular cases.

I Problems in constructing theory

Discussion of any kind of responsibility on the part of individuals and organisations is necessarily grounded in a theory of agency, which seeks to identify and explain the role and character of these entities and a justifiable allocation of responsibility to them. But a glance at the existing literature on the subject suggests that such theoretical and conceptual discussion is difficult and opaque, especially since it is spread across a number of disciplines in a way that has not been well linked together. The debate on individual and organisational agency, identity and responsibility has been bedevilled by differences in vocabulary and conceptual description, and by a tendency for writers to have different focal points for their discussion.

Thus, to illustrate the first problem, it soon becomes evident to the reader that concepts and definitions may slip between terms such as 'agency', 'identity' and 'personality'; between the description of actors as 'collective', 'group' and 'corporate'; and between different descriptors of categories of responsibility. Fundamental terms such as 'natural', 'metaphysical' and 'moral' may bear a similar but not precisely the same meaning as between different disciplines and different authors.

To illustrate the second point, it is clear that a discussion of 'organisational'[1] actors may encompass a range and variety of entities, as diverse as States, companies, non-governmental institutions, gangs, and crowds, to name just some.[2] But different disciplines will naturally focus upon certain main types. Thus, there is quite a substantial literature in economics and business studies which has as its focal point the role of the corporate business entity commonly known as the 'company' or 'firm'. Legal discourse on the other hand naturally emphasises the main categories of legal personality, which in the context of organisational actors usually means the State and the company. Then again, recent international relations (IR) discussion which has taken an interest in matters of organisational responsibility has a rather different focus, on States and intergovernmental institutions. It is principally in the context of moral philosophy that we encounter a more broad-minded review of a wider range of organisational actors.[3] But the basic point remains, that for epistemological reasons underlying theoretical discussion is elusive and fragmented. Intriguingly, also, in terms of English language writing, it is largely North American in its provenance. It is also perhaps revealing that a leading American writer on the subject, in one of his later works, was persuaded to jettison a chapter on the theory of corporate responsibility, on the ground that it would be of interest only to a minority of readers ('professional philosophers').

---

1 On how to understand this term, see the discussion in Chapter 2 above. Thus the term 'organisation' is used generally and neutrally in this book to describe any entity comprised of human actors who are organised together in a purposeful way so as to give that entity a certain identity in the view of external observers. There is, confusingly perhaps, a temptation to refer descriptively to such organisational entities as 'non-human actors' even though they are made up of human beings. But the term 'non-human' is still useful as a shorthand description of a main distinction between 'individual' human and organisational actors. Already, therefore, we are beset by definitional agonising!

2 As demonstrated by the typological discussion in the previous chapter.

3 See, for instance, the anthology edited by Larry May and Stacey Hoffman: *Collective Responsibility: Five Decades of Debate in Theoretical and Applied Ethics* (Rowman and Littlefield, 1991). The papers here consider the role of a number of actors, ranging through the corporation, the State, governments, professional associations and crowds. On a point of epistemological description: is this a work of 'moral philosophy' or (in the words of the editors) 'theoretical and applied ethics'?

The author's discussion then proceeded on the assumption that corporations *were* morally responsible actors.[4]

Nonetheless, any debate concerning the appropriate allocation of responsibility to organisational actors requires a clear sense of *why* and *how* an entity may be regarded as a responsible agent. It is also important to recognise that the discussion requires a clear anchorage in terms of epistemological location. In particular, we need to be aware of the possibility that the same subject matter may be discussed as a matter of both *moral agency* and *legal personality*, and that it is not difficult or indeed uncommon for these two dimensions of the subject to be debated independently. For instance, much of the writing on the subject in the context of philosophy, business studies or IR is predominantly concerned with an *ethical* dimension in that the corporate or organisational actor is investigated as a potential moral agent, accountable in terms of ethical rather than legal norms.[5] On the other hand, jurists and legal writers would naturally think in terms of responsibility as derived from the norms of a legal order, and use such legal ordering as a term of reference, whatever the relationship, if any, of the relevant legal norms to any moral principles. Discussion within such epistemological boundaries and in particular the way in which legal discourse may be carried out in a self-contained fashion is well illustrated by the dictum of Hans Kelsen, arising from a discussion of criminal responsibility:

> Can a criminal delict be imputed to a juristic person? ... Imputation to a juristic person is a juristic construction, not the description of a natural reality. It is therefore not necessary to make the hopeless attempt to demonstrate that the juristic person is a real being, not a legal fiction, in order to prove that delicts and especially crimes can be imputed to a juristic person.[6]

---

4 Thomas Donaldson, *The Ethics of International Business* (Oxford University Press, 1989), at p. xii.

5 See for instance the approach taken in the two edited collections: May and Hoffman, note 3 above; and Toni Erskine (ed.), *Can Institutions Have Responsibilities? Collective Moral Agency and International Relations* (Palgrave Macmillan, 2003).

6 Hans Kelsen, *General Theory of Law and State* (Russell and Russell, 1945), at pp. 104–5. Kelsen here uses the term 'juristic person' to refer to an entity which comes into *legal* existence through a constitutive legal act: typically, for instance, a company via the relevant legal process of incorporation.

A different position will be taken in this discussion, however: it will be argued that we cannot understand fully the allocation of criminal responsibility to different types of actor without an appreciation of the sociological and ethical underpinning of that process of legal ascription. Admittedly in one sense criminal responsibility is a matter of law and what may be decided through legal rules within any particular legal order. In a Kelsenian 'pure' legal world, it is for international law to decide that States are the primary form of legal person, while national legal orders say the same of the human individual, and there the matter ends. But to leave the discussion at that point does not in any way enable us to understand how or why the two legal orders seek to manage the issue differently or, more generally, what informs any decision regarding the identification of an entity as an agent and the ascription of responsibility, or kinds of responsibility, to an agent. The basis for the discussion here will therefore not be juristic, but more broadly philosophical and will involve some exploration of our understanding of agency and responsibility in the widest sense, before moving on to consider more specifically the ascription of legal and criminal responsibility in Chapters 4 and 5.

This is not to say, though, that we should engage in what Kelsen describes as the 'hopeless' task of attempting to demonstrate the 'reality' of the juristic (or non-human, organisational, corporate) person. We might agree with Kelsen that in one sense the question of the reality of different actors is the subject of an endless ontological debate. On the other hand, there is a certain empirical starting point for discussion in the observable phenomena of persons in social interaction, either as individuals *per se* or as individuals acting within organisational structures. Moreover, organisational structures are as real as the human individuals who act within them.[7] The task then is to interpret this *real social activity* in terms of agency and to decide how far we may meaningfully proceed in the identification of organisational agency for purposes of the attribution of responsibility.

---

7   As Bertolet argues: the statement 'Pegasus is a winged horse' does not refer to something which does not exist (a winged horse) but to a Greek myth; statements 'about Pegasus' can have a meaning which is independent of the existential status of Pegasus itself (Rod Bertolet, 'Reference, Fiction, and Fictions', 60 (1984), *Synthese*, at p. 433).

2 Actors and identities: reality and social ascription

As already noted, theoretical discussion of agency in the social sciences tends to be beset by an inconsistent use of conceptual vocabulary, which in turn obscures the substance of the debate. In particular, in much of the discussion a distinction is not always explicitly or consistently drawn between two kinds of social action, between 'action' and 'agency', although this distinction is frequently at the basis of a good deal of the argument. This lack of clarity is not surprising when the definition of 'agent' is often given as 'one who acts', so that action and agency are then sometimes used interchangeably and loosely.

For purposes of the following discussion, it is suggested that a distinction be drawn between an entity as an *actor* and an entity as an *agent*. The basis of this distinction resides in different ways of viewing and talking about action: on the one hand, to do so descriptively, as a matter of empirical observation; then, on the other hand, to do so interpretatively, by assigning meaning and purpose to the action in question. In this way we can talk about an *actor* as an empirically observable fact, as in, for example: 'the man made a speech'; 'the government issued an ultimatum'; or 'the company made a bid'. But then we might invest these factual observations with particular meaning and in doing so use the language of *agency* in that the actions become purposeful and consequential, and so calling for some evaluation. Thus the observable facts could be coloured with meaning, for instance of the following kinds: 'the man made a *defamatory* speech'; 'the government issued an ultimatum *that it would declare war*'; 'the company made a bid *so as to effect a merger with the other company*'. Here, we have moved on to an interpretation of action within various normative contexts, rendering the actor purposeful within a context of established expectations, and in this sense we often refer to the matter as one of agency rather than simple action.

Such a distinction lurks in much of the theoretical literature. For instance, it would appear to equate with the following classification made by French:

> It is important to distinguish three quite different notions of what constitutes personhood that are entangled in our tradition: the metaphysical, moral and legal concepts.[8]

---

8 Peter A. French (1979) 'The Corporation as a Moral Person', *American Philosophical Quarterly*, 16: 207; reprinted as Chapter 9 in Larry May and Stacey Hoffman, *Collective Responsibility*, note 3 above, at pp. 133–4.

Although French is here using the term 'personhood', 'person' and 'agent' are often used to cover much the same, and what is of particular interest is his reference to three domains of action. French does not himself expand very much on the definition of the metaphysical, but it would seem to convey a basic and non-evaluative sense of action, of the actor simply as an intelligent and rational person (thus defined as 'agent' in his terminology). French's term would appear to correspond for instance with Dennett's understanding of metaphysical as 'roughly the notion of an intelligent, conscious, feeling agent',[9] or in another context, with John Rawls' idea of a party in 'the original position' (a kind of pre-moral and pre-legal position).[10]

French's moral and legal personhood on the other hand clearly refers to the actor in a more responsive sense, since the action gives rise to accountability within some kind of normative context. In Dennett's explanation, this is the 'moral notion', or 'roughly the notion of an agent who is accountable';[11] or, in Locke's language, this is personhood as 'a forensic term, appropriating actions and their merit'.[12] Thus, if A kills B, in a metaphysical sense this is simply a rational and intelligent action on the part of A. In a moral or legal sense, or in terms of A's moral or legal agency, the act of killing is further qualified in relation to moral or legal norms, no doubt as a prohibited or wrongful act in those contexts of agency. What is fruitful in this classification is the description of agency in terms of contexts or domains of action, which colour and characterise our interpretation of the metaphysical action, and so bequeath on the actor different identities.

There is no set number of such domains of activity or, as we may say, types of agency – we may go beyond the moral and legal, for instance to talk also in terms of 'political' agency[13] or agency

---

9 Daniel Dennett, 'Conditions of Personhood', Chapter 7 in Amélie Oksenberg Rorty (ed.), *The Identity of Persons* (University of California Press, 1976), p. 176.

10 See for instance: John Rawls, *A Theory of Justice* (Harvard University Press, 1971), at p. 146.

11 Dennett, 'Conditions of Personhood', note 9 above, at p. 176.

12 John Locke, *An Essay Concerning Human Understanding*, Book II, Chapter XXVII.

13 In international relations discourse, for instance, action may well be evaluated in terms of political principles which may be very different from and independent of legal or moral norms.

within some religious order.[14] It is useful to see action in terms of these normative domains, since to do so uncovers the fundamental question of this discussion: whether an actor in the metaphysical sense may qualify as a moral or legal agent in the sense of being able to respond to moral or legal norms. This is clearly not the 'hopeless' question of whether the State or the company are *real* actors, agents or persons. Rather it is the question of whether, as actors, they are capable of moral or legal accountability and so achieve identity as a moral person or agent, or legal person or agent. This discussion will therefore proceed on the assumption that entities such as States and companies are real in the sense that they may be empirically observed as actors of some kind. The problem is then that of establishing the criteria for their moral or legal agency or identity.

In talking about different kinds of agency or identity in this sense, it should be appreciated that no one kind of agency is logically and formally dependent on or derived from another. French, for example, refers[15] to the way in which some theorists, such as Locke, have assumed some primacy for the juristic concept of personhood, perhaps because in the legal domain the concept of personality and accountability is highly developed. But in a formal sense, these normative domains are independent of each other (indeed as legal positivists assert in relation to the legal domain). However, in an empirical, or it may be said sociological sense, they may well, and do, interact. For instance, for practical and social scientific purposes, we may need to enquire about the 'moral basis' or 'political legitimacy' of a particular law. Conversely, we may describe something as politically necessary or wise, though morally or legally questionable. It is then important to recognise this *cohabitation* of normative domains,[16] especially for purposes of discussing responsibility, where discussion of the desirability of or need for legal responsibility may be influenced by arguments concerning moral responsibility. In this way, as French asserts,[17] a discussion of moral agency will therefore usually come before one of legal agency.

---

14 Thus an act of killing may be independently a breach of a broad moral code, the law of a particular legal order and religious norms, as set down for instance in the Old Testament or the Koran.

15 French, 'The Corporation as a Moral Person', note 8 above.

16 This may be seen as a way of short-cutting the large debate on the relationship of law and morality; it is, rather, to recognise that there is an important relation, without further probing the ramifications of that relationship at the present point.

17 French, note 8 above, at p. 134.

Once we have this clearer sense of what is involved in the idea of either moral or legal agency (or, acting within the moral and legal domains) – that is, the idea of the agent as an accountable actor – the concept of responsibility appears central. For, then, the search for moral or legal agency is the search for the morally or legally responsible actor, and more specifically the criteria for saying that an actor is thus responsible. Within that broader quest, we can then locate the main concern of the present discussion – whether an organisational entity may qualify as a moral or legal agent, as a basis for the use of criminal responsibility in relation to such actors.

The outcome and ramifications of identifying an entity as a responsible actor will be further considered in the following chapters. More immediately, the test of such agency needs to be more fully explored and first of all it would be useful to say something more about the ontology of persons and the longstanding debate between proponents of individualism and holism.

3 Does an organisation possess agency? 'Individualism' versus 'holism'

Let us return for a moment to the ontological issue of seeking to identify a 'real' person, the *ding an sich*, in the discussion of social action. In a society which appears, at least at first sight, to be made up of individual human beings, it may be easy to take for granted the 'reality' of human actors and the 'unreality' of non-human actors, such as corporate entities, as the constructions of human enterprise. Such is the assumption of the school of thought usually referred to as individualism.

As a philosophical tradition and as guiding principle in social scientific research, individualism is well entrenched in Western thought. The primacy which it allocates to the role of the individual human being in society is rooted in both intuition and empirical observation, viewing organisational and collective activity as the product of human action and so always reducible to human activity. It is an approach that appeals in particular to the practical lawyerly mind, and is displayed frequently in judicial opinion. A classic statement is the following dictum of a British judge:

The artificial legal person called the corporation has no physical existence. It exists only in contemplation of law. It has neither body, parts, nor passions. It cannot wear weapons or serve in the wars. It can be neither loyal, nor disloyal. It cannot compass treason. It can be neither friend nor enemy. Apart from its corporators it can have neither thoughts, wishes, nor intentions, for it has no mind other than the minds of the corporators.[18]

Or, to quote another leading British judge, in a more recent (and less militaristic) opinion:

a reference to the company 'as such' might suggest that there is something out there called the company of which one can meaningfully say that it can or cannot do something. There is in fact no such thing as the company as such, no ding an sich, only the applicable rules. To say that a company cannot do something, means only that there is no one whose doing of that act would, under the applicable rules of attribution, count as the act of the company.[19]

These statements reveal a commitment to an anthropocentric sense of identity, dependent upon the characteristic human qualities of intellect and emotion, and also a reluctance to escape from the 'trap' of human construction of corporate persons. Certainly for purposes of legal argument, therefore, the individualist view remains dominant. The outcome has been summarised by Dan-Cohen in the depiction of the individual human being as 'the paradigmatic legal actor, in whose image the law is shaped and then applied to corporations and other entities',[20] while Wells has commented that 'the extent to which stereotypes of criminal behaviour rely on images of individual offenders is nowhere seen more clearly than in the doctrinal explanations of the criminal law.'[21] In the context of criminal responsibility, it remains for many lawyers self-evident that the criminal actor is a human individual and that criminality is a

---

18 Buckley L.J. (dissenting) in the Court of Appeal, in *Continental Tyre and Rubber Co. v. Daimler* (1915) 1 QB 893, at p. 916.
19 Lord Hoffmann, for the Privy Council, in *Meridian Global Funds Management Asia Ltd v Securities Commission* (1995) 2 AC 500, at pp. 506–7. See also: H.L.A. Hart, *Definition and Theory in Jurisprudence* (Clarendon Press, 1950), at p. 21.
20 Meir Dan-Cohen, *Rights, Persons and Organizations* (University of California Press, 1986), at p. 13.
21 Celia Wells, *Corporations and Criminal Responsibility* (2nd edn, Oxford University Press, 2001), at p. 63.

human characteristic which cannot be meaningfully used in relation to non-human entities, which possess neither emotion nor rationality in the human sense.

In philosophical terms, the main opposing school of thought is commonly referred to as 'holism'. The main terms of the debate between individualism and holism are neatly summarised in this account given some time ago by Brodbeck:

Can 'crowd hysteria' be defined in terms of individual behaviors or is it an undefinable quality of the crowd itself? The denial that there are such undefinable group properties or such superentities is the view usually known as *methodological individualism.* Its contradictory is *metaphysical holism.* It is called 'holism' because its proponents generally maintain that there are so-called wholes, group entities which have undefinable properties of their own. The property of the whole is thus also said to be emergent from the properties of its parts ... Philosophically, the holist assumption that there are group properties over and above the individuals making up the group, their properties and the relations among them is counter to empiricism. For the latter holds that all terms must ultimately refer to what is observable, directly or indirectly, and that what we observe are people and their characteristics, not supraindividual groups and their characteristics ... Culturally, holism is intimately connected with hostility toward the liberal political individualism of the Western tradition. If 'states' have wills and purposes of their own ... who is to divulge the 'will of the state'? The answers are, alas, only too familiar. The will and wisdom of the state reside in a privileged class or caste.[22]

From this account, we can then deduce three main objections to the holist argument. First, there is a logical objection: groups or organisations are necessarily formed and operated by human individuals. Secondly, there is an empirical objection: we observe, in reality, humans in action in groups. And thirdly, there is a cultural and in some senses an ethical objection: to talk in terms of a collective will invites the risk of an undemocratic abuse of power.

This overview of attempts to resolve the issue of the corporate actor in terms of traditional oppositional individualism and holism should

---

22 May Brodbeck (1958), 'Methodological Individualisms: Definition and Reduction', *Philosophy of Science*, 25(1): 3–4.

illustrate the limitations of a dogmatic approach. The philosophical opposition between these two approaches has its parallel in the juristic debate on legal personality, as between adherents of the 'fiction' theory and those following the 'realist' theory (to be explored in the next chapter), while also shadowing major dividing lines in the sociological debates already referred to in Chapter 2 above. This opposition in argument presents a major stumbling block for progress in this discussion. But on the other hand, an approach which recognises the dynamic character of individual human interaction within organisational structure may enable us to penetrate more clear-headedly the conundrum of organisational agency.

4 Human interaction as a key to organisational agency

A way out of the individualist–holist impasse may be, first, to shake off the anthropocentric mindset which pictures organisational agency as a derivative form, in some way aping human agency, and secondly, to recognise nonetheless the significant contribution of human *interactions* to the emergence of organisational agency. On the one hand, then, Fisse and Braithwaite, drawing upon Michael McDonald's 'personless paradigm',[23] urge that:

> Granted, corporations lack human feelings and emotions, but this hardly disqualifies them from possessing the quality of autonomy. On the contrary, the lack of emotions and feelings promote rather than hinder considered rational choice and in this respect the corporation may indeed be a paradigm responsible actor.[24]

Then, it should also be recognised that the process of organisation in itself, and of individuals engaging in a group activity, may generate an autonomous activity which does not have to be identified either in anthropocentric terms, or as just the sum of its parts. This argument is concisely expressed by May and Hoffman:

---

23   Michael McDonald (1987) 'The Personless Paradigm', *University of Toronto Law Journal*, 37: 212.

24   Brent Fisse and John Braithwaite, *Corporations, Crime and Accountability* (Cambridge University Press, 1993), pp. 30–31.

The decision-making capacity of certain groups melds the individual intentions into a corporate intention that is often different from the intentions of any of the members of the group. In addition, while the corporation cannot act except through its individual members, these acts are not understandable unless they are conceptualized as part of a larger process. Because act and intention are best attributed to the group and not to the individual members, responsibility can also be attributed to the whole group.[25]

Or, as Galbraith has concisely expressed the idea: 'From [the] interpersonal exercise of power, the interaction ... of the participants, comes the *personality* of the corporation.'[26]

In this way, a convincing argument for identifying a distinct organisational agency may be based upon an organisational or group rationality, a rationality of a different kind and character from that associated with individual human actors, but deriving from a structure of human interactions. Such a view of organisational action allows for the emergence of an organisational autonomy, despite the organisation having necessarily been established, and operated, through human action. This approach combines the force of both holist and individualist argument. On the one hand, it requires an effort of imagination which conceptualises rationality and action in a non-human form. But it also acknowledges the human contribution to the construction of this different kind of agent. It visualises the metamorphosis of the 'collective of individuals' into

25 Larry May and Stacey Hoffman (eds), *Collective Responsibility*, note 3 above, 'Introduction', at p. 3. Indeed, this part of the argument draws very usefully on May's contribution to the debate, and his ideas on the subject are perhaps most fully presented in his *The Morality of Groups: Collective Responsibility, Group-Based Harm and Corporate Rights* (University of Notre Dame Press, 1987). May, in turn, in working out his 'middle position' (between individualist and holist argument), draws upon Richard De George (1983) 'Social Reality and Social Relations', *The Review of Metaphysics*, 37: 3 and David Copp (1984) 'What Collectives Are: Agency, Individualism and Legal Theory', *Dialogue*, 23: 253; (1979) 'Collective Actions and Secondary Actions', *American Philosophical Quarterly*, 16: 177.
26 John Kennedy Galbraith, *The Age of Uncertainty* (BBC/Andre Deutsch, 1977), p. 261.

the 'corporate', or, in French's terminology, from the 'aggregate' into the 'conglomerate'.[27]

Let us take a relatively straightforward example of how this kind of transformation may occur. Assume that a scholar, working for a university, has an idea for a research project. At this initial stage, it is very much an individual enterprise, dependent on the ambition, intention and action of this one person. But after some reflection, she decides that the project could be better achieved in collaboration with a second scholar. This second person is willing to collaborate, so the research proceeds as a joint project, melding their ideas and knowledge, already acquiring then a team character. They then decide that the project could be further developed with the participation of a range of other experts, spread around the world, and also aided by financial support from a research funding body. There are then negotiations with a publisher for publication of the research findings, so that the whole project has become transformed into a large collective enterprise with a number of participants and 'stakeholders' with interests of different kinds in the success of the project. The ultimate form of the project is thereby transformed and no longer dependent on the contribution or wishes of any one individual participant, but upon an amalgam of the interests and actions of a range of actors within the overall enterprise. The project will require a representative management and direction, which will reflect the joint contribution and the support provided from a number of sources, whether directly participant or as stakeholders. Although originating in and based upon the initiative of one person, the activity has been transformed into a collective enterprise with its own momentum, character and objectives which transcend that original foundation. The originator may remain a key participant and driving force; but equally, in the event of some disagreement, the founder could be expelled and the project continue in her absence.[28] The collective interest has taken over from the original individual interest.

---

27 See in particular: Peter A. French, *Collective and Corporate Responsibility* (Columbia University Press, 1984). French's work has proven to be an influential challenge to the 'anthropocentric bias' of the individualist position, and centres upon a distinction between an aggregate collectivity as 'merely a collection of people', and a conglomerate collectivity, which is 'not exhausted by the conjunction of the identities of the persons in the organization'.

28 There are examples of, for instance, business entrepreneurs or political leaders who have subsequently been ousted from companies or political

This example could be extended by analogy to numerous other contexts, and should serve to illustrate the genesis and development of many types of organisation, whether business, cultural, political, religious or of other kind. A way of understanding this process of 'organisation emergence' is to view the matter in terms of the interaction and contribution of individuals: each contributes and thereby helps to fashion eventually a distinctive whole. The only mystery in the process is the location of the 'tipping point', at which the balance shifts from an individual (one or more) to collective centre of gravity, or, to express the matter another way, at which the collective identity 'takes control' of the enterprise. This is the point at which any individual participant, including any leading initiators for the enterprise, in effect have to concede that the collective view will now prevail.

A useful interpretation of the way in which organisational identity may be achieved is provided by Coleman when he referred to the 'irrelevance of persons'.[29] This idea conveys the fact that particular individuals have become irrelevant to the survival or operation of an organisation; what is important is that the organisation has positions which can be filled by suitably qualified individuals. The significant leap forward in social terms is the 'social invention which created a structure that was independent of particular persons and consisted only of positions'.[30] Thus, whatever the arrival and departure of particular individuals as office-holder (whether it be president, CEO, club chairman, general secretary, reigning monarch, vice-chancellor, head of department), however charismatic such individuals may be, the endurance of the organisation through changes of individual membership may be evidence of a separate identity. Moreover, this

---

organisations which they have founded, and serving then as dramatic examples of this process of corporate maturing. Or, as a slightly different illustration of the same point, Anita Roddick, having established and developed the successful 'ethical' business The Body Shop, endorsed the sale of the company to L'Oréal, thereby, in the view of some, jeopardising its future commitment in that respect.

29 James S. Coleman, *The Asymmetric Society: Organizational Actors, Corporate Power and the Irrelevance of Persons* (Syracuse University Press, 1982).

30 *Ibid.*, at p. 29. Perhaps an interesting test case for this process, when it may be argued that a particular individual human membership remains decisive regarding the identity of the whole, is provided by the rock group. Could the Beatles, or Queen, ever be anything than their original members? *Sed quaere* The Rolling Stones.

identity may also manifest itself as a controlling ethos in relation to the conduct of individual members, who may then act out an organisational role different from their 'natural' role as individuals. May has asserted, for instance, that:

> Sociologists have also documented the fact that members of highly structured organizations develop different norms and mores as organization members than they would hold, or do hold, outside of a given organizational setting. Gordon Donaldson and Jay W. Lorsch contend that 'all of the beliefs of each company are a tightly interrelated system' which is best characterized as a 'fabric' or pattern of beliefs 'which do not exist in isolation as discrete principles. Rather they are closely interwoven in managers' thought processes'. Donaldson and Lorsch explain that this 'fabric' of beliefs has a very strong impact on any manager that comes under the sway of a given company's organizational structure.[31]

We shall return later to these ideas of both enduring structure and controlling ethos, in the discussion of criteria of organisational identity and agency. For present purposes they may be retained in mind as outcomes of this social phenomenon of individual interaction. Here, in short, we are referring to a crucial synergy through which two plus two are indeed equal to five. It cannot happen without that essential human individual participation and interaction. But the latter may acquire its own momentum and energy, and this remains in some ways a 'mysterious' part of the process, since it may be planned or unplanned. For example, what we now know as the European Union was not planned as such in 1957. The individual founding Members States did not establish the organisation as something *sui generis*, which would at some point begin to determine its own identity, irrespective of what any of the Member States might feel about the matter. How the EU was able to achieve what is now recognised as a distinctive identity as an international organisation remains a metaphysical matter, for instance, evidenced by rather than resulting

---

31 Larry May, *The Morality of Groups*, note 25 above, at p. 68, referring to Gordon Donaldson and Jay W. Lorsch, *Decision Making at the Top: The Shaping of Strategic Decision* (Basic Books, 1983), pp. 81–82. On the impact of a controlling corporate ethos, see also the discussion of research by Maurice Punch, in *Dirty Business: Exploring Corporate Misconduct* (Sage, 1996), Chapter 5.

from transformative judgments of the European Court of Justice.[32] But this provides a nice example of component interactions producing something more than the sum of their parts.

5 The criteria of organisational agency (and of organisations)

What has been done so far has been to sketch a possible theoretical foundation for asserting a distinctive organisational identity, as a basis for the moral and legal agency of organisational actors separate from that of their individual human components. Having made a case for showing how such agency may come about, as a result of individual interaction within the organisational structure, the question remains of how to identify such agency in particular cases. What are the grounds, for example, on which it may be asserted (as some writers have done) that such agency may be found in the case of the corporation[33] but not a crowd,[34] or in the case of the State but not the nation?[35] Put another way, when more precisely do the interactions referred to above result in a condition of agency, in the sense of a capacity to respond to norms and so be regarded as a *responsible* actor?

Those writers who have turned their attention to issues of individual and collective action and responsibility have tended to focus on criteria relating to structure and rationality in any attempt to justify a separate collective or group agency and responsibility. Larry May usefully summarises much of the debate in saying that:

---

32 On the evolution of the EU's novel legal identity, see: Christopher Harding, 'Legal Subjectivity as a Fundamental Value: The Emergence of Non-State Actors in Europe', Chapter 8 in Kim Economides *et al.* (eds), *Fundamental Values* (Hart Publishing, 2000).

33 For instance, among others, Peter A. French, 'The Corporation as a Moral Person', note 8 above.

34 For instance, Stanley Bates (1971) 'The Responsibility of "Random Collections"', *Ethics*, 81, reprinted as Chapter 7 of May and Hoffman, note 3 above. Larry May draws some detailed distinctions between crowds and mobs, in *The Morality of Groups*, note 25 above, Chapters 2–4.

35 For instance, Toni Erskine, 'Assigning Responsibilities to Institutional Moral Agents: the Case of States and "Quasi-States"', p. 25 in Erskine (ed.), note 5 above.

In contemporary moral theory and social philosophy, the prevailing wisdom is that it only makes sense to talk about collective action when the members of a group are linked by means of a strong organizational apparatus, and where the individual acts can be directed through some explicit decision-making structure.[36]

In argument that has become a reference point for much of the discussion, Peter French has drawn a key distinction between the 'aggregate' and the 'conglomerate' as collective actors, in order to argue for the attribution of agency to the latter but not the former. For French, the conglomerate group actor is more than a sum of its parts, and this is indicated by a decision-making capacity and an identity over time – this enables the collectivity to be regarded as an intentional actor in a way that is distinct from its human components. French states, for instance:

> I shall argue ... that a Corporation's *Internal Decision* Structure (its CID Structure) is the requisite redescription device that licenses the predication of corporate intentionality.[37]

The approach taken by French has been influential. For instance, taking up the issue of institutional agency in the context of IR discussion, Erskine has based herself on French, although also adding to his list of criteria:

> I want to suggest a related criterion that is implicit in the way French requires agents to conceive of themselves as having an identity over time: to be candidates for moral agency, collectivities must be self-asserting ... [to have] a conception of itself as a unit.[38]

(As an aside, a point which may be made now about the emphasis on a collective rationality in much of this argument concerns the way in which 'collectivists' appear to be often haunted by an

---

36 May, *The Morality of Groups,* note 25 above, at p. 32.
37 French, 'The Corporation as a Moral Person', note 8 above, at p. 141. French's key text in this argument is *Collective and Corporate Responsibility,* note 27 above.
38 Erskine, 'Assigning Responsibilities to Institutional Moral Agents', note 35 above, p. 24.

anthropocentric paradigm of rationality, so that French, for example, in using the concept of the CID Structure, appears to be imputing to the corporation something very much analogous to the human mind. May, on the other hand, usefully suggests, as we have seen, that the individual interactions within a group structure may produce a rationality which is quite different from that of any of the individual human components. Certainly, it would seem preferable to avoid human metaphors (especially of mind, soul and body) in this debate.)

Clearly, however, much of this argument provides a useful ground for the enterprise of establishing criteria of organisational agency. At the very least, there must be a sense of enduring structure and a capacity for rationality and intention. Erskine's criterion of self-awareness – the organisation's conception of itself as a unit – is also helpful, in contributing a distinctive sense of identity. But it will be argued here that a useful approach would be to organise these criteria of agency into two main types, one relating to *structure and capacity for autonomous action*, and the other relating to *role*.

(a) Structure and capacity for autonomous action

The identity of a separate (and therefore autonomous) organisational actor and agent naturally requires elements of recognisable and stable structure. This is necessary for purposes of recognising the organisational actor in the 'real' or material world, and to give cohesion to its role as an actor. This is the element which links together the individual human components of the organisation in purposeful activity, supplying an overall infrastructure of persons, other material elements, and a network of relations. It is this which, in the argument of a number of writers, would serve to distinguish, for instance, the corporation from the crowd or random collectivity. Such a structure also implies something like French's internal decision-making process, as a necessary prerequisite for purposeful action and outcomes. Once we have a sense of an enduring structure of this kind, the identification of many of the widely agreed candidates for moral or legal agency follows quite swiftly: various types of corporation, the State, non-governmental organisations, and intergovernmental organisations. But also, more 'informal' and delinquent organisations might be considered as agents in this way, since certain types of criminal and terrorist organisation in practice may possess sophisticated structural and decision-making features and an enduring character. The decision-making process is an essential but not sufficient part of this element of agency, for it needs to be located within a recognisable material and representational infrastructure in order for the agent to relate fully to other actors and act purposefully. In crude terms, the State requires territory as well as a constitution;[39] the company requires a logo and premises as well as its board of directors; and a university requires a timetable and curricula as well as its charter. In another sense, such an identifiable infrastructure also contributes to what is referred to as more than the sum of the individual human parts of the organisation, since it is that which brings together those parts and provides the opportunity for some kind of collective expression. This package of structural conditions therefore comprises what various writers have listed as a decision-making process, organisational apparatus, and an identity over time, characterised by an irrelevance of persons (in Coleman's terms), and producing a functional autonomy of action.

(b) Role criteria

Thus far in this discussion of organisational agency, two basic questions have been addressed: *how* such agency may come about, and *what form* it may take. This, however, leaves another important question: *why?* Or, this last question may be rephrased as, what purposes are served by such organisational agency? This takes the discussion into a consideration of something that is missing from the focus on structural criteria – an examination of the role of the organisation.

Naturally, any organisation is established for defined purposes (typically, for instance, governance in the case of the State, economic activity in the case of the company) and perceived as an appropriate and efficient form for carrying out such purposes. Another way of expressing these self-evident points is to say that organisations represent certain interests, and may do so *more effectively* than individuals acting alone, or even as a collective unit (a Frenchian 'aggregate') without the distinct identity which has the been the subject of the preceding discussion. The advantage of stressing this *representational* aspect of organisational identity, and including it as one of the criteria of organisational agency, is that it enables us to

---

39 It is interesting then to compare such criteria with the normally listed attributes of statehood, for purposes of legal personality under international law: territory, population, government and a capacity to enter into relations (the famous list in the Montevideo Convention on the Rights and Duties of States 1933).

appreciate on the one hand what might be described as the driving force and ethos of the organisation, and on the other hand how the organisation may present itself as a *legitimate* actor in relation to others. Governments of States may justify their existence by asserting that they are in the best position to protect the interests of their citizens.[40] Companies may assert the same regarding their shareholders, universities likewise for their students and academic staff, trade unions and professional associations for their members, NGOs for the special interests they represent, and intergovernmental institutions for their State members. Thus enquiry into the role of organisations, and in particular into their representation of certain interests, provides a further clue regarding the transition from individual to collective and organisational action. When the commonplace observation is made that the world is increasingly dominated by organisations, this is to some extent a reflection of the complexity of life which renders sensible working together in groups rather than individually. Organisational agency is then a reflection of the need for collective activity, and then perhaps the allocation of responsibility at the group rather than the individual level.

It may be that such role criteria coincide with what Erskine has referred to as the organisation's conception of itself as a unit, if this may be seen as a self-awareness arising from the organisation's sense of its own mission. This more purposive element of identity also provides some substance or colour to the structural shell of the organisation discussed above. It helps us to understand the behaviour of the organisation in so far as this may be distinguished from that of any of its individual members. In this sense the collective role or mission may produce a culture or ethos, a pattern of behaviour and expectations within the organisational structure. This element of culture or ethos, as a further aspect of 'role identity', may be particularly helpful at the stage of discussing organisational responsibility, since it is something which may be used to inform an evaluation of collective or organisational behaviour, and how that may relate to the behaviour of the human actors within the organisation.

Thus it is being argued here that a combination of structural and role criteria enables us to identify an organisational actor as a moral or legal agent, in the sense that it would be appropriate and meaningful to consider such an entity responsible for certain actions,

---

40 Or at least this may be so in the context of democratic governance, within which governments are accountable to their citizens regarding the management of the latter's interests.

whereas it would not be appropriate to attach such responsibility to any individual human beings within the organisation. A point has been reached at which identity, agency and responsibility shift from human actors, either individually or cumulatively, to the organisational entity. For both ethical and practical reasons there is more sense in referring to the organisational actor rather than any of its individual members. This point of argument is nicely expressed by Virginia Held, saying about a collectivity that:

> judgments about the moral responsibility of its members are not logically derivable from judgments about the moral responsibility of a collectivity. 'The Democratic Party is morally responsible for the nomination of Humphrey,' and 'The United States is morally responsible for sending its planes to bomb North Vietnam,' may well be valid judgments, but from such judgments alone one cannot conclude that Democratic Party member M or U.S. political-system member N is morally responsible for the acts in question.[41]

As Held explains, an important reason for this ascription to the collectivity but not to the individual is identified by Gellner in arguing that reductionist translations from the collective to the individual would be 'clumsy, long and vague where the original statement about an institution … was clear, brief and intelligible'.[42] In Held's examples, the Democratic Party, acting as such, has both the functional ability and the role for purposes of selecting a presidential candidate, and the State, as such, possesses the same qualities for purposes of attacking another country. But it would not make sense to ascribe either action to either a single individual or to an aggregate of individuals.

Finally, the value of the structural and role criteria identified above may appear from some concrete examples which may be especially

41   Virginia Held (1970) 'Can a Random Collection of Individuals Be Morally Responsible?' *The Journal of Philosophy*, 68, reprinted as Chapter 6 in May and Hoffman (eds), *Collective Responsibility*, note 3 above, at p. 93. Her examples of course reflect an earlier age. Hubert Humphrey was the Democrats' presidential candidate in 1968. The Vietnam War naturally excited considerable debate in the late 1960s and early 1970s.
42   Ernest Gellner, 'Holism vs Individualism', in May Brodbeck (ed.), *Readings in the Philosophy of the Social Sciences* (Macmillan, 1968), at p. 258.

relevant to the issues of moral and criminal responsibility. Two cases may be taken: of the corporate business delinquent, and the governmental State delinquent.

Let us first take the statement that 'Company A decided to join an illegal price fixing cartel'. In the normal case, such a company would be a large corporate person, comprising a sophisticated structure of personnel with allocated roles, and decision-making procedures. While it may be true that a particular executive, marketing manager B, played an important role in discussing the details of prices with executives from other companies, it is unlikely that B's role in itself would be sufficient for the company to engage in the cartel. In the first place, membership of the cartel (with all that entails) is legally a corporate act of the whole company, not just B's agreement of certain prices. Secondly, there is a wider, corporate awareness of what it means to become involved in the cartel, and B's specific role is based on an organisational structure and policy. And thirdly, the price fixing arrangement serves the economic interests of the whole company, not B's personal interest (although B may incidentally benefit from his role, for instance through an increase in salary, or promotion). In this way, B is a cog in the system – necessary but nonetheless only a part of the whole machine. It may be appropriate to hold B accountable for his share in the action – his 'technical' role of participating in a meeting and calculating certain prices. But the membership of the cartel is a corporate matter, depending upon corporate identity, deliberation and action, and thus appropriately attributable to the company as such. As Galbraith expressed the matter:

> In the corporation, power must be shared. All but the most elementary decisions require the information, the specialised knowledge or experience of several or many people. It is a world .... where there are no great men, only great committees.[43]

Secondly, let us take the statement that 'State X decided to send its armed forces against State Y in an illegal act of force under international law'. Again, in the normal case, such a State would comprise a sophisticated structure of persons, in positions of governance, acting through procedures of governance. It may be true that a particular individual, General Z, the head of the armed forces of X, issued the command for those forces actually to be deployed against Y. But once

---

43 Galbraith, *The Age of Uncertainty*, note 26 above, at p. 259.

more, Z's order is a necessary but not sufficient element of the act of aggressive warfare. It is necessary to take into account the broader political and military infrastructure of activity, the broader official and governmental knowledge and awareness of the nature of the act, and the wider interests of the State, as distinct from any of Z's individual interests, which may have motivated this act of aggressive warfare. Once again, we should describe Z as an important cog in the system, who again may be appropriately accountable for a share of the illegal attack, but no more than that. The primary agency should be located within the organisational entity of the State, or at least the organs of governance of that State.

In both examples, a consideration of both the functional structure and the representational role of the company and the State supplies a convincing basis for talking about both as autonomous and responsible agents.

6 From agency to responsibility

At this stage it may be useful to reprise briefly this discussion of agency, before taking on the associated concept of responsibility. Agency is used here to refer to the situation of an actor capable of responding to relevant norms within a normative domain, such as the moral or the legal. The moral or legal agent is thus an appropriate bearer of responsibility within those domains. Whereas the individual human being is taken as the paradigm moral or legal agent, the qualifications of any organisational entity for such a role have been disputed, particularly on the basis of individualist argument that any claimed organisational agency reduces to that of its individual human components. This is the basic conundrum of organisational agency: how can an organisation, originating in and composed of human actors, be regarded separately from those human components? Yet at the same time a great deal of activity may only be understood in terms of organisational action. A persuasive argument in favour of distinct organisational agency may be grounded on the idea of such agency as the outcome of human interactions within an organisational structure. The resulting agency would be identifiable with reference to structural criteria on the one hand (notably an enduring decision-making capacity and an infrastructure of autonomous action) and role criteria on the other hand (indicative in particular of distinctive representative role). Such criteria would explain the candidature of certain key organisations in contemporary society for some kind of moral and legal agency – the State, the corporation (business or otherwise), representative non-governmental organisations, and intergovernmental bodies, among others. It will also have been noticed that this identification of the organisational agent dovetails with the sociological definition of organisation put forward in Chapter 2. A convincing theory of agency and responsibility requires a sound sociological basis for purposes of the moral and legal ascription of responsibility.

Chapter 4

Legal routes to responsibility

Having provided some kind of definition and typology of organisation in social terms, and suggested some criteria for the moral and legal agency of organisational actors, it is next necessary to examine the ways in which either individuals or organisations might be held legally accountable and criminally responsible as a matter of legal process. At this stage the argument may start to appear quite tricky, as we move into normative territory. The important point to grasp is that, whether we are talking about individuals or organisations, there may be different routes by which either may be taken to the point of some kind of legal accountability. On the one hand, an individual may be seen acting simply as an individual and judged accordingly. This would lead to what might be termed 'classic' individual responsibility, based simply on an evaluation of that individual acting alone. The same may happen to an organisation, once that organisation's moral and legal agency has been established. This is to deal with the individual qua *individual, or the organisation* qua *organisation. But matters may not be so simple. An individual may also act as part of a group which does not itself qualify as a single organisational actor. An organisation may do the same, although perhaps less frequently, but we could refer for instance to the examples of companies acting as part of a cartel, or States acting within an alliance, or Mafia families combining in a loose federation. This raises the question of some kind of collective responsibility, whereby the individual members of the group are ultimately held responsible as individuals, but their responsibility is based upon membership of the group. Two main forms of collective responsibility may be identified. The first arises simply from membership and leads to an imputed responsibility for each member in respect of the acts of other members or of the group as a whole. A historical example is the Norman frank-pledge system. This is sometimes referred to as a 'collective' or 'vicarious' responsibility and in modern criminal justice is frequently open to ethical objection. The second form arises from involvement in the group and a contribution to the group's enterprise and is rather a 'distributed' responsibility for that contribution to the collective act. Feinberg describes this as 'the responsibility of individuals in joint undertakings'. This kind of responsibility has become significant in contemporary legal process, for instance in the form of the 'joint criminal enterprise' and in the context of cartel regulation, and is examined in more detail later. All this leaves us with three main contemporary routes to legal responsibility: individual as individual, organisation as organisation, and individual (or perhaps organisation) as a participant in some collective or group activity.*

I Moving into a legal landscape

So far our discussion has traced the idea of organisational action through its sociological aspects and then through the ethical arguments relating to the attribution of agency to an organisational actor, bearing in mind all the while the conundrum that human individuals remain a necessary constituent of such organisations. Building upon the view that those collectivities with a degree of social cohesion and purposiveness, which then satisfy in ethical terms criteria relating to structure and role, may be sensibly attributed agency for moral and legal purposes, it is next necessary to examine the way in which such agency may be used in the calculation of legal responsibility. In this part of the exercise it must be remembered that the context remains one where the choice between individual and organisational responsibility lies in a situation in which individual and organisational actions are interactive: individuals contribute to organisational action and the existence of organisation has an impact on individual conduct. This circular process of interaction (Figure 4.1) should thus inform the way in which legal responsibility may be allocated between individual and organisational agents.

Also, it should be remembered that the step from that of identifying agency to that of allocating responsibility necessarily involves the exercise of a choice. The discussion of agency has led us to identify two principal types of agent in contemporary social life: the individual and the organisation. Decisions regarding responsibility relate to the accountability of one or the other, or both, for purposes of applying norms: which is more appropriately answerable for breaches of norms

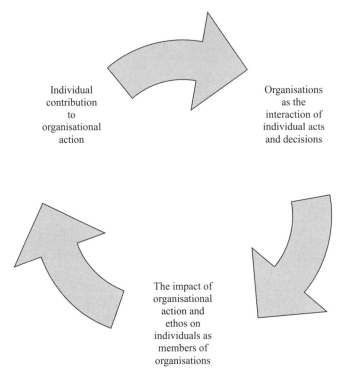

Individual
contribution
to
organisational
action

Organisations
as the
interaction of
individual acts
and decisions

The impact of
organisational
action and
ethos on
individuals as
members of
organisations

Figure 4.1 The interaction of individuals and organisations and the construction of organisational identity

and standards, so becoming the site for the application of sanctions and other measures? It may be helpful to think of the making of this choice as opting for a particular *route to responsibility*. Such routes will lead ultimately to one of two destinations, either individual or organisational responsibility, based upon the two paradigms of agency. But, as will be explained below, there may be more than one route to these two destinations, leading through a map of organisational activity and reflecting the actual complexity of the spectrum of individual and collective action. In particular, there is more than one route to the destination of individual responsibility and liability. What may be thought of as intermediate routes on the overall map – navigating involvement in organisational action but leading to a form of individual responsibility – contribute in a significant way to the argument and conclusions of this study, especially regarding the idea of 'joint criminal enterprise', which is the subject of discussion in Chapter 10 in particular.

2 Individuals, collectivities and corporate actors

Much of the 'classic' discussion of moral and legal responsibility, such as that of H.L.A. Hart in his seminal text, *Punishment and Responsibility*,[1] takes as a paradigm the individual human actor. As Nicola Lacey has commented,[2] Hart's idea of criminal responsibility was founded on human capacity and agency; when Hart referred to roles and capacities, and pondered causal relations, he was thinking about human action and the human mind and, for the most part, human beings acting autonomously as individuals. And, as already noted, this has also been the paradigm on which much criminal law itself has been based, drawing upon that perception of the world often described as 'individualism'.[3] However, one of the main questions being considered in this work is the extent to which this model is appropriate for a society in which collective action and organisations play a significant role. How should we work out issues of responsibility in a context of group rather than individual action, and how do we evaluate the impact of collective action on the role of the individual?

Taking a broad view of individual and collective activity in contemporary society, there would appear to be three main models of action and thereby routes to responsibility to consider.

First, there is the *human individual* acting conventionally and simply as an individual, as the most obvious unit of human society. This is what would be seen as the most appropriate model of agency for many interpersonal relations, when the individual's identity as such is a governing dynamic. In terms of criminal law, this is likely to remain the most appropriate paradigm for a large part of the subject which is concerned with violent action (most of the 'offences against the person'), and conversely explains the difficulty in securing legal acceptance of a concept such as 'corporate manslaughter'.[4]

Secondly, there is the model of individuals acting collectively as a group, but nonetheless still as individuals within a group, so

---

1 H.L.A. Hart, *Punishment and Responsibility: Essays in the Philosophy of Law* (Oxford University Press, 1968), Chapter IX. Hart's analysis is discussed in greater detail in Chapter 5, below.
2 Nicola Lacey, *A Life of H. L. A. Hart* (Oxford University Press, 2004), at p. 281.
3 Chapter 3 above, at p. 62.
4 See the discussion by Celia Wells, *Corporations and Criminal Responsibility*, (2nd edn, Oxford University Press, 2001), p. 70 *et seq.*

that their identity as individuals remains a significant determinant of the collective action. This corresponds with French's concept of the aggregate as no more than the sum of the parts,[5] and the term *collective* (in the sense of individuals acting together) may be appropriate to describe this model of agency. In a modern criminal law context, this type of action is perhaps most clearly manifested in the phenomenon of conspiracy, with its connotation of significant individual contribution to a group action. It is also evident in other forms of joint activity, in which one party supports another in the realisation of a criminal goal (as in the case of offences of aiding, abetting and inciting, as secondary forms of collusion). The important feature of this model is that, despite the group context and an important sense of collective enterprise, individual identity and autonomy remain decisive, so that any resulting responsibility for the action in question is seen as a *collection of individual responsibilities*. But it is also important to bear in mind that this route to responsibility has a historical antecedent in a significant form of collective liability which involved a different conception of the individual, as will be discussed further below.

The third model, however, takes the analysis of group action a stage further, to the point at which the group or collective dynamic predominates and a *corporate* identity (in French's terminology, a conglomerate) supplants that of the individuals who make up the group. In terms of both identity and responsibility this (as has been seen already) is the most contestable form, because it brings about a metaphysical shift and reconstitutes agency. In that it implies a reality for the corporate actor, which is distinct from, or 'over and above', that of the human members of the corporate organisation, it challenges conventional perceptions of action in the world. But this is the case in which responsibility would vest in the collective or organisational agent, and not in any associated individuals.

Another way in which to explain and understand these three main models is to draw an analogy from sport and teamwork.[6] Let us compare: an individual tennis player in a singles tournament, a national athletics team in the Olympic Games, and a football team. The tennis player performs as an individual, and his personal identity

---

5 See the discussion of French's analysis in Chapter 3 above. For a summary of his argument, see: Peter A. French (1979) 'The Corporation as a Moral Person', *American Philosophical Quarterly*, 16.

6 I am grateful to Uta Kohl for suggesting the use of a sporting analogy in this part of the argument.

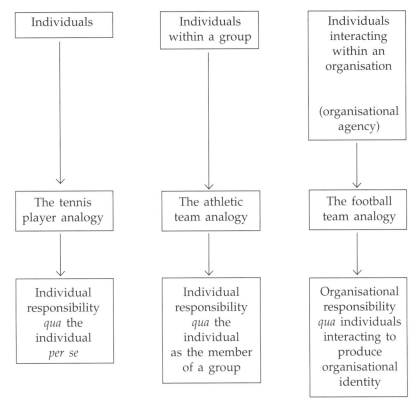

Figure 4.2 Three routes to legal responsibility

and role are crucial to the event: take away that particular player and the match fails. The members of the team of athletes individually take part in different events within the Games and although the team performance as a whole is ranked at the end, individual members are allocated medals or score points. Moreover, if one member of the team, such as the javelin thrower, drops out of the competition, that will not affect the viability of the team as a whole in the Games. But in the case of the football team, the team must consist of a certain number of members with allocated and interrelated roles. If a member is injured, a substitute takes that player's place; the roles endure irrespective of the personal identity of the players. Moreover, the performance of the team as a whole decides the game. In this way the tennis player, the athletics team and the football team provide sporting analogies for the individual, collective and corporate forms of responsibility in the legal context.

This outline should supply a basic mapping of agency and responsibility and provides a template for much of the later argument in the book. These three models may now be considered in turn, as to what each may imply for purposes of allocating responsibility and deciding on particular forms of liability.

3 The nature of individual responsibility

By its nature, the route to individual responsibility and liability may appear (in contemporary society) as the most straightforward, since the individual human agent falls to be considered by him or herself. Moreover, since this kind of agency is the paradigm, at least in Western society, for purposes of ethical, political and legal argument, many of the established concepts and rules have been worked out with the human individual in mind. There is a 'body to kick' and a 'soul to damn'.[7] In the tradition of individualism, the human being is then the subject *par excellence* of both criminal and civil liability, and of moral debate.

However, care should be taken not to take the primacy of the paradigm of individual responsibility for granted. Areas of difficulty and argument endure, especially in relation to the 'inner' working of the human mind for purposes of determining issues of capacity, and the paradigm in itself has been subject to some doubt. In particular, a combination of hermeneutic scepticism and behaviourist critique would lead to the argument that mental states are non-existent or inaccessible and that behaviour is determined from an observer's interpretive position. This kind of argument undermines one of the main justifications for allocating responsibility to the individual human actor, certainly in moral and often in legal terms – the exercise of rational choice by such an actor. The quandary then is to determine the exercise of that choice, and for legal purposes, proving it: it may be argued that the insistence on the part of modern criminal law on the presence of certain subjective mental states, usually expressed in the language of intentionality, is no more than a reliance on deductions from externally observed action. To put the matter crudely, how are we able to read infallibly the mind of another, or even know for sure our own minds? Discussion of *mens rea* in criminal law may appear

---

7 From the famous quotation about corporations that there is 'no soul to damn, no body to kick', by Baron Thurlow.

as an 'interminable debate about subjective and objective mental elements'.[8] The less problematical part of individual responsibility is the latter end of the process, in the application of sanctions, since there is an easily identifiable 'body to kick'. The more difficult part remains the earlier allocation of responsibility to the individual in general and to particular individuals, as autonomous and rational actors.

This difficulty is perhaps inherent in the fundamental problem of understanding human action. On the one hand, it is characteristic of the reflective aspect of human nature that humans seek meaning and purpose in their own actions. This point was made forcefully by Hart:

> Human society is a society of persons; and persons do not view themselves or each other merely as so many bodies moving in ways which are sometimes harmful and have to be prevented or altered. Instead, persons interpret each other's movements as manifestations of intentions and choices, and these subjective factors are often more important to their social relations than the movements by which they are manifested or their effects.[9]

Indeed, it might be added that a great deal of intellectual endeavour is concerned with just this business of making sense of human action by finding intentions and choices behind the movements and effects. This may be a purpose of art, literature and history as much as law.[10] Yet at the same time, there is a residual recognition that this is a matter of deduction and interpretation rather than full knowledge. This is the point made poignantly by Michael Collins, suggesting that 'maybe we should not give evidence to have ourselves judged against, that the historical moment, and the crimes of which we stand charged cannot be fully comprehended.'[11]

---

8   Celia Wells, note 4 above, at p. 74.
9   *Punishment and Responsibility*, note 1 above, at pp. 182–183.
10 For instance, as Lisa Rodensky has remarked in relation to nineteenth-century writing: 'Literary and legal representations of the criminal act, and particularly of the internal component of the criminal act, did not occur in a vacuum but rather formed a part of the body of Victorian writing about the workings of the interior self, and – more broadly – about personal identity, no small topic in the nineteenth century.' Lisa Rodensky: *The Crime in Mind: Criminal Responsibility and the Victorian Novel* (Oxford University Press, 2003), p. 8.
11 Michael Collins, *The Resurrectionists* (Phoenix, 2003), p. 360.

It may then be relevant to enquire whether alternative paradigms of responsibility – collective, corporate, or whatever else – would provide a fuller or more ascertainable comprehension of action and its results. It has been shown, for instance, how conceptions of corporate or organisational agency also rest upon a process of rationality. Is it easier to understand and make legal use of the rationality which informs a company or government's decision-making? Given that entities such as companies and governments have a more clearly defined (and arguably more limited) role compared to human individuals, and carry out that role unaffected by emotional responses, it may be argued that their behaviour is thereby more transparent and so easier to judge. In fact, some theorists have gone so far as to argue that the knowledge resource of some corporate actors combined with a clearly defined rationality render them paradigm moral and legal agents. Thus McDonald argues:

> Not only does the organization have all the capacities that are standardly taken to ground autonomy – viz., capacities for intelligent agency – but it also has them to a degree no human can. Thus, for example, a large corporation has available and can make use of more information than one individual can. Moreover, the corporation is in principle 'immortal' and so better able to bear responsibility for its deeds than humans, whose sin dies with them.[12]

And this leads Fisse and Braithwaite to comment that:

> Granted, corporations lack feelings and emotions, but this hardly disqualifies them from possessing the quality of autonomy. On the contrary, the lack of emotions and feelings promote rather than hinder considered rational choice and in this respect the corporation may indeed be a paradigm responsible actor.[13]

This kind of analysis therefore provides some comparative basis for the evaluation of these main 'routes' to responsibility.

---

12 M. McDonald (1987) 'The Personless Paradigm', *University of Toronto Law Journal*, 37(212): 219–220.
13 Brent Fisse and John Braithwaite, *Corporations, Crime and Accountability* (Cambridge University Press, 1993), pp. 30–31.

4 Collective responsibility: all for one and one for all[14]

Individual/human responsibility and corporate/organisational responsibility, in the terms described above, are both forms of responsibility which reside in a single entity, the one an individual human actor, the other an individual corporate actor. In one sense the allocation of responsibility as between these two types of agent is a matter of choosing between two forms of individual agency. The middle category, described above as collective, is rather less tidy. On the one hand the collective nature of the conduct is crucial, since that is how the action in question is being judged. On the other hand, the role of the individuals within that collective framework is also a significant determinant of responsibility. As a model, it occupies a middle position, but in practical terms its coexistence with the other models or routes to responsibility may be complex.

The matter is further complicated by the fact that it may be possible to move along the route of collective responsibility in divergent directions, at least in terms of the ultimate decision about liability. The outcome may be liability for the *group as a whole* or liability *for each individual member* of the group. This requires some explanation.

A shared liability attaching to the group as a whole is sometimes described as a collective or vicarious liability. Liability attaches to the group and individuals within the group suffer the liability as members of the group. This kind of liability has a number of significant historical illustrations. Feinberg has provided a useful critical discussion of this kind of arrangement, which he defines in the following terms:

> Collective liability, as I shall use the term, is the vicarious liability of an organized group (either a loosely organized or impermanent collection or a corporate institution) for the actions of its constituent members ... Under certain circumstances, collective liability is a natural and prudent way of arranging the affairs of an organization, which the members might well be expected to undertake themselves, quite voluntarily. This expectation applies

---

14 'The spirit of "all for one and one for all" is not merely a useful device; it is imposed by the very nature of the enterprise': Joel Feinberg, *Doing and Deserving* (Princeton University Press, 1970), at p. 235. (Also reprinted as 'Collective Responsibility', Chapter 4 in Larry May and Stacey Hoffman (eds), *Collective Responsibility* (Rowman and Littlefield, 1991).

only to those organizations (usually small ones) where there is already a high degree of *de facto* solidarity.[15]

Feinberg refers to historical examples of family or kinship responsibility in earlier societies, such as the Norman frank-pledge system.[16] But he warns against an easy condemnation of such a concept of collective responsibility, for offending against 'modern sensibilities', as a 'barbarous expedient of primitive people who had no conception of individual justice':

> The frank-pledge system was a genuine system of criminal law: there was nothing arbitrary, *ad hoc* or *ex post facto* about it. It was also a system of compulsory self-policing in an age when there was no professional police. Moreover, it reinforced a pre-existing group solidarity the like of which cannot occur in an era of rapid movement like our own. And most important, the system worked; it prevented violence and became generally accepted as part of the expected natural order of things.[17]

This provides an important perspective on the subject and serves as a reminder that the issue of allocating responsibility is both historically and culturally contingent.[18] On the one hand it is now easily agreed that collective liability in the form of wartime reprisals against civilian communities is ethically and legally beyond the pale (and would be clearly now in violation of international law).[19] But collective

---

15 *Ibid.*, at p. 233.
16 A system of surety, replacing the Anglo-Saxon tithing – a locally based association of ten men forming collective bail for the appearance of any one of them before a court. See: W.A. Morris, *The Frankpledge System*, Longmans and Green, 1910).
17 *Doing and Deserving*, note 14 above, at p. 239.
18 Compare for instance the prevailing views on responsibility for war crimes respectively at the end of the First and Second World Wars (the collective responsibility of the German nation being emphasised in 1919, while the role of the individual offender was more to the forefront in 1945). For a critical summary, see Christopher Harding and Richard W. Ireland, *Punishment: Rhetoric, Rule and Practice* (Routledge, 1989), pp. 169–172.
19 As 'grave breaches' of the 1949 Geneva Conventions. See Antonio Cassese, *International Criminal Law* (Oxford University Press, 2003), pp. 55–56. The moral objection to such collective sanctions is similar to that against hostage-taking and many forms of terrorist action, in which

responsibility based on kinship is not such an alien notion outside the context of Western culture with its particular emphasis on the role of the individual.[20] As Feinberg concludes, it is rather because of the conditions of modern life than because individual liability is an eternal law of reason that collective responsibility is now a less attractive model in contemporary society. There are a number of surviving forms of such collective responsibility in contemporary legal life: for instance, the concept of the business partnership in which all risks and liability for the joint activity are shared equally by two or more persons, and the concept of collective ministerial or cabinet responsibility in the context of British government. Moreover, the idea of State responsibility in international law (as discussed further in Chapter 7 below) is in one sense a form of collective responsibility in so far as it is in practice borne by everybody within the State regardless of their individual contribution to or support for the action giving rise to responsibility. However, much of the contemporary (Western) objection to collective or vicarious liability resides in the individualistic notion that it is neither fair for one individual to suffer for the independent actions of another individual, nor conducive to deterrent efficacy in an individualistic culture.

Individual liability for each member of the group in respect of collective action on the other hand is a different outcome of a similar collective responsibility, and is more relevant in many respects to the contemporary allocation of responsibility. This is sometimes described as a 'distributive' liability. However, it is not a kind of vicarious liability, as in the previous case, in which a non-culpable member of the group could become collectively liable simply through

---

'innocent' persons suffer through an association with the political target of the action.

20 African and Asian culture both emphasise community and collective rights and responsibilities to a much greater degree than in Western culture. Cobbah notes, for example: 'In the same way that people in other cultures are brought up to assert their independence from their community, the average African's worldview is one that places the individual within his community.' J. Cobbah (1987) 'African Values and the Human Rights Debate: An African Perspective', *Human Rights Quarterly*, 9(309): 323. See more generally, on African traditions, Douglas Hodgson, *Individual Duty Within a Human Rights Discourse* (Ashgate, 2003), p. 123 *et seq.*

membership of the group.[21] In this situation, each individual is culpable, in respect of an act which necessarily finds its expression in a collective arrangement. As noted already, a paradigmatic example of this species of collective responsibility arises from the concept of a conspiracy, in which the individual participation in a collective act constitutes the offending conduct – it is the collusion which in itself gives rise to liability, and a liability which is distinct from that for the specific object of the collusion (the 'predicate offence', such as a killing in a conspiracy to kill). This model of responsibility will be further discussed in later chapters in relation to such contemporary examples as business cartels and organised crime, in which such arrangements may provide a collective framework for a number of individual liabilities. Although, at the end of the day, it is a matter of individual liability, this nonetheless represents a distinctive route of responsibility, since the organisational framework for action is a necessary part of that route. In this way, it may be seen as a distinctive third model of responsibility, raising particular practical and ethical questions which deserve further exploration (see Chapter 10 below).

The phenomenon of collusion is in itself a significant and potentially revealing topic for purposes of investigating ideas of both moral responsibility and legal liability. At one level, the imposition of individual liability for participation in a collective act raises some questions of principle, including the justification for allocating responsibility to individual members rather than the group, raising in turn questions about the identity, legal and otherwise, of the group as such. At another level, the final allocation of responsibility to each individual member raises more specific questions, again well summarised in Feinberg's discussion:

---

21 The distinction may be expressed as the difference between a liability based on membership of a group and one based on a certain kind of participation in the group's activity. See the discussion in Christopher Harding (2005) 'The Offence of Belonging: Capturing Participation in Organised Crime', *Criminal Law Review*, 690, and the discussion in Chapter 8 below. But the distinction between responsibility based on membership and that based on participation may not always be clear-cut. For instance, Woodrow Wilson in 1919 justified the imposition of reparations on Germany in the following terms: 'The nation permitted itself, through unscrupulous governors, to commit a criminal act against mankind, and it is to undergo the punishment … It must pay for the wrongs it has done.' (Woodrow Wilson, *Messages* (Doran, 1924), p. 807.) Is this a case of collusion, or vicarious responsibility?

Part of the problem of determining degrees of responsibility of individuals in joint undertakings, where the responsibility is not vicarious, is assessing the extent of each individual's *contribution* to the undertaking. This involves the assessment of various incommensurable dimensions of contribution – degrees of initiative, difficulty or causal crucialness of assigned subtasks, degrees of authority, percentage of derived profit, and so on. Although these matters cannot be settled in any mathematical way, rough and ready answers suggest themselves to common sense, and the legal categories of complicity have proved quite workable. The more difficult problems require estimates of *voluntariness*.[22]

Such issues will be explored further below in relation to the example of business cartels, delinquency in government, and participation in organised crime, and this leads in turn to some consideration of the increasingly significant legal concept of 'criminal enterprise'.

5 Corporate responsibility: the autonomous organisation

In referring to an organisational agency and responsibility which is clearly distinct from that of any human components of the organisation, viewed either individually or collectively, it is important to emphasise again that this implies an acceptance of a *distinct and autonomous identity*, whatever the human origins of and participation in the organisation. It has been shown that recognition of such distinct and autonomous identity has been a matter of debate, summed up in the sceptical assertion, in relation to corporate actors, that there is no *ding an sich*,[23] and that any form of corporate legal liability is nothing more than a legal attribution to a legal construction: the company, as a person, exists in law and nowhere else. But in so far as a distinct organisational identity may be accepted as a fact of the material world, it is important to be clear what this implies regarding the responsibility of such an agent.

---

22 *Doing and Deserving*, note 14 above, at p. 216.
23 For instance, the assertion by Lord Hoffman in the Privy Council, in *Meridian Global Funds Management Asia Ltd v. Securities Commission* (1995) 2 AC 500, at p. 506.

Indeed, one of the main purposes of asserting the 'reality' of organisational agency is to bring about a shift in the allocation of responsibility.[24] The thrust of the argument is to enable the organisational agent to displace the individual human agent, through the allocation of responsibility to the former rather than the latter. An argument was put forward in the previous chapter to provide a basis for such a shift in responsibility. In such cases the company, State or other organisational actor is seen as the determining agent for certain outcomes. As will be argued below in Chapter 5, and using Hart's analysis of responsibility,[25] the organisation may be seen as possessing a relevant and distinct role and capacity for purposes of certain action, and acting autonomously causes certain outcomes to happen, in relation to which some accountability should be established through a process of deciding on liability. For instance, in fairly simple terms it might be said that a distinctive decision-making process and culture within a company or State structure was the main cause of an outcome which should then be most appropriately attributed to that organisational actor, rather than, for example, any implementing human agents. Thus corporate manslaughter might then be seen as a more appropriate form of liability than individual homicide. Or, in another context, as Erskine argues, 'the individual soldier can be expected to uphold the duty not to shoot at a civilian intentionally; he cannot reasonably be burdened with the duty not to engage in a war of aggression.'[26]

While argument continues about this kind of attribution to companies, it is intriguing to reflect that in some contexts it has been comfortably accepted in relation to the State, as a paradigmatic agent of governance. The modern system of international law is predicated upon the existence of the State as a real and indeed the primary type of agent. For instance, that impressive legal protection system usually referred to as the law of human rights for the most part envisages the State as the main site of responsibility. It is not clear that Lord

---

24 As Wells argues: 'If [the corporation's] liability is based on nothing more than an artificially constructed responsibility it is easier for it to evade the implications of that responsibility. The fiction theory can be an accomplice in the corporation's lack of accountability': *Corporations and Criminal Responsibility*, note 4 above, at pp. 82–83.

25 *Punishment and Responsibility*, note 1 above.

26 Toni Erskine, 'Assigning Responsibilities to Institutional Moral Agents', Chapter 1 in Toni Erskine (ed.), *Can Institutions Have Responsibilities?* (Palgrave Macmillan, 2003), at p. 26.

Hoffman[27] would say of the State as an organisation or corporate actor that there is no *ding an sich*. At a number of levels (national, supranational and international) there is a well-established acceptance of the State's identity as an entity of the material world, and one that has engaged legal responsibility for a wide range of activities, without any conscious legal process of deriving that responsibility from constituent human activity.[28] In short, there is a strong tradition in *legal* discussion of attribution of State responsibility, although in the context of international relations discourse, with a focus on moral responsibility, there appears less certainty.[29] It is interesting to speculate whether the *legal* definition of statehood, which incorporates an element of physical 'reality' in the form of a 'defined territory', has enabled international lawyers to accept more readily the metaphysical character of the State.

While the 'no *ding an sich*' argument is ontological, the other main objection to corporate agency and responsibility is based on more pragmatic considerations: 'no body to kick, no soul to damn'. This oft-quoted but anthropocentric view of the issue encapsulates in particular the legal reluctance to embrace organisational responsibility. The outcome is explained by Wells:

> Two effects of the individualistic bias of criminal laws can be identified. One is that concepts about individual liberty, responsibility, and accountability are applied unaltered to organizations such as corporations. Secondly, and following on from that, insufficient thought is given to how criminal law should address itself to the corporate offender in terms of liability and sanction.[30]

---

27 See note 23 above.

28 Writers on international law, for instance, appear to be quite comfortable and unselfconscious in talking about the 'motive' or 'intentions' of States. See, e.g., Ian Brownlie, *Principles of Public International Law* (Oxford University Press, 6th edn, 2003), at pp. 426–7.

29 Erskine, note 26 above, comments: 'The question when, if ever, a collectivity is a moral agent is not one that has commanded attention among theorists of international relations' (at p. 21); and she refers to the paradox 'that states have often been presented as *the* agents in international relations even as they have evaded any attribution of moral agency' (at p. 26).

30 Wells, *Corporations and Criminal Responsibility*, note 4 above, at p. 74.

Thus it may often be assumed that a corporate person is less, or sometimes not, susceptible to moral or legal enforcement since it lacks the human characteristics that such enforcement was designed to target. Such a circular mode of reasoning may be seen as the product of not only a failure of ontological imagination, but also of practical legal imagination.[31] Companies, States and other corporate actors are without doubt susceptible to sanctions, but clearly and logically these sanctions may take a different form compared to those applied to individual human persons. However, it may not even be necessary to think about different forms of sanctions, but simply to adapt existing forms.

In this way more adventurous legal orders (for instance, in the United States) have begun to employ types of sanction which may openly bear such descriptions as 'corporate probation' or 'corporate imprisonment'. It is possible to construct a catalogue of sanctions, beyond the familiar range of financial penalties, which could be applied to corporate offenders with promising deterrent or retributive effect: corporate dissolution (equivalent in one sense to the 'capital' punishment of humans); corporate 'imprisonment', in the sense of prohibiting certain types of role or activity; corporate probation, which could include a variety of measures, such as agreed internal restructuring, continuing monitoring of conduct, or self-reporting on future activity; and adverse publicity.[32] Similarly, some of the same forms could be appropriately adapted in the field of international relations to deal with State delinquency – indeed such methods have been and are used in practice, although they may be described in such a way as diplomatically to preserve the façade of State sovereignty.[33]

In short, the philosophy underlying the aphorism 'no body to kick, no soul to damn' is caught in a trap of its own making. It begins with a categorical and limited concept of responsible agent (the individual human actor) and so conceives of penality and sanctions only in

---

31 But it is not only lawyers whose imaginations may be bound in this way by experience within a certain field of knowledge and practice. Consider, for instance, the tendency of those working in the field of international relations to treat the subjects of their discussion as political (rather than, say, legal) actors, or for economists to talk about companies as economic (rather than, say, ethical) actors.

32 See generally the discussion in Wells, *Corporations and Criminal Responsibility,* note 4 above, at pp. 31–39.

33 To take just one example: consider the range of measures taken internationally in relation to the State of Iraq since 1990.

terms of such agency. The resulting problem is nicely conveyed in the argument of Fisse and Braithwaite:

> The design of sanctions against corporations is fundamentally affected by the designer's conception of corporate responsibility and blameworthiness. If one takes the view that corporations are merely machines or vehicles for maximising the interests of individuals, it is difficult to see the point of trying to create a corporate sanction of comparable potency to imprisonment … By contrast, if corporations are taken to be blameworthy responsible actors, there is a need to devise sanctions that can express corporate blameworthiness and impose punishment in a way that impresses upon corporate defendants the fact of their responsibility.[34]

The key, then, to working out appropriate and effective sanctions in relation to the corporate actor lies in the idea of responsibility itself. Such sanctions will naturally derive from the way in which the corporate agent is considered to be responsible, which in turn derives from the identity (or to use a legal term, personality) of that agent.

6 Incorporation as a legal process

Finally, in this discussion of the routes to legal responsibility, it may be useful to say something about the formal process of incorporation and its significance in relation to questions of agency and responsibility. It should be clear from the discussion above in this chapter that there are two principal legal outcomes in determining responsibility for action within an organisational context. The first outcome is that, notwithstanding the collective or organisational nature of the activities of the individuals concerned, responsibility and liability are allocated to and borne by those individuals (as for instance in the case of the conspiracy, or the partnership). The fact that the individuals have acted in concert is a relevant consideration but does not ultimately deflect responsibility to a separate organisational agent. The second outcome is that the organisational nature of the activities in question is regarded as so significant as to appropriately transfer agency and hence responsibility to a distinct organisational actor with a clearly accepted identity (such as a company, or State). In this

---

34   Fisse and Braithwaite, note 13 above, at p. 83.

second case, where the route leads to a distinct and single corporate or organisational agency and responsibility, the journey along that route may be facilitated by a formal process of incorporation of the organisational actor, so as to establish clearly the latter's identity and agency.

The process of incorporation is thus practically useful for legal purposes of allocating responsibility to an organisation and indicating that individuals acting within that organisation are not to be regarded as responsible for the organisational action in question. For such purposes, incorporation provides evidence of a separate agency and supplies a legal basis for determinations of responsibility. But it is important to understand that as such incorporation is a legally *facilitating* device rather than a *necessary* condition of organisational agency and responsibility, and that the fact of incorporation does not answer all questions relating to responsibility. Or, put another way: organisations do not need to be incorporated in order to possess moral agency and be subjects of legal responsibility in the sense discussed above – there are examples of non-incorporated organisational actors who may bear a responsibility which is distinct from that of their individual members. This point takes us back to arguments arising from individualism, discussed in Chapter 3 above, and in particular raises conflicting 'fiction' and 'realist' theories in relation to the process of incorporation.

The subject of incorporation, and the creation thereby of corporate legal personality, was a favourite topic of legal theory some hundred years ago,[35] largely triggered by the emergence of companies as common and significant economic and legal actors.[36] In those jurisprudential debates the battle lines were largely drawn between

---

35 See, for instance: Ernst Freund, *The Legal Nature of Corporations* (1897); Otto von Gierke, *Political Theories of the Middle Age* (transl. F.W. Maitland, 1900); F.W. Maitland, *Collected Papers* (Vol. III) (ed. H.A.L. Fisher, Cambridge University Press, 1911), 'Moral Personality and Legal Personality, at p. 304; Arthur W. Machen Jnr (1911) 'Corporate Personality, Part I', *Harvard Law Review*, 24: 253; F.W. Maitland, 'The Sidgewick Lecture 1903' (Newnham College Cambridge); Harold J. Laski (1916) 'The Personality of Associations', *Harvard Law Review*, 29: 404; George F. Canfield (1917) 'The Scope and Limits of the Corporate Entity Theory', *Columbia Law Review*, 17: 128; Bryant Smith (1928) 'Legal Personality', *Yale Law Journal*, 37: 283.

36 See: Gregory A. Mark (1987) 'The Personification of the Business Corporation in American Law', *University of Chicago Law Review*, 54:

advocates of the 'fiction' theory of incorporation and opposing 'realists', but this was in many respects a replay of the philosophical argument between individualism and holism regarding the nature of agency and personhood already described in Chapter 3 above.

Essentially, the 'fiction' theory of incorporation rested on the individualist assertion that the company or any other incorporated person had no existence (there was no *ding an sich*) apart from the act of legal incorporation. For instance, in H.L.A. Hart's argument, we should 'put aside the question "What is a corporation?" and ask instead "Under what types of conditions does the law ascribe liabilities to corporations?"'[37] Following from this, a company or other incorporated actor could only act in so far as legal rules allowed and had no existence outside the legal fiction of its creation.[38] Or, it might be said, an entity such as a company existed in the legal realm, but nowhere else.

The opposing 'realist' position asserted on the other hand the pre-existing and independent existence of such organisational actors in the 'real world', so that a legal process of incorporation merely confirmed and defined, for legal purposes, that existence. In Ferran's recent summary of the argument:

> The realist view of the company is that the company is a real person brought into existence by the actions of a group of individuals acting together for a common purpose. As a real rather than a fictitious person, its existence does not depend on state intervention. As a real person, the company is deemed to have organs to think and act on its behalf.[39]

1441; John P. Davis, *Corporations: A Study of the Origins and Development of Great Business Corporations* (Capricorn Books, 1961); Jeffrey Kaplan, *The Short History of Corporations* (Terrain, 1999).

37 H.L.A. Hart, *Definition and Theory in Jurisprudence* (Clarendon Press, 1950), at p. 24.

38 As Lord Hoffmann stated in his opinion for the Privy Council in *Meridien Global Funds Management Asia Ltd v. Securities Commission* (1995) 2 AC 500, at pp. 506–7: there is no such thing as the company, 'only the applicable rules'.

39 Eilís Ferran, *Company Law and Corporate Finance* (Oxford University Press, 1999), at p. 12. Note how Ferran's summary analysis refers to both the interaction of individuals as a key element in the emergence of organisational identity (as discussed in Chapter 3 above) and to a purposive role, stressed as an important element in the definition of organisation (Chapter 2 above).

Or, in Mark's description, underlying a confusion of argument concerning corporate personality lay a single crucial question: 'whether corporations … were natural outcomes of human social life or derivative and sterile creations of positive law'.[40]

The realist approach has a rich pedigree in theoretical writing of the later nineteenth and earlier twentieth centuries. Seen as very much promoted by the work of the German theorist Otto von Gierke,[41] there was also a large support for this position in English language writings.[42] For example, the British constitutional lawyer Dicey famously stated that:

> It is a fact which has received far too little notice from English lawyers, that, wherever men act in concert for a common purpose, they tend to create a body which, from no fiction of law, but from the very nature of things, differs from the individuals of whom it is constituted.[43]

Much of this realist argument deplored the preference of lawyers for the fictional account of corporate personality and Jethro Brown perceptively commented on a general inconsistency in maintaining the 'fiction' of the corporation while accepting the 'reality' of the State. Brown argued:

> While lawyers admit the existence of 'personality which is a fiction' in the typical corporation, other people are loudly affirming the existence of 'a personality which is no fiction' in the state. The historian who sees in the state a growth, the scientist or sociologist who holds it an organism, the political philosopher who talks of social solidarity, or social consciousness,

---

40 Mark, 'Personification', note 36 above, at p. 1468.

41 For a classic statement of von Gierke's argument, see: *Die Genossenschofstheorie* (Berlin, 1887).

42 Note 35 above.

43 A.V. Dicey, *Law and Opinion in England,* (2nd edn, Macmillan, 1914). See also Dicey's argument in (1894–5) *Harvard Law Review*, 8: 511. Similarly, the legal historians Pollock and Maitland argued: 'Every system of law that has attained a certain degree of maturity seems compelled by the ever-increasing complexity of human affairs to create persons who are not men, or rather (for this may be a truer statement) to recognise that such persons have come or are coming into existence.' (Sir Frederick Pollock and F.W. Maitland, *History of English Law* (Cambridge University Press, 1898), Book II, Chapter II, Section 12).

conscience, will, and intellect – all alike bear testimony to the power and growth of a perception in the presence of which political philosophy and political science acquire a new meaning and value.[44]

This dispute concerning the reality or otherwise for legal purposes of organisational agency (which, as seen from the discussion above, has its underpinnings in both sociology and philosophy) has been productive of some uncertainty and confusion in the legal field. For instance, the logic of the 'fiction' theory suggests that a separate organisational agency may only occur through some formal legal process of creation, such as those incorporating procedures by which companies come into legal existence.[45] Yet, at the same time, courts may recognise the legal personality (and distinct legal responsibility) of an unincorporated person, a good example being the trade union under English law.[46] It is difficult in such cases to maintain that the organisation is wholly a 'fictional' creation of legal process, although admittedly the more precise delineation of its rights and duties will be a matter of legal decision (but the same is true of human actors, who of course are not seen as fictional).[47]

It may be helpful to view many of these arguments concerning the nature of the legal personality of incorporated persons, and the extent of their legal rights and obligations, as being not so much concerned

44 W.J. Brown (1905) 'The Personality of the Corporation and the State', *Law Quarterly Review*, 21: 365, at p. 376. This argument, which we may refer to as 'Brown's razor', will be revisited later in this work, for instance in Chapter 7.
45 There are of course a variety of formal incorporating processes; for instance: the 'charter' (a concession by State authority); modern bureaucratic procedures of company registration; recognition of new States under international law; the constitutional establishment of State or public bodies.
46 See the judgment of the House of Lords in *Taff Vale Railway Co. v. Amalgamated Society of Railway Servants* (1901) AC 426.
47 The case of the trade union may be seen as analogous to that of the State under international law. In the case of States, 'constitutivists' have argued that they come into existence through the *legal* process of recognition by other States, while the 'declaratory' theory accepts the prior political and social existence of States, saying that recognition then 'declares' or confirms that existence. At the same time, the process of recognition, by setting up a series of legal relations, helps to identify the more precise legal situation of the recognised entity.

with the separate existence of a corporate person, but whether or not a certain kind of responsibility should be allocated to the corporate person or its human individual components. Thus, the seminal ruling in *Salomon v. Salomon*[48] is usually cited to demonstrate the separate legal personality of the corporate actor (or the company as distinct from its human shareholders). But the recognition of personality still does not tell us whether it proceeds from a fictional legal creation or a real independent existence. The ruling is in fact concerned with an allocation of responsibility: in this case for the payment of debts, and deciding that the matter is the responsibility of the organisational actor (the company) rather than any human individuals who participate in the company's activities (here, shareholders). The fact that in *Salomon v. Salomon* the company and the sole shareholder were in another (material) sense the same person is a fortuitous circumstance which ought not to interfere with the reality of the difference between a company and a shareholder. For not only are these distinct entities in economic and legal terms, but also in a material and physical sense, despite any apparent identity of human and non-human actors, since the company will have a material infrastructure which distinguishes it from a single human shareholder. Similarly, the First World War judgment in *Continental Tyre and Rubber Co. v. Daimler Co.*[49] is also about allocation of responsibility as an enemy alien in a wartime context. In that litigation there were different decisions: the Court of Appeal allocated responsibility to the company (as a foreign-owned company), while the House of Lords fixed the responsibility on the human components in the form of directors and shareholders. In such examples, it becomes clear that much depends on 'what the rules say' (or more precisely, on what the courts say). But the rules presuppose the separate existence by some means of an organisational agent as one possible recipient in the exercise of allocating responsibility.

Rules of law (and thus also the process of legal incorporation) therefore do not provide final answers to questions concerning identity, agency or even responsibility. For the world is not a product of legal system; rather the latter has to reflect the world in which it is located. As Mark has argued in relation to the legal personification of the business corporation:

---

48 *Salomon & Co v. Salomon* (1987) AC 22.
49 (1915) 1 QB 893. See: David Foxton, 'Corporate Personality in the Great War', 118 (2002) *Law Quarterly Review*, 428.

The corporation's ability to operate successfully depended on its legitimacy in society at large. Legitimacy, in turn, hinged upon the ability of the theory [of corporation] to describe the corporation accurately enough to make it a legal unit fully equivalent to its place as an economic unit.[50]

Legal description should therefore base itself on the social, the economic and the political and not undertake a misleading role of (original) legal creation. The dangers of reading too much into (or, in an odd way, starting to believe in) legal fictions may be gauged from a closer examination of Hart's argument. Having demoted the process of definition to one of legal ascription, he then seeks to adopt the same approach in relation to the 'moral personality of organised groups', when he argues:

> ... we are tempted to ask, 'What *is* a Church, a Nation, a School?' 'What is any association or organized group?' But here too we should substitute for this ever-baffling form of question the question: 'Under what conditions do we refer to numbers and sequences of men as aggregates of individuals and under what conditions do we adopt instead unifying phrases extended by analogy from individuals?'[51]

But in the non-legal context, the very question 'under what conditions?' suggests that there is a process at work which is more than just a matter of creating a fiction, since it is a distinctive feature of the moral realm that it does not possess the legal machinery or the constitutive authority for creating such fictions. In short, there are limits to the explanatory power of this 'fiction theory', in that it can convey a lawyer's view of the legal world, but does not help beyond that point, at which the only explanation for the existence of an organisation is the 'reality' of the matter.

---

50 Mark, 'Personification', note 36 above, at p. 1465.
51 Hart, *Definition and Theory*, note 37 above, at p. 24.

Chapter 5

Models of responsibility

It has been argued so far that individuals and organisations may be seen as social actors and agents, capable of an autonomous reflective response to normative requirements. As such they may be held accountable as individuals, as organisations, or as either, acting within a group on the basis of their participation in that group activity. But what more precisely does it mean to say that they are being held accountable or responsible for their actions? Responsibility is a device for fitting actors and their actions into a normative framework: in so far as norms and standards impose obligations, the idea of responsibility is used to attach these obligations to particular actors within the normative order and work out more precisely the consequences of not fulfilling these obligations. In this way responsibility links a particular agent with a particular obligation and determines the consequences of thus linking the two together. A classic exposition of the working of responsibility has been provided by Hart and this now provides a key reference point in most discussion of the subject. Hart's analysis is developed in this chapter by linking together more explicitly the four senses of responsibility identified in his account. Hart's 'role-responsibility' may be seen as referring 'externally' to the actor's place or office in social organisation, while his idea of 'capacity-responsibility' provides the 'internal' intellectual and psychological attributes of agency. Hart's 'causal-responsibility' links the role and capacity of the agent with the event giving rise to questions of responsibility – it is the factual basis for that agent's responsibility in that instance. Finally, Hart's sense of 'liability-responsibility' refers both to the process by which responsibility is established and the end result of that process: the determination of responsibility (and so liability to sanctions) in a particular case. Organising the four senses, role (x) and capacity (y) responsibility are respectively the social and psychological foundations, and causal responsibility (z) the factual basis, for the allocation of responsibility as liability responsibility (r). Thus, (x + y) × z = r. Criminal responsibility is that kind of responsibility which is used to respond to the socially and morally serious problem of deliberate challenge to and undermining of crucial social ordering and cohesion.

Building on the discussion in the last chapter, it should be possible now to explore more fully the idea of responsibility, in both a moral and legal context, with a view to considering more specifically the criminal responsibility of individual and organisational actors. The concept of agency outlined in Chapter 3 supplies the basis for this discussion in that an agent is seen as an appropriate entity for the allocation of responsibility. In itself, responsibility should be understood as a social mechanism which enables meaning and effectiveness to be given to norms and standards, and is thus a crucial element within any normative ordering. In so far as norms or standards necessarily impose obligations, responsibility is the allocating device which attaches such obligations to particular persons or subjects of the order in question. It is frequently pointed out[1] that responsibility means literally *accountability* or *answerability*, and this etymology conveys readily the sense that the concept is used to identify the person who is to answer for the performance or non-performance of an obligation. In this discussion, therefore, the idea of agency has been used to indicate the capacity to be a responsible actor, while responsibility indicates more specifically the role of that agent within a particular normative context. But the process of working out this role – that is, determining responsibility – is carried out in a number of stages, and in this way the term may be used to refer to a number of different elements within this process.

I Hart revisited

This multiplicity of meanings is conveyed very clearly in H.L.A. Hart's classic exposition of four distinct senses of responsibility: role-responsibility, causal-responsibility, liability-responsibility and

---

1 See for instance, H.L.A. Hart, *Punishment and Responsibility: Essays in the Philosophy of Law* (Oxford University Press, 1968), at p. 265: 'the original meaning of the word "answer" … was not that of answering questions, but that of answering or rebutting accusations or charges.'

capacity-responsibility.[2] These four senses may be simply understood by using straightforward examples:

- As the master of the ship I am responsible for ensuring its seaworthiness.[3]
- As the person who shot and killed X, I caused and am responsible for his death.[4]
- As the employer of Y, I have a supervisory relationship with him and am legally liable for his conduct as an employee.[5]
- As a rational and able person I am responsible for my own behaviour. It is appropriate to assume that I was aware of and in control of my behaviour, that I had some choice in the matter

---

2 H.L.A. Hart, *Punishment and Responsibility,* note 1 above, Chapter IX. The relevant part of the chapter was first published in the *Law Quarterly Review,* vol. 83 (1967). It is important to read the notes to the chapter at p. 264 *et seq.* of the book.

3 What Hart refers to as responsibility arising from the occupation of 'a distinctive place or office in social organization, to which specific duties are attached'. Such a 'distinctive place or office', Hart explains, is usually associated with the performance of duties that are relatively complex and extensive, requiring care and attention over a protracted period of time (*Punishment and Responsibility,* pp. 212–13.) This leads him to distinguish responsibility as a required role from a specific duty.

4 Of the four senses, this stands apart in some respects from the other three senses. It is less concerned with the character and social position of the agent, and instead refers to the agent's factual position within a chain of events. It is a necessary element within the process of allocating responsibility, by connecting the agent with the norm-violating or standard-breaching outcome for which accountability is sought. Hart argues: 'in the case of causal responsibility the notion of answering questions seems not to be involved' (*Punishment and Responsibility,* p. 265). Hart has also contributed to another classic text on these causal questions: H.L.A. Hart and Tony Honoré, *Causation in the Law* (Oxford University Press, 2nd edn, 1985).

5 Hart is concerned to express 'liability-responsibility' primarily as a legal concept, as indicating a state of affairs that will come about within a legal system (*Punishment and Responsibility,* p. 215 *et seq*). Although it is not usual to talk in terms of 'moral liability', logically there seems no reason why the term should not be applied in a moral rather than a legal context. The essential thrust of 'liability' would appear to be 'liable to sanctions' (e.g. punishment, or to pay compensation) and sanctions are as significant in moral as in legal ordering. At a later stage (p. 225) Hart agrees that there may be 'moral liability-responsibility', stating that 'the

and should be accountable for exercising that choice in a particular way.[6]

Hart's taxonomy remains a valuable guide to understanding the complex psychological and social process of allocating responsibility, and will be used here as a framework for discussion.[7] In his account, Hart does not engage in a detailed ordering of these senses of the term, but does, in his notes, accord primacy to liability-responsibility.[8] This appears to be mainly on etymological grounds, tracing responsibility to answerability in its paradigm legal form. However,

---

striking differences between legal and moral responsibility are due to substantive differences between the content of legal and moral rules'.

6   This is now a widely used sense of the term. Hart points out that, although it is a crucial element of moral responsibility (indeed, as a component of what he describes as 'retribution in the distribution of punishment', in Chapter 1 of *Punishment and Responsibility*), legal systems may be selective in their recognition of capacity-responsibility in calculating legal liability. Capacity responsibility is derived from an amalgam of psychological and ethical theory. As Hart explains: 'the capacities in question are those of understanding, reasoning, and the control of conduct: the ability to understand what conduct legal rules or morality require, to deliberate or reach decisions concerning those requirements, and to conform to decisions when made.' Significantly, of course, such intellectual capacity has already appeared in the discussion above in Chapter 4 concerning the qualifications for agency. For a discussion of the way in which the conception of capacity-responsibility has evolved since the eighteenth century, moving from ideas of character to a sense of capacity based on cognition and volition, see: Nicola Lacey (2001) 'In Search of Responsible Subject', *Modern Law Review*, 64: 350.

7   Hart's analysis of the concept of responsibility, pointing out these four main senses of the term, remains a reference point in the literature. Forty years after being written, *Punishment and Responsibility* continues to be an influential text. Lacey refers to the work as 'one of the cornerstones of both penal philosophy and the burgeoning field of criminal law theory … Its idea of criminal responsibility as founded on human capacity and agency is the inspiration for or counterpoint to almost all serious scholarship in English in the field published over the last 35 years.' (Nicola Lacey, *A Life of H.L.A. Hart,* Oxford University Press, 2004, at p. 281.) Interestingly, however, Hart did not develop his ideas in the work very much further, despite some self-confessed dissatisfaction with some of the argument contained in the essays in the collection (see Lacey, *op. cit.*, p. 282 *et seq.*).

8   *Punishment and Responsibility,* at p. 265.

there is a sense in which liability-responsibility is the last stage of the process, and itself has to build upon the other three senses of the term – there should be no liability to sanctions, no requirement to answer, if the agent does not possess the role and capacity to be responsible, or could not be considered as a cause of the outcome to be answered for. In terms of ordering the allocation of responsibility *as a process* it may seem more logical to talk first of (a) role- and capacity-responsibility (related together) and (b) causal-responsibility as equally prior elements, on which liability-responsibility is founded. Another way of expressing this argument is to say that role (*x*) and capacity (*y*) responsibility are respectively the social and psychological foundations, and causal-responsibility (*z*) the factual basis, for the final allocation of responsibility as liability-responsibility (*r*). Thus:

$$(x + y) \times (z) = r.$$

The discussion will proceed on that ordering of the senses of responsibility, and consider the four Hartian senses of the term in relation to the idea of agency discussed in Chapter 4 above.

2 The agent in a social role: role-responsibility

The first element in the allocation of responsibility is that of associating an agent with a social role relevant to the performance of the obligations in question. As Hart explains, establishing role-responsibility as a matter of 'place or office in social organisation' may not always be an obvious or clear-cut matter. Some cases will be clear enough. The master of a ship will be responsible for its seaworthiness, but not the passenger travelling on the ship, and similarly the driver of a motor vehicle for how it is being driven, but not a passenger in that vehicle. But it does not take long to reach the uncertain margin area surrounding 'core' roles: in Hart's words, 'the idea of a distinct role or place or office is, of course, a vague one, and I cannot undertake to make it very precise. Doubts about its extension to marginal cases will always arise.'[9] Thus the master of the ship has a clear role in ensuring its seaworthiness, but in this sense is he the sole agent? May we not say that the owners of the ship, or the official carrying out regular inspections have some role? It

---

9 *Punishment and Responsibility,* p. 212.

may easily be seen that already the example has taken the discussion into the topical and controversial realm of responsibility for purposes of 'corporate manslaughter' – those well-known 'disaster' cases in which ferry boats sink, trains crash or buildings catch fire, and the debate concerns the possible allocation of responsibility between the more immediate person in the controlling role (the captain, driver or manager of the building) and persons with a less direct role in ensuring standards of safety (such as the transport operator, usually a corporate person).[10] Or, taking another topical situation, it is possible to question the respective 'place or office' of the police officer physically perpetrating acts of torture and of the senior official requiring or authorising torture as part of systematic policy. In short, roles are identifiable but what may prove more difficult is the drawing of limits between, and assessing the relative impact on each other of, related roles.

Thus while role allocation is important for purposes of drawing the boundary around a zone of responsibility, it is likely in some cases to be a contestable process, based upon an arguable evaluation of an individual agent's position within society. The issue is dependent upon a social reading of the situation, and this is something which may be subject to change over time, as between cultures and on the basis of information about and understanding of social interactions. Most importantly for purposes of the present discussion, it is something which may be significantly affected by the way in which social ordering has become a matter of organisational structure as much as individual action. How are individual roles constructed within organisations such as companies and States, and to what extent do such organisations themselves supplant individual roles? A point which will be taken up in greater detail later in the discussion concerns the disaggregation of individuals and organisations for purposes of legal liability, for instance, as between company executives and corporations (in relation to cartel offences) or as between heads of state and States (in relation to human rights violations and war crimes). Such disaggregation is essentially a process of redefining roles as between different agents. An important part of this process is the recognition of the distinct role(s) which may be undertaken by

---

10 See generally the discussion by Celia Wells in *Corporations and Criminal Responsibility* (2nd edn, Oxford University Press, 2001), at p. 46 *et seq.*, referring to the *Herald of Free Enterprise* disaster in 1987 and the Southall train crash in 1997.

organisational actors, especially in representative terms, as discussed above in Chapter 3.

Such reflection would suggest that it may be difficult to be categorical or 'legalistic' about role identification and allocation. So much may depend upon variable social ordering, unless it may be demonstrated that there is a clearly defined and expected performance of a particular role. Historically, social trends and ethical argument may produce such a definite sense of role. For instance, the normative hardening of the rejection of the defence of superior orders during the twentieth century has served to confirm the role-responsibility of certain agents, by denying the possibility of transferring or sharing their role with those in a superior position. It is important therefore to understand that much discussion about the allocation of responsibility is essentially concerned with the definition of roles, and whether particular agents may fall within the scope of such definitions.

3 The psychology of agency: capacity-responsibility

If role-responsibility may be regarded as supplying the external boundaries of an agent's responsibility, capacity-responsibility, with its concern with psychological and intellectual attributes, provides the internal qualifications of the responsible agent. The argument here is that, for the agent to perform a role meaningfully, there has to be a subjective appreciation of that role and some awareness of the consequences of its performance. In conventional criminal law terms, this attribute manifests itself in the idea of *mens rea*,[11] as a shorthand conceptualisation of a bundle of intellectual and psychological capabilities, or 'inner facts of mental life' – awareness, understanding, knowledge, rationality and autonomous decision-making. Without such capacity-responsibility, there is a well-established ethical reservation concerning the imposition of liability. The agent lacks autonomy in the sense of having control over his or her conduct, and this undermines, both in ethical and utililitarian terms, the justification for allocating responsibility. The insistence on such intellectual and psychological capacity as a pre-condition of responsibility is summarised usefully by Hart in these terms:

> It is characteristic of … all advanced legal systems that the individual's liability to punishment, at any rate for serious

---

11   Deriving from the maxim: *actus non est reus nisi mens sit rea.*

crimes carrying severe penalties, is made by law to depend ...
on certain mental conditions ... the individual is not liable to
punishment if at the time of his doing what would otherwise
be a punishable act he was unconscious, mistaken about the
physical consequences of his bodily movements or the nature
or qualities of the thing or persons affected by them, or, in some
cases, if he was subjected to threats or other gross forms of
coercion or was the victim of certain types of mental disease.[12]

It may be appreciated that it is this aspect of responsibility which
relates most closely to the idea of the responsible agent as a human
agent, since these cognitive and volitional characteristics are drawn
from the model of the human mind. As has been seen already, this has
led to one of the main objections to an autonomous organisational,
non-human agency, especially in the context of criminal law: that
corporate actors, lacking any 'real' cognitive or emotive capacity,
cannot in themselves be counted as rational actors, and are not
therefore qualified for responsible agency.

To some extent, this argument has been addressed in Chapter 3,
with reference to the attribution of decision-making structures and
processes to organisational actors, through the recognition of a non-
human model of rationality. In this way the corporate actor may
validly be regarded as an agent distinct from its human components
and an appropriate site for separate responsibility. For instance, a
'delinquent rationality' which may be attributable to a corporate
culture and processes of decision-making, and not attributable to
specific individuals within the organisation, may provide the basis in
this way for a corporate responsibility.

It is particularly through the discussion of organisational agency,
such as that of corporations and States, that the close relation between
role and capacity becomes evident. The argument in Chapter 3
concerning the qualifications for organisational agency emphasised
the combination of structural and role criteria, and that argument
rehearsed this part of the discussion of responsibility. In this way,
Hart's concepts of role and capacity may be seen as forming the
essential core criteria of responsible agency. But this is a kind of
prima facie responsibility. In particular instances, it is necessary to

---

12 *Punishment and Responsibility*, p. 28. Chapter II of Hart's book ('Legal
Responsibility and Excuses') explores both the ethical (retributive)
and utililitarian bases for the insistence on conditions of capacity-
responsibility.

link such responsibility in principle to a particular outcome (in the form of a breach of a norm or standard) through a demonstration of a causal link. Hart's causal-responsibility is then the link between being responsible in terms of role and capacity and being liable to the application of sanctions.[13]

4 Responsibility in the instant case: causal-responsibility

Causal-responsibility is an essential prerequisite for both moral judgment and legal liability, in providing the necessary factual basis for such conclusions. At first sight causation might appear to be clearly distinct from the more evaluative processes of deciding upon role and capacity and to be an evidential matter of tracing a chain of events. Simester and Sullivan comment:

> Some causal relationships are very mechanical, and present no problems for the law. This sort of causation occurs when the action leads to a relevant consequence through the ordinary workings of physics, biology and the like … the connection between D's shooting V and V's consequential death is normally just as straightforward, something that a pathologist might be able to discuss in technical rather than, say, legal or moral terms.[14]

However, it is well known as a matter of both philosophy and law that some chains of causation may be more complex, involving a number of causal factors which are sufficiently proximate to the result as to raise questions as to the 'main' or operative cause.[15] The simple example of D shooting V can soon be converted into a more complex

13 As Hart expresses the matter in his notes: 'So a person who causes harm by his action or omission, and possesses these capacities, is responsible in the liability-responsibility sense' (*Punishment and Responsibility*, p. 265).

14 A.P. Simester and G.R. Sullivan, *Criminal Law: Theory and Doctrine* (Hart Publishing, 2nd edn, 2003), at p. 88.

15 Such problems of causation thereby become a common feature of criminal and tort case law and are dealt with in textbook discussion in both those areas of law. Hart and Honoré's general work on causation remains a primary reference point and provides an exhaustive account. For a more recent critical analysis of issues of causation in English criminal law, see A. Norrie (1991) 'A Critique of Criminal Causation', *Modern Law Review*, 54: 685.

causal pattern. For instance, assume that D2 pushes D as the latter is holding the gun and this causes D to fire the gun at V – is the cause of V's death the act of D or D2? Alternatively, assume that D3, as D's superior, orders D to shoot V – is the cause of V's death the act of D or D3? These simple alterations of the facts not only render the causal question more complicated, but show how, after all, causation may not be wholly distinct from questions of capacity and role. For in the case involving D2 it might be questioned whether D in fact had the requisite capacity for purposes of responsibility (he lacked bodily control over his act), while in the case involving D3 it might be argued that role-responsibility should be transferred to D3 on the ground of superior orders. In this way, the issue of causation may not be just a technical and factual separate aspect of responsibility, but may be intermeshed with issues of capacity and role, and so a matter also of evaluation, in terms of ethics and policy. Norrie illustrates this complexity of causation very effectively by taking an example from the Scarman Report into the inner city riots in Britain in the early 1980s. In his report, Lord Scarman argued:

> Deeper causes undoubtedly existed, and must be probed: but the immediate cause of Saturday's events was a spontaneous combustion set off by a spark of one particular incident.[16]

Norrie then takes up the question of causal analysis by asking:

> Which factor 'makes the difference', 'the deeper causes' or the 'immediate cause'? If those 'deeper causes' (relating to poor social environment, racial discrimination, police harassment) are part of the 'normal' conditions of life in late twentieth century England, are they *for that reason* excluded from our account of what caused the riot?[17]

Once again this example impinges on matters of capacity and role. To what extent was the rioters' capacity (to do otherwise than engage in riot) affected by these 'deeper causes'? Or to what extent may the riot be seen as an outcome attributable to the role of other persons and agencies in society?

Such causal complexity may be seen very clearly in a situation involving both individual and organisational actors. In a

---

16 *The Brixton Disorders, 10–12 April 1981*, Cmnd 8427, p. 37.
17 Norrie, 'Critique of Criminal Causation', note 15 above, p. 691.

straightforward case of a price fixing cartel, it might be asked, as a matter of causal-responsibility: what was the operative cause of the illegal price fix – the meeting of marketing managers which calculated the agreed prices, or the companies' agreement to enter into a cartel? As an issue of responsibility this is not only a matter of causation, but also of role, and perhaps capacity. The general truth underlying this argument is expressed in the following way by Hart and Honoré:

> ... the narrative of history is scarcely ever a narrative of brute sequence, but is an account of the roles played by certain factors and especially by human agents. History is written to satisfy not only the need for explanation, but also the desire to identify and assess contributions made by historical figures to changes of importance.[18]

5 The determination of responsibility and application of sanctions: liability-responsibility

A moment's reflection suggests a significant difference between the three senses of responsibility discussed so far – role, capacity and cause – and Hart's fourth (and in his discussion, primary) sense of the term, liability. In any particular case, role, capacity and cause need to be identified within some process of discussion and evaluation. This process is implicit in the fourth sense of the term and the point of the process is to come to some determination on that question of liability. The process is one of enquiry: is this particular agent in this particular case responsible in the sense of having the requisite role and capacity, and being the cause of the outcome for which liability should be established? 'Liability-responsibility' therefore encapsulates the process through which responsibility is established, while also referring to the end result of that process in the determination of liability, whether the latter be moral or legal,[19] and whatever the

---

18 *Causation in the Law* (second edition), note 4 above at p. 63.

19 A good part of Hart's discussion of liability-responsibility is preoccupied with the distinction between the legal and the moral: see pp. 215–227 of *Punishment and Responsibility*. This is part of the discussion where he does address some criticism made of the argument in the earlier publication. A particular theme, or concern, in Hart's discussion is the extent to which legal liability may extend beyond the scope of moral liability, particularly in so far as the latter may be rooted in blameworthiness,

sanctions which might follow from that determination. Logically, it might be said, the discussion of role, capacity and cause would not exist without the aim of establishing liability, and in this sense Hart is correct in assigning liability-responsibility some priority in the ordering of the senses of the term. But at the same time liability in itself is derivative, in being worked out from a discussion of the other elements of responsibility.

The focus on liability-responsibility serves as a reminder that discussion of responsibility generally is about giving effect to norms and standards. Why are we interested in establishing responsibility for any act and its outcome? The answer appears to be that the act and its outcome are a cause for concern as a breach of a norm or standard and some reaction to that occurrence is necessary in order to confirm the value of that norm or standard. This is the point of any sanction and the application of the latter, to be meaningful and effective, should attach to the 'responsible' agent.

In this way, we can understand the function of responsibility as a social, ethical and legal device, with an essential role to perform in any system of normative ordering. Equally, determinations of responsibility inevitably point to the application or non-application of sanctions – logically there appears to be little purpose in the business of considering responsibility without some conclusion as to liability to sanctions. The latter issue then appears as the necessary second part of the discussion of responsibility, since it constitutes the *realisation* or *manifestation* of the process of allocating responsibility. Without the determination of liability and decision on sanctions, we *do not see* responsibility.

The remaining discussion within this chapter should therefore analyse further this latter end of the process, by returning to a consideration of different types of agency and how the responsibility of the latter may be realised through different forms of liability and sanctioning. We thus return to the key point of discussion concerning individual and organisational agency and how such different forms of agency may fit within schemes of liability. In particular, this will involve some consideration of the distinctive role and features of that category of liability which is contained within systems of criminal law.

---

whereas the former may extend to instances of 'strict' and 'vicarious' liability. This relates to the question of agency and will be taken up again in the discussion below.

6 Criminal responsibility and liability

As indicated above, the final stage in the working out and allocation of responsibility comprises the process of holding a particular agent responsible in a particular case; and, in the context of legal ordering, this is usually described as a matter of imposing *liability*. Such liability is, in short, the final expression of responsibility. Typically this will take the form, first, of a process of ascription (which may be formal in character, such as a judgment or conviction) and secondly be reinforced by the imposition of a sanction, which is the material expression of the consequences of a finding of responsibility. However, in the legal context, such imposition of liability may take different forms.

This difference of form may be presented at two levels. Most obviously, at the more specific level involving a choice of sanction, there is the difference between the various measures which may be adopted in response to particular cases of breach of a rule or standard. Typically, in a legal context, such sanctions will include such measures as compensation,[20] required performance of or restraint from certain acts,[21] forfeiture of assets, and a range of penalties which usually attach to the assets or person of the offending party.[22] Naturally the choice of particular sanctions will depend to a large extent on the nature of the breach and frequently these measures will have a practical purpose in achieving some rectification. But the form of liability is also determined at another level, which is more expressive and less material in nature. It is common in many modern legal orders to categorise liability as an *expression of the strength of condemnation* of the breach, and the main distinction which is drawn in this respect is to classify liability as either *civil* or *criminal* in nature. These two classifications are not necessarily exclusive: some breaches may give rise to both civil and criminal liability and in this way result in the application of more than one sanction. Thus a personal assault may amount to both a tort or civil wrong and a crime, giving rise to both

---

20 Different terminology may be used: typically, 'damages' in the context of contract and tort claims, 'compensation orders' following criminal injuries, 'reparation' in the context of international law.

21 For instance, specific performance of a contractual obligation, injunctions, and a range of restraining, exclusionary, and prohibitory orders.

22 For a general and theoretical discussion of the range of punitive measures, see Chapter 10 in Harding and Ireland, *Punishment*, note 18, Chapter 4 above.

an award of compensation and the imposition of a criminal penalty. In such a case the two sanctions may appear similar in material terms – for instance both might involve the payment of a sum of money – but they will have different purposes, reflecting their civil and criminal character. The difference between civil and criminal is often conveyed and understood in terms of the outcome of the legal process, that is, in terms of the choice of sanction. But, as the above example demonstrates, sanctions in themselves may not indicate clearly the difference, which is essentially related to a *symbolic* representation of the kind of responsibility attaching to the breach.[23]

It might be tempting to think of this difference as being one of seriousness of the breach: that a criminal wrong is regarded as a more serious violation than a civil wrong. However, such an analysis provides only part of the explanation. In a material sense – or more exactly, in terms of the damage inflicted – it may be possible for a civil wrong to be more serious than a crime. This last observation provides an important clue to the vital difference, which is concerned not so much with the outcome of the breach, but with the manner in which it was committed. A greater degree of condemnation or moral censure attaches to a crime compared to a tort since the commission of the crime involves a more objectionable attitude and state of mind.[24] The simple illustration of this difference is to say that an intentional breach is open to stronger censure than a negligent breach, since the former entails a deliberate choice to break the rules.

---

23 In seeking to understand the distinctive character of criminal condemnation, it may be useful to make the comparison between taxation and criminalisation. The point has been made for instance by Coffee: 'A world of difference does and should exist between taxing a disfavoured behaviour and criminalizing it. We tax cigarettes, but outlaw drugs. Both are disincentives but the criminal sanction carries a unique moral stigma. That stigma should not be overused, but, when properly used, it is society's most powerful force for influencing behaviour and defining its operative moral code … the message needs to be clearly communicated that there is no price that, when paid, entitles you to engage in the prohibited behaviour.' (J.C. Coffee Jnr, Statement to US Sentencing Commission, Hearing, New York, 11 October 1988.)

24 The focus on attitude rather than outcome may be seen as a crucial indicator of what is understood in the concept of the 'criminal'. The argument is made by Fisse and Braithwaite, discussing corporate and individual responsibility, in the following way: ' … allocating [criminal] liability … is not a matter of expedient recovery of damages or penalties

Thus the responsibility is of a different order, since the deliberate violator *undermines social ordering and cohesion* in a more damaging fashion than the careless violator. Even in cases when negligence is a basis for criminal liability, it will usually be regarded as a lesser order of such liability (for instance, in English criminal law, manslaughter rather than murder).

The dichotomy between civil and criminal is not the sole classification of responsibility in such expressive terms. A number of legal systems, for example, make use of the category of 'administrative' liability. This is usually done in the context of rules of public interest ordering, where the values being protected do not reflect the kind of fundamental societal interest associated with criminal censure and liability, but where broader public rather than private interests are served by the system of regulation. However, this is in some senses a less certain and clear-cut classification in terms of its purpose compared to the civil–criminal dichotomy. This fuzziness is reflected in some of the language and terminology employed. Thus English law resorts in some instances to a kind of administrative liability although using the term 'civil penalties',[25] but then in other situations uses formal criminal law while the offences are informally described as 'regulatory', in order to distinguish them from 'proper' criminal offending. At the same time, the penal aspects of administrative liability may in substance be difficult to distinguish from criminal liability, in terms of both the procedure adopted and the nature of the sanctions.[26] Another context in which the civil–criminal

---

sufficient to reflect the financial cost of the offences. The focus is more on preventing unwanted conduct and on finding a balance of individual and corporate responsibility sufficient to impress the need for compliance on people and their organisations. There is an incentive structure here, but it is not merely a financial one. Weight is attached to the imposition of responsibility because the blameworthiness of the relevant actors – individual or corporate – is an integral part of the unwantedness of the criminally proscribed behaviour.' Fisse and Braithwaite, note 13 above, at p. 85. Attitude and outcome will be discussed further in relation to cartel collusion in Chapter 6 below.

25 For instance in relation to competition offences as committed by companies (under the Competition Act 1998). See the discussion in Chapter 6 below.

26 For instance, the EC procedure for dealing with competition law violations, as laid down in Regulation 1 of 2002, and which has been considered as analogous to criminal procedure for the purpose of working out defence rights; again see Chapter 6 below.

categorisation has not been widely used is in relation to the responsibility of States under international law, where the less determinate term 'State responsibility' is usually employed. This is to some extent a result of the decentralised nature of the international legal order, with the result that the outcome of State responsibility is on the whole more suggestive of civil liability (a breach of a treaty provision as a breach of contract, reparation as compensation)[27] than criminal liability. But there have been some tentative attempts to establish a regime of criminal responsibility on the part of States,[28] for instance in relation to the 'crime' of aggression. Overall, it is difficult to escape the sense of the civil–criminal dichotomy as fundamental for purposes of categorising in an expressive way the nature of legal responsibility.

If criminal responsibility and liability should therefore be understood as something related in particular to the attitude and state of mind of the relevant actor, this again has an important bearing on the discussion of organisational agency. Put in such terms, some of the reluctance to allocate criminal responsibility can be appreciated as the problem of finding the 'mind' of the non-human actor. Conceptually, it may then appear easier to impose an 'administrative' liability on companies, or to talk in terms of a more generalised responsibility on the part of States. The solution, as argued above, is to avoid a directly anthropocentric analysis of organisational agency, and to ground a convincing case for such agency in the human interactions which produce a distinct organisational identity. The criteria of organisational agency discussed in Chapter 3 are thus

---

27 Brownlie comments for example that 'there is no acceptance of a contract and delict (tort) dichotomy. However, the emphasis of the duty to make reparation does present a broad concept akin to civil wrongs in municipal systems'. (Brownlie, *Principles of Public International Law*, note 28, Chapter 4 above, at p. 421.)

28 For a useful overview, see Crawford's critical discussion of the relevant section of the International Law Commission's Articles on State Responsibility: James Crawford, *The International Law Commission's Draft Articles on State Responsibility: Introduction, Text and Commentaries* (Cambridge University Press, 2002). Crawford enquires: 'If crimes of State as defined in article (19) had been real crimes and not merely a pejorative way of describing serious breaches of certain norms, the question was then what sort of regime they should entail. What should be expected of international law if it contained a regime of State crimes in the proper sense of the term?' (at p. 18). See also the discussion in Chapter 7 below.

crucial for purposes of any meaningful allocation of criminal liability to organisations. The structural and role criteria referred to in the earlier discussion provide the functional equivalent to the mind and attitude of the human actor, which have traditionally supplied the main reference points for the allocation of both moral responsibility and criminal liability in the context of human action.

Using these models of agency and responsibility, the discussion may now be taken forward to consider the allocation of criminal responsibility to organisational actors, or as between human and organisational actors, in relation to a number of paradigmatic examples: the company, the State and the delinquent organisation.

Part II

Contexts: paradigmatic sites for individual and organisational interaction

Introductory note

The discussion in the following section of the work will apply the theoretical argument just deployed in the first section in a number of contexts of contemporary significance regarding the interplay of individual and organisational actors and the consequent allocation of responsibility to such actors. As outlined in the first chapter, the three chosen contexts within which to explore the argument may be regarded as useful paradigms for this purpose: considering issues of responsibility in relation to the phenomena of business delinquency, delinquency in governance and finally 'organised criminality'. This approach enables a range of organisational types to be studied (we may say for convenience: the firm, the State and the crime organisation), although these main types should not be regarded as inhabiting wholly separates sites of activity or as mutually exclusive in their forms. In practice, business and government are not always clearly distinct, and in so far as their operation takes on a delinquent character, they also merge with the type usually referred to as a crime organisation.

The choice of these three main types is also intended to enable some comparative evaluation and in particular the identification of any common or similar legal developments as between these contexts of activity. In some respects, the exercise carried out and reported in these three chapters embodies a common approach. In each case there is an enquiry into the interaction and relationship between individuals and organisations and the legal choice of allocating responsibility in respect of the actions of these two types of entity. The questions regarding responsibility are therefore pervasive: to what extent is it sensible to talk about a distinct organisational agency and responsibility, where should any dividing line between individual and organisational responsibility be drawn, and what is the impact of the organisational environment on the role and behaviour of individuals?

In terms of what is revealed by the following comparative analysis, it will be seen that two points of argument in particular emerge from the discussion. The first concerns the significant impact of enforcement imperatives: the way in which the interests of enforcement and the activities and perceptions of enforcement agencies actually drive legal developments. In that sense, actual outcomes in terms of responsibility may reflect such practical dynamics of enforcement rather than comprise the implementation of a carefully thought through and coherent model. This should then serve as some explanation for outcomes which have provoked critical comment.

The second point, rather differently, relates to an emergent legal development which interestingly may be found in each of the three contexts explored in this section. This is the move towards a concept of 'criminal enterprise' as a facilitating device for establishing a form of individual responsibility which is based not so much on classical individualist ideas of human behaviour as on involvement and participation in an organisational structure of action. Strikingly, whether the context is that of a business cartel, a paramilitary arm of governance, or a crime organisation, and across a number of jurisdictions, the concept of a criminal enterprise has appeared as a significant legal vehicle for resolving some challenging conceptual and practical issues regarding responsibility. The significance of the emergence of this concept, and its location within the overall scheme of criminal responsibility, will be separately and more fully explored in Chapters 9 and 10.

It would also be helpful to note at this point two lines of argument which are being significantly exploited in the analysis within these three contextual chapters. Both are being used to address the quandary of individual and organisation and how the two relate to each other for purposes of ethical and legal evaluation.

The first relates to the idea of the distinct organisational agent for purposes of constructing a meaningful and convincing idea of organisational responsibility which is separate from any individual responsibility within the same field of action. This argument builds in particular on the idea, explained in Chapter 3, of combining structural and role criteria for the identification of an organisational agency, as the product of human interactions within an organisational context.

This is put forward as a persuasive basis for talking sensibly about the distinct responsibility which may be allocated to, for instance, a company, a governmental entity or a crime organisation.

The second line of argument follows the 'third' route to legal responsibility outlined in Chapter 4 – that which leads to a species of individual responsibility but is the product of participation in group activity, and is therefore the theoretical basis of the emergent concept of criminal enterprise referred to above. Indeed, this third 'route' in effect seeks to resolve the relation between the individual and the organisational – or more exactly, resolves a number of theoretical and practical problems in understanding and interpreting that relation – and ultimately provides a third solution to this question of criminal responsibility for contemporary legal orders. We are then able to talk about the responsibility of the individual in the classic sense, that of the organisational actor as a genuinely distinct form of responsibility, and then also that of the individual through participation in a joint enterprise, or it might be said, the individual as an organisational person.

Chapter 6

Human or corporate? Allocating responsibility for business conspiracy

Business conspiracy in relation to anti-competitive practices such as price fixing and market sharing provides a significant contemporary context for the investigation of individual and organisational interactions and the way in which responsibility is allocated for such practices. The contemporary business cartel is a complex organisational structure within which both corporate and individual actors may be seen as planning and implementing illegal activities. Is such conduct human or corporate, or both? Taking the example of US and UK law (both important systems of regulation in this context), it may be seen that these systems of legal control allocate responsibility to both companies and the individuals working for these companies, although in rather different ways. Thus, in the prosecution of business cartels both individuals and companies may be the subject of legal process and the imposition of sanctions, but in relation to activity which is legally categorised as a single cartel, or conspiracy or unlawful agreement. Yet at the same time, on one view, these companies and their executives may be regarded as the alter ego of each other. It may then be asked whether the approach taken by either of these legal orders is logically or ethically defensible – for instance, is there not then a double counting in terms of identity, agency and responsibility? More generally, how should a process of legal regulation address such a complex interaction of individual and organisational activity, for purposes of allocating responsibility, separating the individual and organisational elements, and determining the way in which organisations may affect individual behaviour? A closer examination of legal policy and practice in this area suggests that varying approaches and outcomes are largely the product of 'enforcement imperatives' and end-of-process concerns about sufficiency of evidence or effectiveness of sanctions. The overall picture therefore resembles a legal patchwork, lacking any coherent theoretical basis in terms of agency and responsibility.

1 Elements of conspiracy

What does it take to have a conspiracy? Presumably a number of conspirators, conspiring to a common end: a number of offenders, committing one offence. But is it always so simple?

Let us revisit the recent case involving Infineon Technologies, referred to already in Chapter 1, as a convenient illustration of the complexity of business collusion. It will be recalled that late in 2004 four executives employed by Infineon Technologies AG, a German company, and its American subsidiary, Infineon Technologies North America Corporation, decided to plead guilty under US criminal law to participating in an international conspiracy to fix prices in the dynamic random access memory (DRAM) market. Each of these individuals (three German nationals and one US national) agreed to pay a $250,000 criminal fine and also serve prison terms of between four and six months in respect of the offences committed by them individually. Two months previously, Infineon AG, the company, had pleaded guilty to a charge of participating in the same conspiracy and had been sentenced to pay a criminal fine of $160 million. All the convictions, fines and prison terms are provided for under Section 1 of the Sherman Act 1890.[1]

Who exactly are the parties and what comprises the offence in this case of criminal business conspiracy (in fact a classic US antitrust case)? To be more precise, the offenders include a number of corporate actors, the Infineon company (actually two companies, the German parent and American subsidiary) and the other companies involved in the price fixing arrangement,[2] and a number of individuals working for those companies. Under American law, this mixed group of corporate and human actors are treated as conspiring together to fix prices.

---

1 US Department of Justice (DOJ) Press Release, December 2004. Proceedings in the US District Court, Northern District of California (San Francisco), *US* v. *Infineon Technologies AG.*

2 The other companies subject to the Department of Justice investigations were Samsung, Micron and Hynix. Samsung and Hynix (both Korean companies) subsequently pleaded guilty and were sentenced to pay considerable fines. See Department of Justice Press Release, 13 October 2005.

More specifically, this latter form of criminal activity involved, in this case: participating in meetings, conversations and communications in the US and elsewhere, to discuss the prices for selling DRAM; agreeing to charge certain prices; issuing price quotations on the basis of that agreement; exchanging information on sales, in order to monitor and enforce the operation of the agreement; and authorising and arranging the participation of subordinate employees in the conspiracy. The offence, under the umbrella heading of 'conspiracy', is therefore more exactly an operational infrastructure for planning and implementation of the price fixing agreement, extending over a period of time and carried out in a number of places.[3]

Not only is this therefore a criminal event of some complexity, but the register of its participants is, in both practical and philosophical terms, a matter of slippery identity. The companies conspired with each other to do a number of things. The executives conspired with each to do (more or less) the same. The companies conspired with the executives to do (more or less) the same. Each are severally convicted and punished for ... committing the same single offence ...? And this offence was committed on a number of occasions in different places, with who present? Both the companies and their executives. But how? Sitting together around the table, in how many chairs ...? Does this single offence of conspiracy occur in the material world, or some parallel juristic universe? It is when we try to envisage in this way the operation of the conspiracy in a material sense that the uncertainty of its legal character and components begins to emerge. It is this uncertainty and complexity of business conspiracy, especially in so far as it entails a combination of corporate and individual participation, that is the subject of the discussion in this chapter.

2 Business conspiracy: participation and identity

The interesting point about this example for purposes of the present discussion is that US law enables two forms of conspiratorial behaviour to be brought together for legal purposes:

- that conducted through the agency of the companies, as corporate actors or 'legal persons';

---

3 July 1999–June 2002, in the US and elsewhere, including the Northern District of California.

- that conducted through the agency of the companies' executives, as individual human or 'natural persons'.

In the legal domain, the distinction between two types of legal person allows the construction of two conspiracies, and so potentially two offences, arising from a single body of activity in a material sense. This differentiation of person and identity therefore offers legal systems a choice of strategy. The Sherman Act in the US adopts the approach of constructing two types of legal person from the conduct, but attributing the same act to those persons, *as co-conspirators*. Thus the companies and their employees juridically combine together in a conspiratorial network of action.

However, another approach would be to differentiate the legal actors, but at the same time disaggregate the offensive conduct into distinct offences. This for instance is the method used at present under UK law, which provides for an *administrative* offence committed by companies under one statute (the Competition Act 1998) and a *criminal* offence in relation to the same anti-competitive conduct committed by individuals[4] under another statute (the Enterprise Act 2002). The two types of actor are not brought together as co-conspirators and indeed the respective offences focus on different aspects of the conduct, the anti-competitive strategy (e.g. price fixing) in the case of the companies, and participating in an agreement to arrange such strategies in the case of the individuals.

SHERMAN ACT 1890

Section One

Every contract, combination in the form of trust or otherwise, or conspiracy, in restraint of trade or commerce among the several States, or with foreign nations, is declared to be illegal. Every person who shall make any contract or engage in any combination or conspiracy hereby declared to be illegal shall be deemed guilty of a felony, and, on conviction thereof, shall be punished by a fine not exceeding $10,000,000 if a corporation, or, if any other person, $350,000, or by imprisonment not exceeding three years, or by both said punishments, in the discretion of the court.

---

4 For a critical discussion of this new 'cartel offence' under UK law, see Christopher Harding and Julian Joshua, 'Breaking Up the Hard Core: the

COMPETITION ACT 1998

Section 36(1)

On making a decision that an agreement has infringed the Chapter 1 prohibition,* the Director** may require an undertaking which is a party to the agreement to pay him a penalty in respect of this infringement.

Section 36(3)

The Director may impose a penalty on an undertaking under subsection (1) only if he is satisfied that the infringement has been committed intentionally or negligently by the undertaking.

* Chapter 1 prohibitions are defined in Section 2 of the Act as certain listed anti-competitive agreements, decisions and concerted practices.

** Director: the Director General of Fair Trading whose functions were subsequently transferred to the Office of Fair Trading (OFT) under the Enterprise Act 2002.

ENTERPRISE ACT 2002

Section 188 Cartel Offence

(1) An individual is guilty of an offence if he dishonestly agrees with one or other persons to make or implement, or cause to be made or implemented, arrangements of the following kind relating to at least two undertakings.

The arrangements are listed in Section 188(2) as price fixing etc.

Section 190 provides for penalties following conviction under Section 188: on indictment, imprisonment up to five years, or a fine, or both.

Prospects for the Proposed Cartel Offence', (2002) *Criminal Law Review*, 933.

Let us consider further the consequences of opting for one or other of these models – choosing on the one hand a 'single conspiracy' model, or on the other hand a 'disaggregated offence' model.

One aspect of this choice concerns the way in which participation in the offending conspiratorial activity is understood in socio-legal terms. Much depends on the kind of relationship within the conspiracy which is identified for legal purposes. Thus the Sherman Act identifies such internal relationships in a multi-dimensional, or more exactly, three-dimensional fashion, linking together the horizontal relation between corporate actors, another parallel horizontal relation between executives representing the companies, a vertical relation between each company and its representative executive, and (theoretically) diagonal relations between each company and the executives of other companies. This set of relations is represented in Figure 6.1 below.

This way of interpreting the working of the conspiracy implies certain modes of behaviour in the material world: that companies communicate with each other as companies, while at the same time, for instance, marketing managers working for companies communicate with each other as such, while companies communicate with their marketing managers, and that all of this may be packaged together as a coherent whole as a matter of organisational and

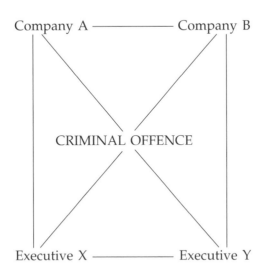

Figure 6.1 The single conspiracy model (Sherman Act)

individual behaviour. There is an underlying assumption that this is a sensible and realistic way of viewing the conduct, for purposes of understanding how it occurred and as a basis for allocating moral and legal responsibility.

The alternative model, as employed by the British legislation, disaggregates the corporate and individual participation, presenting the matter legally as two separate lines of horizontal relations. Thus, for the Competition Act 'administrative' offence, companies deal with each other and individuals do not enter the picture. For the Enterprise Act criminal offence, individuals deal with each other and the companies do not come on the scene. This is represented in Figure 6.2.

Under this model, the companies' dealings belong to a corporate or 'non-human' domain, relating to (some may say) abstract (or legally constructed) dealings on the part of abstract entities. The individual dealings are located in a 'material' world of flesh-and-blood actors, inhabiting 'real' time and space, displaying the human attribute of dishonesty, and engaging in criminal relations. The two sets of relations reflect parallel versions of the same conduct, but each version is constructed differently in socio-legal terms, for instance in

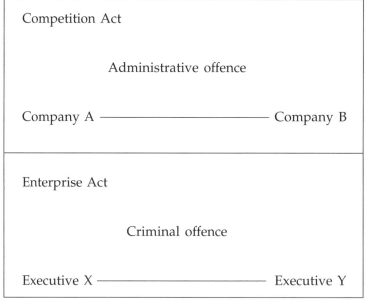

Figure 6.2 The disaggregated offence model (Competition and Enterprise Acts)

terms of the nature of what is agreed, how the offensiveness of the behaviour is characterised (criminal or not), and what penalties may be imposed on the actors.

Both models construct parallel dealings between corporate actors at one level, and individual human actors at another level. In one model these parallel dealings are brought together into a single network of collusion; in the other model they are kept distinct. But both approaches raise questions about the way in which a single body of conduct is apportioned as the activity of two types of actor.

3 Double counting: offences, persons and jeopardy?

A cartel conspiracy – for instance, a price fixing or market sharing arrangement typically dealt with by Section 1 of the Sherman Act, Article 81(1) (ex-Article 85(1)) of the EC Treaty, or the British Competition and Enterprise Acts – is a collusive anti-competitive activity entered into by business competitors. In most cases, and certainly if the collusion is of economic significance, this is an arrangement between companies: suppliers having a corporate identity. Since these companies have a legal personality as such, this corporate identity may be the target of any legal regulation of this kind of anti-competitive conduct. Thus the companies, as legal persons, may be identified as the relevant legal actors (often referred to then as 'undertakings' – the favoured EC terminology), the subjects of the relevant legal process and sanctions, such as orders and penalties. On the other hand, the companies do not in the most obvious material or physical sense carry out the acts in question. In arranging and implementing something like a price fixing agreement, the companies are necessarily represented in the physical world by their appropriate employees or executives – typically marketing managers. In the words of the Infineon indictment:

> Whenever in this Information reference is made to any act, deed, or transaction of any corporation, the allegation means that the corporation engaged in the act, deed, or transaction by or through its officers, directors, employees, agents, or other representatives while they were actively engaged in the management, direction, control, or transaction of its business or affairs.

It is these executives who meet or communicate with each other, as the companies, in order to plan, put into operation and monitor the collusive arrangement. In this sense companies and executives are performing the same act, as alternative *personae* or the *alter ego* of each other in relation to a single body of conduct. But it is also possible, as a matter of legal analysis, to go a stage further and argue that what appears at first sight as a single act may in fact be divided into different acts, as carried out by the different actors, the companies and executives. Both approaches are jurisprudentially feasible but clearly may have different legal consequences.

(a) Single conspiracy: unity of act, diversity of actors

As noted above, the first approach is employed by the Sherman Act. By describing the anti-competitive collusion simply and generally as a 'contract', 'combination' or 'conspiracy' the legislation envisages a single course of conduct which may simultaneously be engaged in by different corporate and individual actors. Two problems arise from this: first, in saying that a company and its executive, as the *alter ego* of each other for legal purposes, may conspire together; secondly, in saying that the inter-company conspiracy and the inter-executive conspiracy, since they relate to the same matter and are committed by legal *alter egos*, may then both be prosecuted. The first is a logical problem, the second is an ethical and legal problem.

(i) Logical difficulties

The problem of vertical company-executive conspiracy arises if it is assumed that the company and its executive serve in this context as each other's *alter ego*. They appear as different ways of expressing *agency* (for purposes of attributing responsibility) in relation to the same act. But in relation to the act itself they possess a common identity: they are the same actor, which logically therefore cannot conspire with itself. In this sense, the Sherman Act provides for an illogical result when it allows company and executive to be charged as co-conspirators.[5]

---

5 But in practice if it was simply one company and the executives of that company a conspiracy would probably not be charged. Plurality has been found to be lacking for instance when a corporation and a person acting as its agent were the only alleged conspirators: *Union Pacific Coal Co v. US*, 173 F. 737 (8th Cir. 1909). Similarly, in EC competition law, if commercial agents or subsidiary companies have no real capacity for independent action on a market, they may be treated as belonging to the same economic unit as the principal or parent company, and so incapable of entering into an agreement with the latter.

It would be different if the relationship between the company and its employee were to be extracted from the course of conduct and defined as a separate element of offensive conduct. For instance, an instruction from the CEO of the company to the marketing manager to organise a price fix could be taken as a separate element of offending conduct – a kind of procuring offence ('OK – I am saying to you that the company is giving you the green light to organise this kind of arrangement'). But it could then be asked whether that kind of conduct should be more appropriately viewed as an inter-executive conspiracy within the company, and thus a matter of individual responsibility.

For much of the time, however, this logical quandary may not be such a problem for purposes of the Sherman Act, since the legislation captures both kinds of horizontal conspiracy (company-company and executive-executive) and that may be practically quite sufficient for purposes of law enforcement and a justifiable criminal conviction. To talk about company-executive conspiracy may then be superfluous.[6]

(ii) Legal and ethical difficulties

The second problem is more significant in legal and ethical terms. Should it be possible cumulatively to prosecute both the corporate conspiracy and the individual conspiracy if they are legal *alter egos* for the same conspiracy? Would this not be a double counting of offenders and as such fall foul of legal principle? The legal principle at issue is the general guarantee against 'double jeopardy' (*non bis in idem*), which guards against proceedings and conviction for an offence already dealt with in the same way. A well-known and significant expression of this principle is the version found in the Fifth Amendment to the US Constitution: 'nor shall any person be subject for the same offense to be twice put in jeopardy of life or limb'. The principle would thus prohibit multiple convictions of the same person for the same offence. But the application of the

---

6 But perhaps not in all cases. If, for the sake of argument, in the case of Infineon only that company and its executive had been charged without the other suspected conspirators being charged, how would the case proceed? It may be sufficient to prosecute and convict just one of a group of offenders for participation in a group offence, if there is sufficient evidence of that one offender's participation, although it does raise the question whether, logically, one conspirator may be convicted if the liability of the other conspirators is not established. Legally, is it possible then to be a 'sole conspirator'?

principle to the situation discussed here depends of course on what is understood by 'same person' and 'same offence', both of which require further legal definition.

As a matter of US constitutional law, this would appear to be an issue of legislative interpretation, since the Supreme Court has for the most part been willing to allow Congress and State legislatures a wide freedom to fashion criminal offences from particular conduct. Regarding the number of offences or offenders which may be carved from a single course of conduct, this may then lead to varying results. So it was observed in the *Yale Law Journal* that:

> We should not be surprised that presenting a forged check to the cashier and accepting the cash, for example, are two acts in Virginia, although they would be one in California.[7]

May Section 1 of the Sherman Act be reasonably construed to provide that the typical price fixing arrangement comprises at the same time a corporate conspiracy and a human conspiracy, interlinked by a common process and purpose, but involving distinct offending acts (of the same kind) by distinct offenders, justifying the separate conviction and punishment of each kind of offender for engaging in the same course of conduct?

American jurisprudence suggests two main tests which might be used to resolve this issue. The first is sometimes referred to as the 'Blockburger Rule'[8]: an evidentiary test which would allow two convictions if they are based on legislative provisions each requiring proof of a fact which the other does not. Applying this to the Sherman Act would appear not to justify multiple convictions since the corporate and individual offending would be based upon very much the same evidence. The second test, sometimes described as 'behavioural', seeks to answer the problem by defining the relevant criminal transaction, so that multiple convictions are barred if the conduct in question constitutes a single act or transaction, motivated by a single intent. This test in practice awards a freedom of definition to the legislator – 'view the conduct as one or more transactions as you see fit'. Conceivably, then, the Sherman Act could be used to interpret the collusive anti-competitive conduct as two transactions,

---

7 'Notes and Comments: Twice in Jeopardy', 75 (1965–66) *Yale Law Journal*, 262, at p. 276.
8 From *Blockburger v. US* (1932) 284 US 299. This is similar to what is known as the 'reciprocal speciality' principle in civilian jurisdictions.

entered into respectively by the companies and their executives at different levels of business activity. To what extent would this prove to be an arbitrary and abstracted reading of the actual business context of the arrangement?

The most convincing justification for establishing separate corporate and individual conspiracy 'transactions' would seem to be one based on different personnel being involved at different levels and performing different roles within the overall conspiracy. Whether this occurs is likely to be a question of fact and as such may vary from case to case. In some cartels, there is a clear hierarchical division of responsibility, whereby for example, senior company executives agree on the principles of anti-competitive cooperation, leaving the details and implementation to marketing managers, such as the self-styled 'Bosses' or 'Heads of State' (higher level) and 'Experts' (lower level) in one cartel dealt with by the European Commission.[9] In such a situation, it would seem quite feasible to talk about significantly distinct elements and perpetrators within the overall body of collusion, justifying an allocation of responsibility to both, which may then be differentiated if appropriate in terms of the formal condemnation and penalty. Thus, the high-level director and the technical number-crunching accountant who draws up the price list may both be charged with their involvement, although the former ('general') may justifiability attract a larger penalty than the latter ('foot soldier'). But in other cases there may equally be a different scenario, in which for example marketing managers act independently of high-level corporate policy, or subsidiaries of that of a parent company.[10] On the one hand this may raise the issue of no vertical conspiracy, if the company is in effect innocent of the behaviour of the 'rogue' executive. Alternatively, it may raise the possibility of negligent management at the higher level, but that again would take the intra-corporate relationship outside the boundary of conspiracy. Actual circumstances, therefore, may render the more precise nature of conspiracy within the company variable and unpredictable. In

9   *LdPE Cartel*, OJ 1989, L 74/21, at pp. 23–4.
10 See for instance the discussion relating to the membership of the Swedish forest products group Stora in the Cartonboard Cartel, dealt with under EC competition law: Commission decision, OJ 1994, L 243/1; judgment of the Court of First Instance, Case T-354/94, *Stora Kopparbergs Bergslag v. Commission* (1998) ECR II-2111. The Stora group of companies operated a relatively decentralised structure and Stora presented itself as a parent company making an effort to 'clean up' delinquent trading practices within the group.

fact, the American approach circumvents this problem by blithely presuming some conspiratorial relation between the company in a more general and undefined sense and particular individuals engaged in the nitty-gritty of collusive discussion and measures.

(b) Disaggregated offence

What might be described as the 'disaggregated offence' model adopted by the British legislation would seem at first sight to have navigated successfully any of the double-counting objections mentioned above. The approach taken together in the Competition Act 1998 and the Enterprise Act 2002 distinguishes between

- different actors (companies, referred to as 'undertakings', and individuals);
- differently defined offences relating to cartel activity; and
- different classifications of offending conduct and resulting processes of enforcement (administrative regulation by the OFT, and criminal prosecution).

The Competition Act offence deals with a company's direct participation in a prohibited agreement or practice (such as price fixing, market sharing or bid rigging), and in this respect runs parallel to the EC process of regulation under Article 81 of the EC Treaty. In effect, this is a regulation of the market outcome of the collusive behaviour embodied in a cartel – the resulting anti-competitive arrangement – and penalises the company (through the sanction of a fine) for its involvement in such an activity, provided that the latter is at least negligent, if not intentional. In many respects, this may be seen as an expression of the historically typical European approach to regulating cartels, replicating the EC model, which is now the standard for national competition enforcement among the EU Member States.

Superficially the Competition Act procedure appears to be an uncomplicated example of administrative penalty. However, its appearance may mask some more tricky issues of accountability and responsibility, especially in relation to corporate identity. An Office of Fair Trading (OFT) decision dealing with a market sharing arrangement between two bus companies, *Arriva and FirstGroup*,[11]

---

11 Office of Fair Trading, Decision of the Director General of Fair Trading, No CA98/9/2002, *Market Sharing by Arriva plc and FirstGroup plc,* Case CP/1163-00, 30 January 2002.

may serve to illustrate some of these more problematical points. Fines were imposed on the two companies for agreeing to share out bus routes in the Leeds area, although both companies benefited from the OFT leniency programme since they cooperated with the investigation and supplied evidence. The factual basis for the penalties was stated by the Director General of Fair Trading in the following terms:

> The meetings at which the agreement between Arriva and FirstGroup was entered into were held in an hotel (one in a private room) and were not reported as contacts with competitors in accordance with internal company compliance procedures, even though other meetings with competitors were reported. Each member of staff involved was at a senior level in their respective undertakings and they had all undergone compliance training. In addition the parties de-registered and registered the bus routes a number of weeks apart, which the Director considers was a device for covering up their anti-competitive behaviour.[12]

While this is not a criminal proceeding, and there was not at that time any possibility of criminal proceedings in relation to the individuals involved (the case pre-dated the Enterprise Act), the decision appears on its face to be a rather too easy attribution of responsibility to the companies. Both companies seemed to take 'antitrust awareness' seriously and the agreement appeared to be in breach of internal codes, of which the individual negotiators were well aware.[13] Since the companies' liability is based on intentional or negligent conduct, there is arguably a case for saying that the companies as such were not responsible in these circumstances. It is not clear from the Decision whether the acts of the individuals were being imputed

---

12 Director General's Decision, *ibid.*, at para. 54.
13 In its submissions, FirstGroup argued that: 'its employees had received compliance training in which market sharing in circumstances similar to those in the infringement had been specified as banned under the Act. FirstGroup took compliance training very seriously and there had been nothing else that it could have done to establish appropriate internal reporting and clearance mechanisms to alert its employees to their responsibilities and obligations under the Act. However, as a result of this case, FirstGroup have reviewed their procedures and improved their monitoring of adherence to compliance.' *Ibid.*, at para. 27.

to the companies,[14] but, if so, that may be something which would hypothetically raise problems of double counting once any criminal liability under the Enterprise Act is brought into the picture.

At the legislative level the Enterprise Act criminal offence is clearly conceived as something distinct from the 'corporate offence' under the earlier legislation. In the report commissioned by the OFT on the proposed criminalisation of cartels (the Hammond-Penrose Report), it was stated that:

> ... it has been suggested to us that it might be 'tidier' if both undertakings and individuals were prosecuted in a single set of proceedings in the criminal court. We do not however favour this approach. By continuing to deal with infringements by undertakings solely under the existing civil process, the OFT will ensure consistency with the approach to undertakings adopted by the EC and we understand that the EC strongly favours the OFT continuing to deal with undertakings under its existing procedures. We also consider that there are advantages of continuing to deal with undertakings under the existing civil law process and therefore, accordingly, we consider that criminal sanctions should be reserved for individuals, for whom the threat of custodial sentences should act as a significant deterrent.[15]

However, this conscious separation of corporate non-criminal and individual criminal offences seems to have been not so much a carefully thought out product of criminal jurisprudence as a result of pragmatic argument. On the one hand, the EC Commission was understandably concerned that the OFT should retain its 'administrative' regulation of cartels at the national level in order to fit into the decentralisation of enforcement contained in the Commission's 'modernisation' policy.[16]

---

14 The decision refers to the staff taking part in the meetings as being at a senior level in their respective undertakings: they were divisional directors and managing directors of subsidiary companies.

15 Report prepared for the Office of Fair Trading by Sir Anthony Hammond and Roy Penrose, *Proposed criminalisation of cartels in the UK*, November 2001, OFT365, para. 6.3.

16 See the Commission's White Paper, *Modernisation of the Rules of Implementing Articles 85 and 86 of the Treaty*, OJ 1999, C 132/1. An important aspect of the modernisation proposals, implemented in Regulation 1/2003, was the delegation of some of the Commission's enforcement role to Member State competition authorities (NCAs), such as the OFT.

On the other hand, the criminalisation strategy appears to have been very much driven by the objective of scaring company executives (the 'deterrence' argument), which in turn was a crucial component of leniency programmes, especially that of the US Department of Justice, in that the prospect of a prison sentence may encourage such individuals to act as whistle-blowers.[17] In short, the emergence of the new British cartel offence may be seen as having pragmatic, enforcement-related origins, rather than as the outcome of principled legal development. But to a large extent the end result may have avoided a number of double-counting concerns, even if this was by luck rather than judgment.

In particular, the two offences are defined very differently. The criminal 'cartel offence' under Section 188 of the Enterprise Act is drafted to cover the more specific individual role in negotiating or implementing the cartel as a whole. Moreover, the *mens rea* for the offence includes a dishonest state of mind in agreeing to make or implement the arrangement or any part of it. The element of dishonesty was included to convey some sense of the seriousness, the 'real criminality', the egregious nature of the conduct. Whether dishonesty is the relevant concept for this purpose may be open to argument,[18] since the state of mind targeted here is rather a contumacious and deliberate disregard for the rules – an attitude often referred to by enforcement agents as 'brazen'. But certainly there is an overall distinction within the legislative scheme between the company's broader economic and market-level participation in the cartel and the individual's executive role in setting up and operating the cartel or parts of it.

In one sense this division of responsibility captures a metaphysical distinction between two domains, one of market activity and one of human activity: one offence is based on the injury to competition and the market, the other is based on a human defiance of rules. Nonetheless, there may be some lingering seeds of double jeopardy

---

17 See Christopher Harding and Julian Joshua, *Regulating Cartels in Europe* (OUP, 2003), Chapters 8 and 9; and Christopher Harding, 'Business Collusion as a Criminological Phenomenon: Exploring the Global Criminalisation of Business Cartels', 14 (2006) *Critical Criminology*, 18. See further the discussion in section 5 of this chapter. The Infineon case provides an example of German nationals serving prison sentences in the US.

18 See the critical discussion of this point in Harding and Joshua, 'Breaking Up the Hard Core', note 4 above, at p. 937 *et seq.*

under this scheme. It is also possible to argue that the corporate and individual activities are inseparable, in that the anti-competitive activity cannot exist without its planning and co-ordination, and the company cannot perform on the market without its human element of participation. This again is the dilemma regarding the separation of corporation and human action in relation to the same subject. Another aspect of the problem concerns the justification for carving a more specific piece of cartel activity from the cartel as a whole and identifying it as a separate kind of conduct and thus offence. The analogy, it may be argued, would be for example, in the case of theft, saying that the planning of the theft, and specific arrangements for the event in which the theft is carried out, could be treated as separate additional offences; or that in the case of robbery, theft is also charged as an additional offence rather than treated as a component of the robbery.

The problem is both philosophical and sociological. On the one hand there is a conceptual question, concerning the definition of conduct and action and the extent to which distinct transactions may be extrapolated in the abstract from a certain course of conduct. But, since the reason for posing the question is to decide on an appropriate allocation of responsibility, it may be that the answer to such questions needs to draw upon the sociology of the conduct – an investigation of how and why the conduct in question takes place. The next stage of the discussion will therefore seek to explore further the sociology of business conspiracy.

4 The attribution of responsibility to corporate business actors

The essential question therefore appears in these terms: is it possible to argue convincingly for a separation of corporate and individual conduct in such cases? This question is relevant to both the legal models discussed above, since the single conspiracy model involves a unitary conspiracy of corporate and individual actors, while the disaggregated offence model depends upon a separation of corporate and individual offending within the same 'cartel as a whole' transaction. In the real world of cartel conspiracies, do companies and their executives carry out distinct roles rather than simply serve as the *alter ego* for each other?

(a) Individual conduct

In some respects, the issue of individual conduct and responsibility for that conduct is more straightforward: in any organisational or corporate context, all action may ultimately be traced to some individual human act. There are two possible problems arising from an attribution of human responsibility in this particular context. One is a practical difficulty of evidence: finding sufficient proof of individual participation in a complex organisational structure of activity involving a large number of human actors. The second problem is ethical and legal: whether it is appropriate to locate responsibility at the individual level, in a context of corporate direction or moulding of individual conduct.

The practical problem of evidence demands practical solutions. This may take the form of enhancing methods of collecting evidence (for instance, in the context of cartels, the use of 'dawn raids',[19] or exploiting 'whistle-blowing' as a part of leniency programmes).[20] Alternatively, a pragmatic 'legal' solution may be to adopt a presumption that a certain actor should be legally liable, by virtue of his or her position and function within the organisation, whatever his or her actual state of knowledge or participation. This is a device of convenience, open to some moral objection (since it penalises a scapegoat, or 'fall-guy'), and is familiar from a number of situations, ranging from ministerial responsibility in the field of governance to vicarious liability in relation to more mundane occupational activities.[21] For purposes of the present discussion, evidential difficulties may give rise to a pragmatic argument in favour of an analogous form of corporate liability. But this would be based upon a 'responsibility of convenience', consciously adopted on grounds of expediency as an exception to normal moral principles of responsibility.

(b) corporate conduct

The second, jurisprudential issue concerning the choice of moral accountability as between human and corporate actors is less easy to

---

19 That is, surprise or unannounced inspections. See Harding and Joshua, *Regulating Cartels in Europe*, note 17 above, p. 165 *et seq*.
20 Harding and Joshua, *ibid.*, Chapter 8.
21 For a further discussion of vicarious liability in English criminal law, see A.P. Simester and G.R. Sullivan, *Criminal Law: Theory and Doctrine* (2nd edn, Hart Publishing, 2003), p. 243 *et seq*, and note the widely held reservations concerning its use, as a matter of principle.

resolve and depends upon further sociological investigation into the nature of organisational conduct. For ethical and legal purposes, such an enquiry could have two more specific objectives. First, it could be asked whether the corporate person should be responsible *in place of* the individual actor. Secondly, it may be asked whether the corporate person should be responsible *in addition to* the individual actor, on the basis of some distinct role or activity.

Discussion is complicated by the need to ensure a clear separation of corporate and human identities and to resist the anthropomorphic temptation to assimilate corporate identity to the controlling individuals within an organisation. It is possible, and may be useful, to distinguish different individual roles and levels of activity within an organisation (for instance, CEO and marketing manager, 'boss' and 'expert', general and captain), in a way that is relevant to questions of individual responsibility. But it is another matter – and it serves to confuse the issue – to distinguish between a lower level of individual responsibility and a higher level of accountability which is labelled 'corporate' but is in fact that attaching to a senior individual. This approach is exemplified by the traditional doctrine of corporate liability under English criminal law, which has attributed to the corporate person the mental state of its controlling individuals:

> A corporation ... must act through living persons, though not always one and the same person. Then the person who acts is not speaking or acting for the company. He is acting as the company and his mind which directs his acts is the mind of the company.[22]

A main criticism of this approach is that the simplistic association of corporate actor and controlling individual fails to capture the reality of complex organisational activity. On the one hand, in reality 'senior' employees may not be very much in control of the corporation as a whole.[23] On the other hand, there may be convincing grounds for

---

22 *Tesco Supermarkets v. Nattrass* (1971) 2 All ER 127, *per* Lord Reid, at p. 131. For a critical discussion of this approach, see: Alan Norrie, *Crime, Reason and History: A Critical Introduction to Criminal Law* (Butterworths, 2001), pp. 93–5.

23 This was the issue addressed by Lord Hoffmann in *Meridian Global Funds Management Asia Ltd v Securities Commission* (1995) 2 AC 500 when he advocated a purposive test of assimilation: whose act or state of mind was intended to count for this purpose as the act etc. of the company?

recognising a distinct, non-human form of corporate personality. It is this last line of argument that is relevant for purposes of the present discussion. The underlying issue is ontological: whether it is possible, contrary to the claims of methodological individualism, to attribute responsibility for conduct to an organisation rather than to its component individuals, whether the latter are identified individually or as an aggregate of individuals. As argued in Chapter 3 above, although it runs counter to our anthropocentric instinct to do so, there may be value in the recognition of a genuinely organisational personality in some contexts. As Fisse and Braithwaite have argued, companies may in some senses be regarded as quintessentially rational actors.[24] Thus, returning to the subject of business conspiracy, it has to be asked whether a company *as such* is able to involve itself in a conspiracy to fix prices or share markets in a way that is operationally and factually distinct from the relevant connected actions of its individual employees, whether the latter may be a CEO or marketing manager. A review of the literature analysing corporate organisation would suggest two crucial elements for purposes of sustaining a distinct corporate identity for such a purpose: a *functional autonomy*, and a *distinct ethos*.

The element of functional autonomy is perhaps most clearly expressed through the idea of a corporation's ability to dispense with human actors, or its capacity for survival irrespective of its human composition. Coleman describes this position as 'the irrelevance of persons':

Persons have become, in a sense that was never before true, incidental to a large fraction of the productive activity in society. This is most evident when the person who occupies a position in a corporate actor is replaced not by another person but by a machine. Then the general irrelevance of persons is clear. But the invention which made this possible was not a technological invention which replaced [people with machines]; it was a social invention which created a structure that was independent of particular persons and consisted only of positions. Once this was done, it became merely a matter of ingenuity to devise

---

24 Brent Fisse and John Braithwaite, *Corporations, Crime and Accountability* (Cambridge University Press, 1993), at pp. 30–31 (building upon the argument of Coleman and McDonald – see the discussion in Chapter 3, above).

machines that could carry out the activities which those positions required.[25]

Coleman has argued that this kind of corporate entity is fundamentally different from other types of collective entity in its independence from *particular* human persons, who simply contributed to the organisation's existence by occupying a position, but who individually could be substituted in that position. Thus universities or companies endure whatever the coming and going of their individual human members and in terms of their form do not disappear with even the departure of the most charismatic vice-chancellor or CEO. In this way, the corporate actor possesses a separate structural and functional identity. But this by itself is a shell and requires something substantive to give expression to the separate identity. This second element may be described in terms of *ethos*, or, as some writers describe the matter, a distinctive *culture*. It is the possession of a distinctive ethos which gives meaning to an attribution of corporate responsibility, since the ethos is a ground upon which to pass judgment on corporate conduct. Thus Bucy[26] has advocated the use of the Aristotelian idea of ethos as a basis for corporate criminal responsibility, and in the Australian draft *Model Criminal Code* a concept of corporate culture is adopted as a means of reflecting the principle of corporate blameworthiness.[27] What is comprised more fully in this idea of culture has been described for instance by Punch in the following terms:

> In its original anthropological sense it refers to patterns of thought and action in a group and, when applied to organizations, it tends to reveal that specific companies, and parts of companies, have often a separate style of doing things manifested in subtle, semi-conscious ways of thinking and acting.[28]

---

25 This idea was discussed in Chapter 3. James S. Coleman, *The Asymmetric Society: Organisational Actors, Corporate Power, and the Irrelevance of Persons* (Syracuse University Press, 1982), p. 29.

26 Pamela Bucy (1991) 'Corporate Ethos: A Standard for Imposing Corporate Criminal Liability', *Minnesota Law Review*, 75: 1095.

27 Australian Standing Committee of Attorneys-General, Criminal Law Officers Committee, *Model Criminal Code, Discussion Draft, Chapter Two, General Principles of Criminal Responsibility*, 501.3.1, 501.3.2.

28 Maurice Punch, *Dirty Business: Exploring Corporate Misconduct* (Sage, 1996), p. 224, following W.G. Ouchi (1985) 'Organizational Culture', *Annual Review of Sociology* 11: 457.

In this way, a corporate ethos or culture is the functional equivalent of attitude, behavioural traits and an outlook on life that in human actors are used as a basis for moral judgment. In turn, these elements of corporate identity may then be used in either an inculpatory or exculpatory manner for purposes of assigning criminal liability.

Thus an inculpatory culture such as to justify an imposition of liability on a company, and relieve or reduce the liability of any relevant human actors, would comprise an established ethos which required or encouraged delinquent action on the part of the company's human agents. Such a culture was identified for example in Conley and O'Barr's study of Archer Daniel Midland (ADM)'s involvement in the Lysine Cartel, dealt with by the US Department of Justice in the 1990s.[29] They summarise the impact of the company's culture in the following way:

> Organizing a price-fixing conspiracy seems to have been an almost natural development in an autocratic, top-down corporate culture that prized influence and control above all else. In the business world, price fixing is the ultimate form of control – control over the vicissitudes of the market. It is the economic equivalent of a sailor being able to control the wind. Regardless of where in the company the scheme originated, it may have seemed like a reasonable idea. If it came from the very top, it probably struck those below as just an incremental step along the continuum of power and influence. If it originated closer to the middle, this was the kind of cultural environment in which it would have been propagated quickly, indeed enthusiastically. It was the sort of thing the company did ...[30]

In such circumstances the ethos may be seen as the key determinant of corporate and also human behaviour in that individual human actors within the company would have found it difficult to resist or question such a course of conduct. American studies of corporate individual and organisational behaviour provide support for the

---

29 On the investigation and prosecution of the Lysine Cartel, see the account in John M. Connor, *Global Price Fixing: Our Customers Are The Enemy* (Kluwer, 2001).

30 John M. Conley and William M. Barr (1997) 'Crime and Custom in Corporate Society: A Cultural Perspective on Corporate Misconduct', *Law and Contemporary Problems*, 60(5): 13.

idea that corporations may effectively in this way direct individual behaviour. Elsen has argued for instance:

> ... I am inclined to agree ... that entity liability or vicarious liability is an appropriate response to unacceptable behavior arising from the corporation's business activities ... There should be more compassion for the middle managers who are forced either to carry out the company's wishes or risk losing their jobs.[31]

The outcome is that the company is inculpated, the individuals exculpated.

But of course, an analysis of corporate culture could work in the opposite direction. If, contrary to the example of ADM, the prevailing corporate culture was legally compliant, any illegal conduct which could be traced to particular individuals suggests 'rogue' behaviour on their part, so exculpating the company and appropriately locating responsibility at the individual level. If a company can demonstrate a genuine and determined policy of inculcating legal compliance at all levels of its organisation and that the personal illegal act of its executive was at variance with its culture, there may be convincing moral and legal grounds for shifting responsibility to the individual. In the case of the *Cartonboard Cartel*, for example, dealt with by the European authorities,[32] one of the participants, the Swedish forest products group Stora, was able to demonstrate such an exculpatory character which was taken into account by the Commission by a large reduction in the amount of fine imposed. Stora had recently acquired two other companies who had previously been engaged in the cartel and so became formally responsible for their past conduct. But Stora's own legally compliant culture was evidenced by its ready co-operation[33] in the Commission's investigation and its earlier active

---

31 Sheldon H. Elsen (1997) 'Commentary', *Law and Contemporary Problems*, 60(87): 88. See also the discussion in Deborah A. Demott's paper, 'Organizational Incentives to Care about the Law', in the same volume of the journal, at p. 39.

32 Commission decision: *Cartonboard Cartel*, OJ 1994, L 243/1; judgment of the Court of First Instance, Case T-354/94 *Stora Kopparbergs Bergslag v. Commission* (1998) ECR-II 2140.

33 Stora readily admitted its responsibility for the allegedly illegal behaviour of its subsidiary companies and provided the Commission with full information, contrasting with the 'vague and anodyne' responses from

corporate compliance programme, established in 1991. The relevant EC rules impose liability only on 'undertakings' and of course have no provision for the application of criminal law sanctions to individuals, so that the option for the Commission was mitigation of the corporate penalty rather than transferring liability to individuals.[34] But a 'good' corporate ethos need not be just a matter of legal compliance in this sense of antitrust awareness; it could also be evidenced for instance by a policy of ethical investment, now actively pursued by some economic actors wishing to convey an impression of being 'good citizens in the marketplace'.[35]

A principled approach to the problem of allocating responsibility for business conspiracy would therefore appear to suggest that a distinction be drawn on the basis of individual responsibility for specific acts of cartel organisation and corporate responsibility for promoting or allowing a culture of delinquency which facilitates such specific illegal action. The kind of identity and legal personality awarded to the corporate actor in this way is analogous to that which has been advocated for corporations in the context of criminal negligence in relation to public safety, the so-called 'corporate manslaughter' issue.[36] The advantage of such an approach is that it disentangles corporate and individual conduct within the same organisational framework and so addresses concerns of double counting discussed above. It also provides some answer to the ethical problem of the 'good citizen' company with 'rogue' executives. However, the adoption of such a 'principled' basis for allocating responsibility may be inhibited, or at least complicated, by a number of strategic considerations, examined below.

---

other firms implicated in the cartel. Stora also provided an example of a loose and decentralised corporate structure, which renders more convincing any claim of not being so well placed to control rogue elements within the group.

34 Similarly, in the British case cited earlier, *Arriva and FirstGroup,* note 11 above, the corporate culture appeared to be legally compliant, and there was also, at that time, no provision for individual criminal liability.

35 Equally and conversely, a recidivist antitrust record would undermine good citizen claims, and all the more so if coincident with compliance programmes, which then appear as cynically adopted measures of subterfuge.

36 See in particular the discussion by Celia Wells, *Corporations and Criminal Responsibility* (2nd edn, Oxford University Press, 2001).

5 The strategic dimension: the enforcement perspective

This part of the discussion considers the way in which enforcement objectives have fashioned significant strategies relating to the choice of corporate and/or individual liability in the context of business conspiracy. Regarding the subject from the perspective of law enforcement, there are a number of arguments which may be put forward in favour of the imposition of either form of liability, or using both together, which possess a largely pragmatic or strategic force. In practice, such arguments may very well determine legal development.

(a) Liability for both corporate and individual actors

As already discussed, this is the approach adopted in a quintessential form under the Sherman Act in the US, which simply sweeps all the relevant companies and their executives into one bag for purposes of prosecution. A widely asserted justification for this policy is its claimed deterrent impact: liability is maximised and the fear of sanctions is spread among both companies and individuals. The totality of this approach avoids some finer questions concerning the nature of the conspiracy. From the enforcement perspective, there is an attractive simplicity, which sidesteps more precise moral questions concerning the specific responsibility of either individual or corporate actors, and ethical qualms relating to the double counting of offenders and offences.

The ability to impose liability on both actors is an important aspect of leniency programmes, now at the forefront of enforcement efforts in the US and elsewhere. Tempting potential whistle-blowers with leniency in order to come forward with crucial evidence depends upon a realistic threat of severe sanctions being applied if they do not come forward in this way. It is calculated that individuals are most vulnerable to this perceived threat if they feel that there is a high risk of criminal conviction and imprisonment. In this way, enforcement agencies are able to target nervous executives in order to score successful prosecution of the company.[37] In addition, the

---

37 Belief in this aspect of deterrence is amply documented in Department of Justice discussion papers. There are a number of informative speeches which can be found on the DOJ website (www.usdoj.gov/atr). See for instance: Gary R. Spratling, 'Negotiating the Waters of International Cartel Prosecutions', 4 March 1999; Scott D. Hammond, 'When Calculating the

publicity attaching to conviction of both companies and individuals is considered to increase the deterrent impact. Werder and Simon, for example, have argued:

> Prison sentences send a special message not conveyed by fines, and they send it much better, because prison sentences for white-collar crimes are much more newsworthy than fines and, thus, will be given more coverage in the media and will be more noted by other businessmen.[38]

Liability for both corporate and individual actors is thus at present a preferred enforcement strategy, especially in the US, although, if analysed more closely, it may be that individual liability is grounded more on deterrent argument, while the corporate liability has a more compelling retributive and restorative justification.

(b) Corporate liability as a priority

An enforcement strategy which targets companies, either exclusively or preferably, may also be seen as having some strategic advantage.

As noted already, this may avoid some of the evidential difficulties associated with establishing the responsibility of particular individuals as actors within a complex organisational structure, resulting in a kind of presumptive or vicarious liability for companies.[39] The underlying difficulty has been described as 'the problem of many hands'.[40] As Bovens explains:

Costs and Benefits of Applying for Corporate Amnesty, How Do You Put a Price Tag on an Individual's Freedom?', 8 March 2001.

38 G.J. Werden and M.J. Simon (1987) 'Why Price Fixers Should Go to Prison' *Antitrust Bulletin*, 917: 933–4. A number of commentators have argued in favour of strong sanctions being applied to individuals: see, for instance, A.L. Lipman (1997) 'The Paper Label Sentences: Critique', *Yale Law Journal*, 86: 619; Wouter P.J. Wils, 'Does the Effective Enforcement of Articles 81 and 82 EC Require Not Only Fines on Undertakings but also Individual Penalties, in Particular Imprisonment?' in C.D. Ehlermann (ed.), *European Competition Law Annual* (Hart Publishing, 2002), p. 4.

39 As Norrie comments: '… the morally central character of the employer-criminal coupled with the practical problems of establishing guilt within the manufactory process conduced to the establishment of a guilt-free form of liability' – Alan Norrie, *Crime, Reason and History*, note 22 above, at p. 104.

40 Dennis F. Thompson, 'Moral Responsibility of Public Officials: The Problem of Many Hands', 74 (1980) *APSR* 905.

It is above all a *practical problem.* For outsiders it is often particularly difficult to unravel who, and in what way, has contributed to the conduct of a complex organisation and who, and to what degree, can be made to account for its actions. In the first instance, it is therefore above all a question of identification and proof.[41]

Such enforcement difficulties are clearly eased by the attribution of responsibility to the organisation as a 'framework actor'. As Calkins points out, it may be difficult to trace all the culpable individuals in such cases:

Even for price-fixing, however, where individuals are indicted and sent to prison, it makes sense to proceed against the entity as well ... the [Department of Justice] currently indicts fewer than one person per indicted corporation. It seems unlikely that price-fixing is the responsibility entirely of sole rogue employees. Other individuals likely participated or assisted (if only by inattention), and entity liability is necessary if there is to be any hope of indirectly punishing them. The government proceeds only against individuals with great responsibility, where the evidence is clear-cut. Lesser wrongdoers also need punishment, and the government can and should work indirectly to cause them to be punished.[42]

More arguably, corporate liability may also be seen as a means of promoting self-discipline and legal compliance within the corporate organisation as a whole. This may be achieved in two ways: (1) providing an incentive for the company to monitor more effectively the behaviour of its employees; and (2) off-setting the possible internal compensation of individuals who are subject to criminal law penalties 'on behalf' of their companies. Regarding the monitoring role of companies, DeMott argues for instance:

Vicarious liability also encourages an organization to use skill in selecting agents. By using care, the organization may avoid hiring would-be agents whose incurable roguishness will be resistant to

---

41 Mark Bovens, *The Quest for Responsibility: Accountability and Citizenship in Complex Organisations* (Cambridge University Press, 1998), p. 46.
42 Stephen Calkins, 'Corporate Compliance and the Antitrust Agencies' Bi-Modal Penalties', 60 (1997) *Law and Contemporary Problems* 127, at p. 144.

the organization's control. In evaluating the effects of vicarious liability, it is helpful to reflect on the actual organizational traits of large business corporations, many of which do not function according to classical models of formal bureaucracy … vicarious liability creates incentives for the organization's senior management to devise systems and patterns of interaction with those lower in the hierarchy that will trump these organizational traits.[43]

Thus it is argued that overall legal compliance may be better assured by imposing a higher standard of corporate supervision on the company as employer. But others doubt the relative effectiveness of internal discipline compared with legal penalties – Calkins, for instance, questions the real impact of the range of corporate disciplinary measures, including dismissal, and points out that many such employees are quite mobile and may soon be out of the range of a particular company's disciplinary action.[44] Then, secondly, in rather different circumstances, corporate liability may undermine furtive corporate support for penalised individuals, as a reward for absorbing some or the whole of the penalty for the violation. But the effectiveness of such strategies for inducing corporate compliance awaits clear demonstration.[45]

Finally, it should be noted that some systems of regulation are still wedded to the idea of dealing with the matter as an instance of market behaviour on the part of economic actors in corporate form. The model provided by the EC Treaty (and now widely replicated throughout the Member States) supplied the paradigm for this approach, focussing on the legal personality of the 'undertaking'. This

---

43 Deborah DeMott, 'Organizational Incentives', note 31 above, p. 43.
44 Calkins, 'Corporate Compliance', note 42 above, at pp. 141–2.
45 But that again is deterrence *theory*. In practice, it may be more difficult to assess the deterrent impact of corporate liability in this respect. Consider the following report in the *International Herald Tribune*, 24 October 2000: 'Robert Koehler returned to his position as chairman and chief executive of SGL Carbon AG in Germany after the company was fined $135 million in May 1999 for fixing the price of graphite electrodes used in the steel industry. Mr Koehler was personally fined $10 million. But SGL shareholders made no complaints about such enormous losses. They presumably had benefited handsomely from the $1.7 billion in electrode sales in the United States during the five years in which manufacturers conspired.'

is a view of business conspiracy which does not easily accommodate the role of the human actor. A characteristic of much 'regulatory' law is a forward-looking, preventive and utilitarian concern with the reduction of harm rather than attribution of blame and responsibility, and this in turn leads naturally to the adoption of administrative techniques of legal control, with a focus on organisational rather than individual actors.[46] But the EC regulatory model (although not its application at the national level) is also to some extent a matter of practical necessity, following on from the EC's lack of criminal law power in the traditional sense.

(c) Individual liability as a priority

The supporting strategic argument for individual rather than corporate liability looks mainly to the perceived ineffectiveness of sanctions as applied to corporate actors. Companies are typically subject to fines as penalties and it is frequently asserted that financial penalties do not in fact possess much deterrent impact, and in practice cannot easily be set at a sufficiently high level to match the illegal profits made by activities such as price fixing. The very fact of widespread recidivism on the part of numerous firms following detection and the imposition of fines in a number of jurisdictions casts doubt on the deterrent impact of such sanctions as such. Research into the impact of corporate fines suggests that these penalties can never be realistically sufficiently severe as to provide a real deterrent.[47] It is also claimed that corporate penalties may indirectly harm innocent parties, such as shareholders, employees or customers. For instance, it has been sometimes asserted that companies in the US may be willing to sacrifice shareholder interests by settling civil cases in order to avoid the imposition of individual liability and so protect friends and colleagues within the company.[48]

---

46 Indeed, it may be argued that this has been the predominant ethos of European (as distinct from North American) competition policy, emphasising the regulation of market *outcomes* rather than the *conduct* of market actors: see Chapter 2 in Harding and Joshua, *Regulating Cartels in Europe*, note 17 above.

47 There is a summary of the research argument in Wils, 'Effective Enforcement', note 38 above. See in particular: C. Craycraft, J.L. Craycraft and J.C. Gallo, 'Antitrust Sanctions and a Firm's Ability to Pay', 12 (1997) *Review of Industrial Organisation*, 171.

48 Calkins, 'Corporate Compliance', note 42 above, at p. 143. Such settlements have been referred to as 'Westinghouse settlements', involving a guilty

On the other hand, enforcement policy in the US certainly considers that individuals are more susceptible to the deterrent threat of penalties, particularly prison terms. Although it is notoriously difficult to measure the relative impact of different types of sanction in this context, especially when the personal impact of prison terms is brought into the picture, so far research findings have not clearly contradicted the anecdotal evidence of apprehension of criminal conviction for individuals. Calkins provides anecdotal evidence that:

> criminal is different. As one CEO told me, if his company pays a moderate civil fine, it is five minutes at a regular board of director's meeting; were the same fine a felony, there is a special board meeting. One CEO worried about customers that would rather not purchase from a tainted source; an inside counsel worried about recruiting new employees; another inside counsel worried about the effect on existing employees.[49]

And Lipman has argued that for the businessman 'prison is the inferno, and conventional risk–reward analysis breaks down when the risk is jail'.[50] Such reasoning reinforces the attractiveness of such sanctions on individuals, especially now as an essential component of leniency strategies, as already noted.

The enforcement perspective therefore centres around the perceived effectiveness of particular sanctions being targeted against different actors. Practice and research argument which suggests a limited impact of corporate fines, and a relatively more powerful impact on the part of prison terms for company executives, has led enforcement agencies to argue more strongly in favour of individual criminal liability, or a combination of individual and corporate liability, as in the present context of leniency programmes. But, as the earlier discussion has demonstrated, the pursuit of such utilitarian enforcement objectives may give rise to jurisprudential difficulties concerning the definition of business conspiracy and the ethical basis for proceeding against different types of actor in this context.

---

plea by the company in return for charges against individuals being dropped.

49 Calkins, 'Corporate Compliance, note 42 above, at p. 145. See also V.S. Khanna (1997) 'Corporate Criminal Liability: What Purpose Does It Serve?' *Harvard Law Review*, 109: 1477.
50 Lipman, 'Paper Label Sentences', note 38 above, at p. 631.

6 The search for legal principle

The above discussion has demonstrated that the legal control of business conspiracy, particularly in the context of cartel activity, is developing significantly across a number of jurisdictions. To a large extent these developments may be seen as driven by enforcement imperatives, as manifested in particular in strategies concerning investigation, the collection of evidence and the imposition of sanctions. Furthermore, a distinctive feature of this area of legal control is the possibility of taking action against both corporate and individual actors in relation to their involvement in the same overall cartel activity. This can be done in different ways. The analysis presented here has identified two leading models: the 'single conspiracy' model (exemplified by the Sherman Act in the US) and the 'disaggregated offence' model (exemplified by the recent British legislation). It is further argued that both models raise ethical and legal issues concerning the double counting of offences and offenders and the allocation of responsibility.

To some extent, the resolution of these questions may depend upon the convincing identification of distinct corporate and individual *personae* and actions within the framework of the cartel conspiracy, so that the two actors are not seen just as each other's *alter ego* but as performing genuinely distinct roles in the material world. This raises the classical dilemma of independent corporate identity: the corporate person as a *ding an sich*. Taking an empirical view of corporate and individual conduct in this context, it is suggested[51] that a combination of enduring structure and an established and governing corporate ethos may confer a meaningfully distinct identity so as to differentiate corporate and individual actors for legal purposes. In this way, some of the logical and ethical dilemma arising from the legal construction of business conspiracy may be resolved. Equally, however, the consequence of such an approach is a *principled* basis for efforts of legal control, which may not always match enforcement

---

51 But in the consciousness that this argument runs counter to the doctrine of 'methodological individualism' much favoured by lawyers. For a classic jurisprudential analysis of this doctrine, see H.L.A. Hart, *Definition and Theory in Jurisprudence* (Clarendon Press, 1950), at p. 21; and for a judicial adoption of this approach, see the statement by Lord Hoffmann in the *Meridian* case, note 23 above, (1995) 2 AC, at pp. 506–7: 'There is no such thing as the company as such, no ding an sich, only the applicable rules.'

imperatives or preferences. The accommodation of legal principle and enforcement policy then emerges as a major task for criminal jurisprudence in this context.

There is another issue arising from the allocation of responsibility for cartel activity, distinct from the choice between corporate and individual responsibility, but relating rather to the way in which either corporate or individual responsibility arises from the collective activity of the cartel. This shifts the focus of discussion away from the members of the cartel to the cartel itself as a collective enterprise, which itself has a bearing on the kind of responsibility which is attributed to its members. This is a subject which will be dealt with further in Chapter 10 below, when concepts such as the 'cartel as a whole' and 'joint criminal enterprise' are examined in more detail, as structures which accommodate a particular form of responsibility arising from participation in a collective action or enterprise.

Chapter 7

Delinquency within structures of governance

The issue of delinquency and criminality perpetrated in the context of public governance presents another significant contemporary site for exploring the interaction of individual and organisational actors. Put simply, when confronting the 'criminal' or 'delinquent State', should responsibility for such conduct be attached to the State or to individuals exercising State authority? It may be observed that during the twentieth century three principal routes emerged towards such legal accountability: that towards the State as a criminal, that towards individuals as criminals, and that towards the State as a human rights violator. After 1945, the third of these routes tended to supplant the first, apparently putting the 'criminal State' in the back seat. It may be asked therefore whether the idea of the criminal State (as another kind of organisational agent) remains relevant or useful.

Employing the model of organisational agency worked out in Chapter 3, it is possible to identify some kinds of activity in relation to which it would be meaningful to impose criminal responsibility (as distinct from responsibility for the violation of human rights) on State actors. However, such a project needs to address a number of issues, or at least surmount some hurdles. First, it is necessary to address a body of scepticism in the field of international law regarding the idea of the State as a criminal actor, as evident for instance in the International Law Commission's debate on the subject of State responsibility. Secondly, an important task is the working out of appropriate offence definitions in relation to the respective roles of the State and the individual in this context. In this respect, the emergence of the joint criminal enterprise (in relation to war crimes and crimes against humanity) as a basis for individual responsibility is a significant development. Thirdly, the desirability of legally disaggregating State and governmental actors (heads of State, governments, regimes and factions) for purposes of the allocation of responsibility should be considered. Two significant outcomes might then be observed: individual responsibility on the basis of joint criminal enterprise, and organisational responsibility on the basis of disaggregating State and government into different forms of governmental actor.

I The delinquent State: in the back seat?

Does it make sense to talk about the State as a delinquent actor – as a moral agent and potential subject of criminal responsibility? Views may appear to differ on this question. A significant and topical context for this discussion is the extreme maltreatment of individuals and groups, which is now commonly converted into legal expression as the violation of such persons' fundamental rights. In relation to this question, consider the following statements. First, in his opening speech as Chief Prosecutor at the Nuremburg War Crimes Tribunal in 1946, Sir Hartley Shawcross argued:

> There is not anything startlingly new in the adoption of the principle that the State as such is responsible for its criminal acts … In fact … the immeasurable potentialities for evil inherent in the State in this age of science and organization would seem to demand, quite imperatively, means of repression of criminal conduct even more drastic and more effective than in the case of individuals.[1]

This argument implicitly accepts the moral agency and legal personality of the State for purposes of allocating criminal responsibility and indeed urges this as an ethical and political imperative, pointing to the growing capacity of the State as a criminal actor. On the other hand, the judgment of the Nuremburg International Military Tribunal itself contains the following statement:

> Crimes against international law are committed by men, not by abstract entities, and only by punishing individuals who

---

1 *The Trial of Major German War Criminals: Opening Speeches of the Chief Prosecutors* (1946), pp. 57–8.

157

commit such crimes can the provisions of international law be enforced.[2]

In contrast, then, the Tribunal's judgment appears firmly to be based on the approach of individualism, arguing that it is functionally necessary to locate responsibility at the level of individual human actors. Thus, within the same legal process set up to deal with the vast swathe of inhumane conduct perpetrated by the Nazi regime, there appears to be a contradiction of philosophy and policy regarding the basic question of agency and attribution of responsibility.

In fact, the Nuremburg trial process was not flawed in this way by self-contradiction and confusion. A more careful reading of the proceedings reveals an underlying policy of resorting to both organisational and individual responsibility, although historically it is remembered more for the way in which it moved forward the latter concept at the international level. As Jørgensen comments:

> It is apparent that after the Second World War, individual criminal responsibility under international law for acts of state became well established while state criminal responsibility, although a key issue, was increasingly viewed as an unworkable concept, and consequently took a back seat.[3]

During the second half of the twentieth century, the 'war criminal' became a familiar figure within the landscape of governmental delinquency, as an especially egregious individual offender. The accompanying eclipse of State responsibility in this context – at least as a criminal actor, though not of course as a human rights violator – is in itself of interest and merits further discussion. Moreover, despite the low profile of the 'criminal State', the involvement of governmental actors in delinquent and injurious conduct is a significant aspect of contemporary organisation, and is a phenomenon worthy of close scrutiny. In particular, the relation between individual and organisational activity and responsibility is within this context (as in that of business activity discussed above in Chapter 6) a subject of complexity, and also a key to understanding the emergence of the model of individual liability within this area.

---

2 Judgment of the Tribunal. See the text in (1947) *American Journal of International Law*, 41: 172.
3 Nina H.B. Jørgensen, *The Responsibility of States for International Crimes* (Oxford University Press, 2000), p. 27.

The plan of discussion in this chapter is therefore to explore further the models of organisational (State) and individual criminal responsibility in relation to delinquent and injurious conduct within the realm of public governance. Something will be said first about the character and substance of the kind of conduct which may qualify as seriously delinquent within this context, and its now significant legal classification as a violation of fundamental human rights. The discussion will then probe the choice between models of State and individual responsibility and what more precisely in legal terms may be entailed in this kind of State responsibility, especially in so far as such responsibility is seen as a matter of international law. Further consideration will then be given to the relation between State and individual responsibility and the idea that respectively they may be taken to represent accountability for different kinds of conduct – broadly speaking, organisational conduct and implementing conduct. Finally, the question will be addressed whether the State is in fact the most appropriate organisational actor for the allocation of any criminal responsibility, and an argument will be made for the disaggregation of the State and more specific types of governmental actor.

2 Governmental delinquency as criminal conduct

It is not difficult to find either historical or more contemporary examples of delinquent and injurious conduct, either on the part of individuals or in an organisational form, arising from the process of public governance. The business of government, at whatever level, necessarily entails an accumulation of power which may then be abused in myriad ways. Following the adage that 'all power corrupts', a certain amount of governmental delinquency might seem to be an inevitable risk of government and indeed a large amount of modern 'public law' is primarily concerned with the containment of the abusive or damaging exercise of power by those in positions of government.

That illegal acts, some of which may qualify as criminal offences, may be committed in the course of government is therefore a commonplace observation. During the later part of the twentieth century there have been two dominant legal responses to such delinquency in public governance, both very much fashioned with reference to the impact on those who are victims of such conduct.

First, the criminal law applicable to individuals has been used as a means of legal control. One approach to the subject is to argue that what is being referred to here is no more than a particular context or circumstance of the commission of familiar criminal offences, whether they involve personal violence, damage to property or financial interests, or other category of injury, by individual human actors in the course of their governmental role. On such a view, while the 'public', 'political' or governmental role of the actor may aid the opportunity for such offending, it is in the final analysis no more than a circumstantial feature: the matter remains one of personal responsibility. This perception underlies the argument that 'crimes are committed by men, not by abstract entities', quoted above; and to the extent that many acts of governance depend upon some human instrumentality or agency, it is difficult to quarrel with such an individualist interpretation.

The second main legal approach has been to cast the injury arising from governmental delinquency, not so much as a criminal act but as a violation of a fundamental right, and in this way hold the State accountable, at either the national or international level, for such violation. Under this method, the State is seen as the responsible actor but not cast as a criminal as such. Sure enough, the State as a fundamental rights violator is seen in general terms as a delinquent actor, but its legal liability in this respect evades categorisation as either civil or delictual on the one hand or criminal on the other hand. It might be argued that this is largely a semantic point: the violation of such rights may well be a matter of serious delinquency and being held to be in violation is like a serious criminal conviction in all but name. Clearly this is so – many human rights violations are the same in substance as war crimes or crimes against humanity. But process and formal descriptions do count for something, especially in political terms. A number of sovereign States may politically be more readily prepared to appear in the dock of a human rights court than that of a criminal court. The legal reluctance to describe States as criminal will be explored further below, but one consequence of this reluctance has surely been the emergence of human rights law as a significant and politically feasible means of achieving accountability on the part of governmental and public authority. During the first half of the twentieth century, particularly in the wake of the two world wars, there had been some idea of imposing criminal liability on States and nations.[4] After 1945 much of that initiative was diverted

---

4 See the account given by Jørgensen, note 3 above, at pp. 9–11, 15–17 and 25–27. For instance, in his election statement in 1918 Lloyd George had announced: 'You may depend upon it that the first consideration in

into the human rights project, which may be understood then, in some senses, as an alternative route for fulfilling a moral and legal vision of State accountability.

Thus governmental delinquency has been very much on the legal agenda from 1945. In effect, at the close of the Second World War, three legal models in particular were on the legal drafting board (see Table 7.1).

It appears that in the immediate post-World War II period, support for the first model, that of State criminal responsibility, declined fairly quickly. This may be gauged from the discussions on the drafting of the Genocide Convention in the late 1940s. The British proposal that:

criminal responsibility for any act of genocide as specified in Article II and IV shall extend not only to all private persons and associations, but also to states, governments, or organs or authorities of the state or government, by whom such acts are committed

Table 7.1 Options Panel 1: three routes to accountability

Criminal responsibility of the State	Criminal responsibility of the individual	Responsibility of the State for human rights violations
e.g. Post-World War I reparations; Post-World War II criminalisation of official organisations (Leadership Corps of the Nazi Party, SS, Gestapo)	e.g. Post-World War II war crimes trials	e.g. Post-World War II human rights protection treaties

the minds of the Allies will be the interests of the people upon whom Germany has made war, and not the interests of the German people who have been guilty of this crime against humanity' (see: David Lloyd George, *The Truth about the Peace Treaties*, I (Gollancz, 1938), at p. 467). In 1946, the French Chief Prosecutor at the Nuremburg Trials, Francois de Menthon argued: 'It is necessary that, after having premeditated, prepared and launched a war of aggression ... After having thereupon piled up the most odious crimes in the course of the war years, Nazi Germany shall be declared guilty ...' (*The Trial of the German Major War Criminals: Opening Speeches of the Chief Prosecutors* (1946), at p. 90).

was rejected by the UN Sixth (Legal) Committee by 24 votes to 22.[5] Later, the US representative to the Committee argued against the British view that 'genocide could be committed by juridical entities, such as the state or the government' since 'in reality genocide was always committed by individuals'.[6] Despite the rise of scepticism regarding State criminal liability, the alternative model of State responsibility as a human rights violator was to gain ground impressively. Moreover, the idea of international responsibility on the part of States for conduct described as 'criminal' as a matter of international law was to revive (although controversially) at a later date, for instance in the earlier discussion by the International Law Commission (ILC) of its *Draft Articles on State Responsibility*,[7] and in the proceedings brought before the International Court of Justice by Bosnia-Herzegovina regarding the *Application of the Genocide Convention*,[8] both of which will be discussed further below.

3 State or individual responsibility?

As the discussion in earlier chapters has shown, responsibility for unacceptable or delinquent conduct may not be just a matter of attributing its physical or material performance to human actors. As in the discussion of corporate responsibility, there may in some situations be aspects of conduct lying beyond the simple act of physical perpetration which justify a different attribution of moral and legal accountability as something more than or different from an assessment of the conduct of discrete individuals. Once again, we are faced with the complication of organisational activity: individuals, in carrying out acts of governance, are (outside the context of very

---

5 Jørgensen, note 3 above, p. 36.

6 Statement of representative Maktos: Official Records of the Third Session of the General Assembly, Part 1, Sixth Committee, Legal Questions, Summary Record of Meetings, 21 September–10 December 1948, 93rd Meeting, 319–20.

7 See Jørgensen, note 3 above, at p 46 *et seq*. The important provision was Draft Article 19, discussed further below.

8 *Case Concerning the Application of the Genocide Convention, Bosnia and Herzegovina v. Serbia and Montenegro*, Order on Provisional Merits, (1993) ICJ Reps 3; Judgment on Preliminary Objections, (1996) ICJ Rep; hearings on the merits began on 27 February 2006 (ICJ Press Release, 2006/9).

simple societies) acting as part of an organisation, and this fact may affect any assessment of the action in question.

In the context of governance, the substance of some activity may be so clearly of a more general and organisational rather than individual character that the role of State organisation is clearly separate from that of its individual human agents. One example of such a situation would be delinquency residing in the failure of State authority, at an organisational level, to supervise and control standards of behaviour on the part of officials. Such a failing or delinquency would be something over and above any specific predicate offences or lapses in standards on the part of individual officials. Or, another example would be conduct that can only meaningfully be carried out as an act of State authority at the organisational level, the classic case usually cited being the waging of aggressive warfare. In its very nature, this is conduct that is based on an institutional rather than individual ethos, policy and decision-making. While there may be predicate instances of aggressive warfare – such as specific orders to attack civilians or use disproportionate methods of warfare – these are conceptually distinct from engagement in a *war of aggression*, as evidenced for instance in a policy of unprovoked military attacks or the occupation of neutral territory. In Hartian language, this is a matter of role-responsibility: something that is within the role of States and governments but not that of individuals. As Erskine argues, using another example:

> The United States can respond to acute environmental crises by upholding the conditions of the Kyoto convention – whether or not it chooses to do so – while the individual citizen cannot. The same citizen might have a duty to live in a way that is environmentally responsible, but she has neither the scope nor the power to coordinate and enforce systemic changes in how goods are produced, consumed, and disposed of.[9]

It is in relation to such activities that are most meaningfully within the role of States or governments that the allocation of responsibility to the State rather than the individual is likely to be most convincing. With reference to delinquent activity, a number of main examples of such action which is typically the role of the State come to mind. Engaging in a war of aggression, as already seen, is a clear example,

---

9 Toni Erskine, 'Assigning Responsibilities to Institutional Moral Agents', Chapter 1 in Toni Erskine (ed.), *Can Institutions Have Responsibilities?* (Palgrave Macmilan, 2003), at p. 35.

and is an established legal concept, listed in the charters of war crimes tribunals and the subject of UN General Assembly resolutions. Linked to such aggression are a number of related types of conduct which may fall short of that which formally qualifies as warfare: in particular, acts which constitute 'threats to peace and security' in the language emanating from the UN Charter, or more specifically, given the present level of legal prohibition, the development and possession of weapons of mass destruction, and also State-sponsored terrorism. Typically, all of these types of conduct exceed the capacity and role of any individual (unless such a person is being identified in a very different way, for instance, as a dictatorial head of state, in which case that individual may be transformed into a 'governmental actor', as discussed below).

Other types of conduct which entail the systematic, serious and large-scale violation of human rights will also typically qualify as such distinctive State or governmental delinquency. Programmes of genocide and ethnic cleansing are likely to head this part of the list, in a sense often representing the 'internal' aspect of the kind of violent, aggressive and discriminatory behaviour described in its 'external' dimension as an act of aggression. Another example, as a species of systematic and injurious discrimination in governance, is the kind of policy now often described under the generic heading of 'apartheid'.[10] Similarly, a policy of governance which is designed to defeat the aspiration towards self-determination on the part of an ethnic or religious group could be seen as falling within the scope of this major branch of governmental delinquency.

What these typically governmental delinquencies have in common, as generic features, would appear to be, first, adoption as an official policy, which then results in a systematic, long-term and widely deployed implementation. As Jørgensen reasons:

> The key distinguishing feature of state crimes within the seriousness test is the element of system. A crime can only be attributable to the state if it is committed by state organs or agents in furtherance of a definite state policy.[11]

Another way of attempting to express the sense of distance between State organisation and human implementing action is to employ the

---

10 See, for instance, the discussion by Jørgensen, note 3 above, at pp. 245–7, and below under section 5(a) of this chapter.
11 Jørgensen, note 3 above, at p. 160.

idea of *anonymity* in relation to action attributed to the State.[12] The term 'anonymous' here conveys the difficulty of associating the action with any particular human actor. This point was made by Charles Dobost, the Deputy Chief Prosecutor for France at the Nuremburg Tribunal:

> Genocide, murder or any other crime becomes anonymous when it is committed by the State. Nobody bears the chief responsibility. Everybody shares it: those who by their presence maintain and support the administration, those who conceived the crime and those who ordained it, as well as he who issued the order.[13]

But it has to be admitted that the subject matter, and theory, of State and governmental delinquency and criminality remains ill-defined. On the one hand, legal definition tends to be tentative, as is evident from the eventual reluctance of the International Law Commission to embrace categorically a concept of international 'crimes' as committed by States and the objection of a number of international lawyers to employing any criminal law terminology.[14] On the other hand, it is now generally accepted that in reality the international community recognises a qualitative difference between different types of internationally illegal conduct on the part of States and also, it may be argued, adopts a 'penal' response to specific State infractions. Pellet, for instance, has argued (on emerging from the ILC debates) that:

> ... the word 'crime' is defensible; it has acquired its legitimacy since 1976 and is very widely used. However, if the analogy with domestic law seems really excessive and repulsive, it may

---

12 This is similar to Coleman's concept of the 'irrelevance of persons', as discussed in Chapter 3 above (James S. Coleman, *The Asymmetric Society: Organisational Actors, Corporate Power and the Irrelevance of Persons* (Syracuse University Press, 1982).

13 *Trial of German Major War Criminals, Proceedings of the IMT,* 29 July– 8 August 1946, pt 20 (1949) 23.

14 See James Crawford, *The International Law Commission's Articles on State Responsibility: Introduction, Text and Commentaries* (Cambridge University Press, 2002), p. 242 *et seq.*; and generally the discussion in J.H.H. Weiler, A. Cassese and M. Spinedi, *International Crimes of States* (De Gruyter, 1989).

be abandoned. But the reality will remain … a genocide cannot be compared with a breach of a trade agreement; it is, by its very nature, different in kind. Call it 'breach of a peremptory norm' or 'violation of an essential obligation', call it 'butterfly' or 'abomination', the fact remains: we need a concept, and a name for this concept.[15]

But the problem with many attempts by international lawyers to define more closely the idea of a State crime resides in the natural tendency of international lawyers to fall back on formal and rather circular indicia and criteria, such as breach of *ius cogens*, breach of an obligation *erga omnes*, breaching the 'conscience of mankind' or 'elementary considerations of humanity, as recognised by the international community', or norms of a sufficient seriousness.[16] This was the approach finally embodied in the ILC's *Articles on State Responsibility* in 2001, when it abandoned the word 'crime' and instead in Article 40 referred to a 'serious breach of an obligation arising under a peremptory norm'. But such an approach shies away from a more direct consideration of substantive characteristics of State conduct, and also misses the important distinctive features of State as distinct from human activity.

On the other hand, social scientific definition tends to be looser, and sometimes verge upon the idiosyncratic. Thus, Geldenhuys, in his work *Deviant Conduct in World Politics*,[17] refers to delinquent States variously as 'pariahs', 'outcasts' and 'rogues' and presents the following list of 'sins of contemporary deviant states': threats to peace, terrorism, stockpiling of armaments, regional aggression, lack of democracy and human rights, crimes against humanity, war crimes, exporting revolution, anti-Westernism, assertiveness, and drug trafficking. While the first part of this catalogue is not contentious, the later part may seem eclectic, selective and sometimes clearly devoid of any normative basis. As Geldenhuys concedes: in relation to 'anti-

---

15   Alain Pellet (1999) 'Can a State Commit a Crime? Definitely, Yes!' *European Journal of International Law*, 10(426): 434. Pellet's discussion is a valuable 'insider' summary of the ILC's internal agonising on the drafting of the relevant part of the 'Draft Articles on State Responsibility'.
16   See the list of criteria discussed in detail by Jørgensen, note 3 above, at pp. 83–131.
17   Deon Geldenhuys, *Deviant Conduct in World Politics* (Palgrave Macmillan, 2004), Chapters 1 and 2. See in particular the section at p. 23 *et seq.* headed 'The sins of contemporary deviant states'.

Westernism', there are 'no settled international norms at stake', while the sin of assertiveness 'constitutes an informal and largely unilateral rule of conduct'.[18] By that stage it is clear that the listing process has strayed too far into the realm of the subjective.

It is necessary therefore to steer a course between the hesitant and formalistic attempts at definition by international law and the looser cannon-fire of international relations discourse. An attempt is made in Table 7.2 below to identify, on the basis of current international practice and the concept of organisational (and thus State) activity presented in the discussion in this book, an outline categorisation of main types of State conduct which would fit a contemporary sense of delinquency in governance, and in turn of State criminality.

Table 7.2 offers a listing of delinquent conduct which may be appropriately attributed to the responsibility of the State rather than to individuals. The first column indicates the underlying values or interests affected by such conduct on the part of the State. The

Table 7.2 The basis for State criminality: delinquency attributable to State governance

Category	Main examples
Procedural	
Failure to supervise the conduct of government agents	Negligent monitoring, or licensing of abusive activities on the part of government agents
Substantive	
Injury or risk of injury to human physical security	War of aggression Threat to peace and security Genocide Ethnic cleansing State-sponsored terrorism Maintaining weapons of mass destruction
Injury to fundamental claims to self-determination	Apartheid Racial discrimination Religious and cultural persecution

18 *Ibid.*, pp. 36–37.

second column indicates in a more specific and substantive way the main categories of action which may be seen as injuring those values and interests. This list in the second column is illustrative and not exhaustive, but is intended to provide some idea of the main categories of conduct which, in our contemporary society, might well qualify as 'State crimes'. The 'procedural' category of delinquent conduct relates to that which is perhaps most easily attributable to the State, and indeed corresponds with a well-established branch of State responsibility under international law. Here responsibility is based on the international obligation of a State to control abusive conduct on the part of its own agents. More traditionally such responsibility related to injury caused to foreign nationals; more recently it has provided the basis for States' obligations to respect certain fundamental rights of their own nationals.

The 'substantive' categories of conduct comprise more directly injurious activities, which because of their systemic and personally anonymous character may be seen as State or governmental conduct rather than that which should be attributed to particular individuals. It should be noted that this attribution of responsibility to the State or government does not imply that individuals are not involved in some way in activities such as genocide, ethnic cleansing or apartheid. What is being argued is that there may be different levels of responsibility for different aspects of the conduct in question – the more general and the more specific, the formulation of policy and particular acts of implementing policy. As in the case of corporate responsibility it is a matter of working out, for both ethical and legal purposes, the best options in allocating responsibility as between different moral agents.[19]

It will be argued here that option 2 in Table 7.3 is an appropriate and viable model for responsibility in the context of governmental delinquency, as indeed in the case of corporate delinquency (see Chapter 6 above). However, before examining further the relation between organisational and individual responsibility in this context, the character of any State responsibility itself needs to be clarified.

---

19 As Jørgensen, note 3 above, argues: 'The criminal responsibility of states, individuals, governments and organizations were all notions that received considerable attention in the aftermath of the two world wars and three possible systems were advocated: first, that of the exclusive responsibility of states; second, that of the cumulative responsibility of states and individuals; and finally, that of the exclusive responsibility of individuals.' (*The Responsibility of States for International Crimes*, p. 4).

Table 7.3 Options Panel 2: the responsible actor

1. The State alone	2. The State and the individual (differentiated responsibility)	3. The individual alone
'Because of the complex structure of the modern State sometimes acts can only be imputed to the whole system.'	'Both individuals and organisations may be regarded as moral agents, in relation to different although related aspects of the same situation.'	'Crimes are committed by men not by abstract entities.'

4 The nature of State responsibility for delinquency in governance: the genie out of the bottle?

Reference has already been made, in Chapter 5 above, to different types of legal liability for rule breaking and delinquent conduct. For example, a primary distinction is drawn within many legal systems, in relation to the conduct of individuals, between civil and criminal liability. A special feature of any kind of State or governmental responsibility is that, for practical purposes, this is a matter which will be formally worked out for the most part as a matter of international law rather than of the legal system of the State in question. While governmental agencies or individuals in positions of government[20] may be dealt with under the law of their own State, there may be a logical problem in the *State as such* being subject to proceedings under the legal system which is part of that State.[21] The international law of State responsibility does not formally categorise such responsibility as 'civil' or 'criminal', and, as noted above, the ILC has agonised for some time over the possible designation of some conduct on the part of States as 'criminal'. The precise nature of international State responsibility for highly delinquent conduct remains therefore a matter of debate.

However, it appears to be generally agreed that there is now a broad distinction drawn in international law between two orders of

---

20 See the discussion below in this chapter on the questions of disaggregating different kinds of governmental actor from the State.

21 Moreover, the doctrine of sovereign or State immunity under international law has similarly impeded States being subject to legal process within the legal orders of other States.

State responsibility: that relating to 'ordinary' or 'normal' breaches of international rules, and that relating to a more serious level of violation, offending against fundamental general rules which embody essential values. This distinction is now encapsulated in the ILC's *Articles on State Responsibility* when reference is made in Article 40 to responsibility 'entailed by a serious breach by a State of an obligation arising under a peremptory norm of general international law'.

Cassese usefully describes this second order of responsibility as 'aggravated' State responsibility.[22] His analysis depicts an 'ordinary' violation as one breaching a 'synallagmatic' obligation concerning the reciprocal interests of two States (for instance, concerning a trade agreement, or the reciprocal treatment of nationals or diplomatic personnel). Such breaches concern bilateral relations, and suggest a 'private' relationship between States, and the analogy of civil liability. On the other hand, 'aggravated' responsibility relates to the breach of a fundamental 'community' obligation and as such is of interest and concern to the international community as a whole: thus the violation is suggestive of a criminal offence in the national context. Cassese explains that following such a breach:

> ... a *'public relation'* comes into being between the delinquent State and all other States or, as the case may be, all the other contracting States. The 'public' nature of the relation lies in that any other State, *regardless whether or not it has been materially or morally damaged by the breach,* can invoke the responsibility of the wrongdoer (this invocation may also be made by a competent international body, either on its own initiative, or at the request of a State). In other words, the States that take action to invoke this class of responsibility *do not pursue a personal or individual interest*; they pursue *a community interest*, for they act on behalf of the whole world community or of the plurality of States parties to the multilateral treaty. In addition, all of the States entitled to demand compliance with the obligation that has been infringed may take a host of remedial actions designed to impel the delinquent State to cease its wrongdoing or to make reparation.[23]

---

22 Antonio Cassese, *International Law* (2nd edn, Oxford University Press, 2005), p. 244 *et seq.*

23 *Ibid.*, at pp. 262–3.

A number of international lawyers, not to mention a number of governments, are very uncomfortable with the idea of 'international crimes of States'.[24] Consequently, as already noted, the ILC has jettisoned the draft of its earlier Special Rapporteur, Roberto Ago,[25] who had used that terminology in Article 19 of the ILC *Draft Articles on State Responsibility*. Yet, Cassese's description of this more serious type of State breach and how it has been dealt with by State practice, strongly suggests a system of proto-criminal law in relation to State conduct at the international level. Certain things may be clearly observed from a review of State practice over the last 40 years or so: a generally perceived seriousness in relation to certain specific instances of norm violation; a concomitant degree of formal disapproval, through tribunal, governmental or United Nations statements; and the application of sanctions with a clear coercive and even punitive objective, going beyond a simple matter

---

24 It is instructive to compare the treatment of this topic by various textbook writers. In contrast to Cassese's detailed and adventurous discussion, other writers appear muted and sceptical. Brownlie, for instance, dismisses the debate in a single line – 'Some jurists are of the opinion that states may bear a criminal responsibility for certain categories of wrongdoing' – and does not bother to supply any references (Ian Brownlie, *Principles of Public International Law* (6th edn, Oxford University Press, 2003)). Another British text, by Gardiner, is rather less brief, but still sceptical: 'The idea that a state as a legal person is responsible because of its failure to comply to a minimum standard led to unfortunate attempts to equate this area of international law with domestic law ... Fortunately, divergence of views has been such that the criminal element of the draft rules has effectively been dropped.' (Richard K. Gardiner, *International Law* (Pearson, 2003), pp. 441–42.) It is perhaps no coincidence that the UK has been one of the States at the forefront of resistance in relation to the idea of State crimes.

25 Ago was a leading proponent of the concept of criminal State responsibility. For a useful discussion of Ago's doctrinal position, see: Georg Nolte (2002) 'From Dionisio Anzilotti to Roberto Ago: The Classical International Law of State Responsibility and the Traditional Primacy of a Bilateral Conception of Inter-State Relations', *European Journal of International Law*, 13: 1083. Nolte pictures Ago as representing 'the recognition after the Second World War that there is a real international community of states which possesses some legal mechanisms to enforce a collective will' (at p. 1084). He also casts Ago as the doctrinal heir of Hersch Lauterpacht: see in particular Lauterpacht's 1937 Hague Lectures, 'Règles générales du droit de la paix', 62 *Receuil des Cours* (1937–IV) 99.

of compensation. Admittedly, this is not a system of criminal law on the familiar national law model,[26] but nor should the exact replication of that model be expected in the international context. The important point is to recognise the substance of this legal development and to take on board the significant *analogy of that substance* with what is elsewhere designated criminal law, and a penal response to conduct widely perceived as delinquent in character. Jørgensen in examining this State practice and international level discussion of the issue has concluded that:

> ... the concept of State criminality is an emergent general principle of international law. The concept has been shown to be juridically sound and it can be transported into the practical sphere ... The international community has come too far to abandon the concept ... The logical development and evolution of the law suggest that the concept will continue to emerge from its post-Second World War 'back seat' position and appear as a workable category of positive law.[27]

It is important to note some of the evidence for what may be described at least as an 'emergent' system of 'proto-criminal responsibility' for States at the international level. In particular, there are two categories of activity which comprise a process of both formal condemnation and enforcement action in relation to identified serious breaches of international rules. First, there is a body of responsive action which may be termed institutionalised collective enforcement, involving forcible or non-forcible (for instance, economic) sanctions, authorised by such international bodies as the UN Security Council or General Assembly, or the EC/EU. For instance, at different times such

---

26 See for instance the Comment by Italy on Draft Article 19: any special regime for serious internationally wrongful acts would have 'nothing in common with the penal sanctions such as those imposed under national criminal laws, and the use of some other term than "international crimes" could perhaps be envisaged'. (A/CN.4/448/Add.2. Comments by Italy under Article 19.)

27 Jørgensen, note 3 above, at pp. 231, 233. In terms of State practice, the strongest and most consistent resistance to employing the concept has been on the part of some Western States, notably the US, the UK and France. Strongest support has come from developing countries, former Socialist bloc States and the Nordic countries among Western States. See Jørgensen's survey, *op. cit.*, at pp. 254–59.

action has been required or recommended in relation to Rhodesia (1966, racial policy); Iran (1980, hostage taking); South Africa (1986, apartheid); France (UN Secretary-General's ruling, 1986, sponsorship of terrorism); Iraq (1990–1, war of aggression); Yugoslavia (Serbia and Montenegro) (1992, aggression, ethnic cleansing); Libya (1992–9, sponsorship of terrorism); Liberia (1993–4, violation of human rights); Haiti (1993, violation of human rights). Secondly, there is now a considerable body of State action, institutionalised and filtered through the formal condemnation of human rights violations under a number of multilateral treaties, and determined in particular by such bodies as the European and Inter-American Human Rights Commissions and Courts, the UN Human Rights Committee and the UN Committee Against Torture. The legal significance of both these forms of response lies in the centrally institutionalised determination of delinquent State conduct, formal condemnation and subsequent imposition of sanctions or other means of enforcement. In addition, there are instances of coercive enforcement action which may lack such authorisation and be undertaken 'unilaterally' by certain States, but nonetheless represent a strong informal conviction of the necessity for responding to manifestly delinquent conduct, such as the NATO intervention in Kosovo (1999, ethnic cleansing and violation of human rights).

While a body such as the ILC has the luxury to consider such questions as the existence of international State criminality over a number of years, a judicial examination of the question would be dictated by the politics of litigation. This question has now been presented to the International Court of Justice (ICJ) in the *Case Concerning the Application of the Genocide Convention*.[28] The proceedings were initially opened in March 1993, when Bosnia and Herzegovina referred to the Court a dispute with the Federal Republic of Yugoslavia concerning the application of the Genocide Convention. The proceedings so far have comprised two requests for provisional measures, a judgment on objections to jurisdiction and admissibility, a further judgment on an application to revise that earlier judgment, and a counter-claim by Yugoslavia. The hearings on the merits opened in February 2006. Since the matter placed before the Court raises directly the question of the responsibility of a State for alleged acts of genocide, there is some possibility that the Court may consider the matters in terms of State criminal responsibility. But opinion within the Court may well be divided on this matter. Judge

---

28 Note 8 above.

ad hoc Kreca has expressed concern that the Court might accept the concept of State criminal responsibility when such a concept 'had not yet found a place within positive international law'.[29] On the other hand Judge Weeramantry has described the present case before the Court in criminal terms.[30]

Much of the reservation of some Western States in accepting a fully-fledged concept of State criminality appears to relate to the potential mischief which may arise from taking on board what is seen as an ill-defined concept. Thus the German Statement on the ILC Draft in 1996 urged that the 'genie of international crimes' be put back into the bottle from which it had been released by the Ago Draft Article 19,[31] and the British Statement in the same year complained that the concept was 'inchoate and lacking in the modalities of implementation'.[32] The Comment presented by Ireland in 1998[33] appeared to summarise some of the major objections: that the national-level concept of crime did not fit into the international context, being essentially concerned with individual criminal responsibility; that proposals for the development of international law ought not to be far removed from State practice; and that the application of penal sanctions to the State may be unjust. In taking the discussion further, it may be useful to address these specific objections, since much of this concern may be met by considering more closely the division of responsibility as between human and organisational actors, and the justification for

---

29 Dissenting Opinion in the Judgment on Preliminary Objections (1996) ICJ Reports, para. 103. Judge *ad hoc* Kreca proposes an individualistic view of criminal responsibility: 'a criminal offence as a phenomenon is reduced to a human action', whereas the criminal responsibility of the State is theoretical, and a 'project' (at para. 102 of his Opinion).

30 Dissenting Opinion in relation to the Court's Order on Counter-Claims, Order of 17 December 1997: 'Crimes must be viewed against the jurisprudential background of the interests and rights of the community … An act of genocide by the applicant cannot be a counter-claim to an act of genocide by the respondent. Each act stands untouched by the other, in drawing upon itself the universal condemnation of the international community.'

31 Statement by B. Simma, Representative of Germany, on Item 146, 7 November 1996.

32 Statement by Ian Brownlie, Representative of the United Kingdom, on Item 146, 7 November 1996.

33 Coments by Ireland under 'Article 19. International crimes and international delicts'. A/CN.4/488, 25 March 1998.

and appropriate location of any kind of organisational responsibility for delinquency in governance.

5 The relationship between State and individual responsibility: distinguishing organisational and implementing responsibility

The idea of attributing and apportioning responsibility for delinquency in governance to and between both individual and State actors is attractive in that it recognises the complexity of determining responsibility in this context. The dogmatic assertion that either the State should be considered wholly responsible – the logical extreme of the 'act of state' doctrine[34] – or that the individual should bear all responsibility – the logical extreme of the principle that crimes are committed by men, not abstract entities – may not serve either the ends of justice or the utilitarian objective of reducing the level of delinquency. However, at the same time, this appeal of the 'dual responsibility' option masks a number of difficulties in the more precise working out of the relative attribution of responsibility between the two kinds of actor.

An underlying question, which has both theoretical and practical significance, concerns the identification and definition of the offending conduct. Does this conduct amount to the same offence (criminal or otherwise), whether committed by individuals or State actors? Of course, this question also arose in the discussion of corporate responsibility in Chapter 6 (for instance in relation to the Sherman Act offences in the US), and has an impact on both the practical delimitation of responsibilities and the ethical justification for proceeding against two separate actors in relation to what may be the same conduct. For instance, it might be contemplated that both a State and individuals could be held responsible for particular genocidal action. At present, the legal definition of genocide as an

---

34 In the context of international law the doctrine of 'act of state' has a particular meaning and purpose: that an individual who is an official of a State should not be personally accountable for an act performed in the exercise of his functions but that responsibility for that act should be attributable to his State as a matter of international law. In effect, this is a kind of immunity at the personal level and an allocation of responsibility at the organisational level (in systemic and jurisdictional terms, it renders the subject a matter of international rather than national law). See generally the summary of this aspect of international law by Antonio Cassese, *International Law*, note 22 above, pp. 110–13.

offence does not distinguish between the role of human and non-human perpetrators. Does that imply that a State and an individual commit genocide in the same way, as co-defendants? If so, there may be two potential difficulties.

- First, would both be held liable as co-defendants (as happens to individuals and companies in the case of Sherman Act conspiracy)? If that were to happen, would such joint liability be justifiable if the individuals were acting in an 'official' capacity (for instance ordering the act in question or following orders), effectively as part of the State apparatus? Such an outcome would appear to involve a double counting of the same one offender, in its abstract and human forms.

- Secondly, if on the other hand, responsibility is to be distributed, either in the alternative or divided as between State and individual actors, where and how is the boundary line to be drawn for this purpose within the same body of offending conduct? While there may be some clear sense of the *basis* for such an exercise, distinguishing between an 'anonymous' organisational responsibility and a more specific responsibility for implementation, how is this distinction to be mapped onto existing legal definitions which do not provide a basis for such differentiation?

The resolution of these questions would appear to require some re-definition of the existing offences to represent more exactly the respective organisational responsibility of State actors and the individual role of human actors. There would be a basis for doing so in the argument already referred to, that (as in the case of corporate actors) there are types of action in governance which are organisational, systemic and personally anonymous and as such justify the attribution of responsibility to an appropriate organisational actor rather than any individual human actor. This approach would achieve a clearer conceptual dividing line between individual and organisational responsibility, but should not, on the other hand, preclude some consideration of the way in which acting in an organisational context might have an impact on individual behaviour, so as to moderate individual responsibility. In other words, and in line with what has already been said in relation to business corporations, while there may be some acts attributable to the organisation rather than the individual, at the same time the organisation should also be taken into account in attributing acts to individuals.

(a) The domain of State and governmental responsibility

There has been some reference already in this chapter to the kind of governmental behaviour which by its nature cannot comfortably be attributed to any particular individuals. This would include such 'systemic' conduct as the general failure to supervise the standard of behaviour of individual officials and political and military personnel, and substantively delinquent conduct exemplified by the development and fostering of policies or cultures of aggression, discrimination and large-scale ill-treatment of individuals or groups. It is in relation to such substantive delinquency that more definitional work would be required to separate the 'meta-level' promotion of delinquent policies and programmes from the more ground-level, 'day-to-day' implementation of the latter by individuals.

A situation which may be seen as a good candidate for organisational or State responsibility in this sense is the former regime of apartheid in South Africa.[35] As a regime, it was clearly a systemic phenomenon, the development and existence of which could not be easily attributed to one or a number of individuals. Moreover, because of this systemic character, the purpose of any individual responsibility for specific acts of implementation may be open to question: individual actions appear to merge into the systematic and pervasive nature of the regime itself. As Jørgensen argues:

> The policy of apartheid was a state policy, and it was the racist regime of South Africa itself which was repeatedly described by the UN as being 'illegitimate'. Only the state could cause the majority of South Africans to live under a system which deprived them of their basic human rights, and the South African system of laws was designed and administered so as

---

35 The South African model of apartheid was defined as a crime under the 1973 International Convention for the Suppression and Punishment of the Crime of Apartheid (for the text, see: (1974) *International Legal Materials*, 13: 50). However, the Convention has only 88 parties. The Statute of the International Criminal Court also list apartheid as a criminal offence within the Court's jurisdiction; Article 7(2)(h) refers to 'inhumane acts committed in the context of an institutionalized regime of systematic oppression and domination by one racial group over any other racial group or groups and committed with the intention of maintaining that regime'. See the discussion by Antonio Cassese, *International Criminal Law*, note 22 above, at p. 25.

to prevent that majority from taking effective peaceful action to alter this condition of fundamental deprivation.[36]

In relation to apartheid, it might be argued that a specific act of implementation, such as an administrative order or court judgment, is not easily separated from the regime as a whole – the essence of apartheid was the institutionalised and systematic concept and programme of discrimination. Significantly, although the 1973 Apartheid Convention casts apartheid as an international crime committed by individuals, there has been no prosecution of individuals for the crime of apartheid as such. Indeed, within South Africa, the post-apartheid regime has eschewed a resort to retributive justice, employing a process of amnesty in relation to criminal and civil proceedings and leaning towards the restorative justice approach embodied in truth and reconciliation commissions.[37] Such 'retreats' from retributive justice have been controversial, especially in so far as they may appear to be influenced by considerations of political expediency.[38] However, the point of argument here is rather different. Truth and reconciliation commissions may be a way of holding a society rather than individuals accountable, and such non-individualised accountability may be valuable in itself. Moreover, it may also be the case that, in the context of policy and political action, individual accountability, even if desirable in principle for retributive purposes, may prove difficult in a more practical sense.

This last point deserves some further comment. One argument in favour of a more general organisational accountability may be that, more negatively, individual accountability may in some circumstances be so difficult to determine. To provide a specific example: it may not be easy, as a matter of criminal law process, to prove that an individual head of government possessed the requisite intention to commit genocide,[39] but on the other hand it may be possible to

---

36 Jørgensen, note 3 above, at p. 245.
37 See, for instance, Ben Chigara, *Amnesty in International Law* (Pearson Education, 2002).
38 In particular, the provision of amnesty has been controversial, especially in relation to prosecution for alleged human rights violations. See Cassese, *International Criminal Law*, note 22 above, at pp. 315–16. Arguably, a distinction may be drawn between blanket amnesties and amnesty linked to a process of truth and reconciliation.
39 See the discussion just below, in relation to the prosecution of Slobodan Milosevic and the idea of joint criminal enterprise.

argue convincingly that a government as a whole failed to control genocidal activity, or even encouraged or abetted genocidal activity within armed forces or paramilitary groups. Such governmental responsibility would relate to a different kind of conduct, based on facilitation and support, rather than direct participation.

(b) The domain of individual responsibility: the impact of organisational structures

Within the context of individual responsibility for acts of governmental delinquency there may be difficult issues of identifying individual roles in complex factual situations, but also in disentangling individual and organisational roles. Historically, a main legal link between governmental and individual agency and responsibility has been the concept and defence of 'superior orders'. In essence, this was a device which could be used to render something a matter of governmental or official rather than individual action: the individual end-perpetrator of the offence was constrained by the duty to obey and therefore had no choice, and so lacked moral agency. However, the scope of the defence of superior orders has been interpreted in an increasingly restrictive fashion, especially in the context of international crimes,[40] and is now largely confined to circumstances of mistaken fact.[41] This has shifted the moral burden down-line to lower ranking individuals, requiring the latter to scrutinise more carefully and rigorously the content of orders passed down to them. In effect, this legal development has widened the field of individual responsibility.

In turn, issues of individual responsibility in this context have become increasingly complex. This is evident from a perusal of the jurisprudence of the International Tribunal for the Former Yugoslavia (ICTY).[42] Many of the cases coming before the ICTY have involved complex circumstances in relation to the chain of command and specific knowledge of action resulting in the perpetration of atrocities.

---

40 See Paola Gaeta (1999) 'The Defence of Superior Orders: the Statute of the International Criminal Court v. Customary International Law', *European Journal of International Law*, 10: 172.

41 See Article 32(1) of the Statute of the ICC.

42 For a full and useful critical overview, see: Allison Marston Danner and Jenny S. Martinez (2005) 'Guilty Associations: Joint Criminal Enterprise, Command Responsibility and the Development of International Criminal Law', *California Law Review*, 75.

Prosecution of the crime of genocide provides a good example. Put very simply, there is a difference between a single and 'normal' act of homicide on the one hand and genocide on the other hand, since the latter comprises the intentional killing, destruction, extermination of a group or members of a group as such.[43] In practical terms, therefore, there may be problems of agency to resolve. It is difficult for one person to carry out genocide in this sense of the term: it will require logistical planning, organisation, systematic violence, killing and terrorisation, and even compliance or support from those who might otherwise intervene – a complex network of joint and co-ordinated activity. The present law provides that within this network of joint activity, a range of individuals may be held responsible for their participation, provided that this happened with the requisite 'genocidal intent'. But a common difficulty in this kind of legal proceeding is that of linking high-level political actors or officials with physically remote 'final' acts (such as rape or killing) in the chain of genocidal causation. It is well known, for example, that Hitler never personally witnessed a genocidal act or wrote down an order to 'kill all the Jews'; in such a case there is only circumstantial evidence which links such a leading actor with the results of a genocidal plan, and this complicates the process of legal prosecution.

Moreover, the actual unfolding and implementation of a genocidal 'programme' may be a matter of considerable complexity. There may be a complex pattern of interactions in terms of 'top-down' planning and 'bottom-up' implementation. For example, in providing evidence of research findings to the ICTY, Ton Zwaan has argued that:

> Once a decision is made that large-scale violence won't be stopped [by state authorities] ... [it] might be ... that groups at the bottom see an opportunity or gain impunity to continue violent crimes ... Many people at the local level will act violently only when they are sure that they can get away with it.[44]

43 The legal definition of the crime of genocide employed by the ICTY is based upon that used in the 1948 Genocide Convention. See also the *Final Draft Text of the Elements of Crimes*, agreed by the ICC Preparatory Commission in June 2000; in relation to the crime of genocide, the focal point of analysis is the method of genocide (e.g., killing, serious bodily harm, prevention of births) rather than issues of agency – the relevant actor is simply referred to as the 'perpetrator', with no further discussion of the mode of perpetration.

44 Evidence to the ICTY in the case of *Prosecutor v. Milosevic*, 20 January 2004, in response to questions by Judge Robinson.

In support of this argument, Zwaan cited the example of local anti-Jewish pogroms in Nazi-occupied Poland, which were ordered by local Polish leaders, but would not have occurred without the support for copying Nazi policies.[45] Such complexities of intention, knowledge and factual opportunity require rigour in the identification of offending conduct and formulation of legal charges. The kind of analysis presented above suggests for example that one act of genocide might comprise an opportunistic killing or rape, while a different act of genocide might comprise the planning of large-scale violence and 'cleansing' but at a number of stages removed from any 'dirty' acts of implementation.

Thus the single generic offence of genocide may be inadequate for purposes of expressing the complexity of conduct, participation and responsibility comprised by what is more appropriately viewed as a network of decisions and actions. In the case of the ICTY there is already evidence of prosecutorial and judicial practice refining the offence classification and modes of participation in order to capture a more sophisticated sense of involvement in such conduct. This is well illustrated by the way in which the case against Milosevic was framed:

> from on or about March 1992 until 31 December 1996, Slobodan Milosevic, acting alone or in concert with other members of the joint criminal enterprise, planned, instigated, ordered, committed or otherwise aided and abetted the planning, preparation and execution of the destruction, in whole or in part, of the Bosnian Muslim … national, ethnical, racial or religious group, as such.

On this basis Milosevic was charged with both genocide and complicity in genocide, the latter being linked to the concept of the 'joint criminal enterprise'.[46] The charge as a whole may be analysed

---

45　*Ibid.*
46　Trial Chamber III of the ICTY has explained Milosevic's potential liability in the following terms: that the defendant could be guilty of genocide in that, first, he participated in a joint criminal enterprise to commit another offence (for instance, forcible expulsion) and other participants in the enterprise committed genocide in a way that was foreseeable by the defendant; or, secondly, as the superior of persons who to his knowledge were about to commit or had committed genocide, which he then failed to prevent or punish. The first 'offence' is thus one of complicity or conspiracy, the second is an individual offence based upon

as a range of offences and modes of participation: (a) the basic forms of individual involvement and complicity; (b) the specific forms of planning, instigating, ordering and directly committing predicate genocidal acts; and (c) the ancillary acts of aiding and abetting. Yet much remains to be clarified and there appears to be in particular some slipperiness as between different heads of substantive conduct and modes of participation. Thus, in attempting to ensure that leading actors are held fully responsible, it seems that the whole idea of 'command responsibility' is being stretched to cover a complex range of mental states and physical activities.[47] More will be said about the concept of the joint criminal enterprise in Chapter 10 below.

The recent practice of the ICTY demonstrates well the problems of working out and specifying for legal purposes the nature of individual responsibility in a particular context of governmental delinquency. There may also be problems in drawing the boundary and clarifying the relation between individual and governmental responsibility. For example, the *Rainbow Warrior* incident in 1986[48] raised directly this issue, once France had admitted responsibility (as a matter of international law) for the illegal destruction of the Greenpeace vessel, and sought then to expunge the criminal liability of its agents convicted under New Zealand law.[49] Once again, the

---

a notion of command responsibility. *Prosecutor v. Milosevic,* Case No IT-02-54-T, 16 June 2004.

47 See also the case of Krstic (*Prosecutor v. Radislav Krstic,* Case No IT-98-33). The Appeals Chamber overturned the finding of the Trial Chamber that Krstic was guilty of complicity in genocide: on the evidence he did not intend to commit genocide, but failed to prevent the use of his troops and resources in contributing to the genocide. As such he was liable on the lesser charge of aiding and abetting the genocide.

48 See the discussion in Chapter 1 above.

49 See: Conciliation proceedings (New Zealand v. France), ruling by the UN Secretary-General, Perez de Cuellar, New York, 5 July 1986; text in (1987) *International Legal Materials,* 26: 1346. Here the French Government invoked the classic statement by US Secretary of State Webster in the *Caroline Incident* (1837) in relation to the individual responsibility of State agents: 'after the avowal of the transaction as a public transaction, authorised and undertaken by the British authorities, individuals concerned in it ought not to be holden personally responsible in the ordinary tribunals for their participation in it' (29 *British and Foreign State Papers (BFSP)* 1137–8; 30 *BFSP* 195–6. On the other hand, New Zealand relied on the 'Nuremberg' rejection of the defence of superior orders, arguing that this had become widely applied in both national and international law.

underlying problems relate to moral agency and offence definition: should the blowing up of the *Rainbow Warrior* be regarded as an act of terrorism on the part of the French Government which violated international rules, or as an offence under New Zealand criminal law committed by individual human agents? Or could it be regarded as both at the same time? It appears to be accepted implicitly by the UN Secretary-General in his ruling that both forms of liability could co-exist, although at the same time this would result in a modification of the penalty imposed under New Zealand law, in that the individual offenders would be transferred into French custody. In effect, a process of offence definition appears to have been carried out in this case. The French Government violated the sovereignty of another State by means of a terrorist attack (which may qualify as an Ago-type 'State crime' or an ILC-type 'serious breach of an obligation arising under a peremptory norm'). The agents committed the offence of manslaughter under New Zealand criminal law. This may be a justifiable allocation of responsibility in relation to different aspects (design and implementation) of a broader delinquent activity (a war of aggression against Greenpeace). Yet, the impact of the organisational context, in that the individual officers were acting as agents of State policy, is also taken into account in the application of the penalty at the individual level.

Both these examples serve to demonstrate the difficulties which may arise in the translation of governmental delinquency into both State (or governmental) and individual responsibility. But this need not, and perhaps often should not, be a simple matter of alternatives. Taking appropriate account of the organisational complexity underlying such delinquency may require both forms of accountability, and perhaps also the third route to individual responsibility based on joint criminal enterprise, but for that purpose may require greater specificity and closer definition of offending conduct and agency in relation to such conduct. Such a task will necessarily be based upon a careful examination of the way in which delinquency in governance arises and is put into effect, and of the interrelationship between a number of both individual and organisational actors.

6 State and government: disaggregating governmental actors

In the discussion so far a broad distinction has been drawn between individual and organisational actors in the sphere of governance, and the organisational actor here has usually been referred to as the 'State'. Thus, as argument has turned to matters of organisational accountability and responsibility, it has been assumed that this attaches to the State as an established and recognised entity within the domains of both international relations and international law. But it may be questioned, as a final point of discussion in this chapter, whether the State is the appropriate signifier and site of such organisational responsibility. There are two principal grounds for such doubt, one based on elements of practical justice, the other concerned more theoretically with the nature of State identity.

In the first place, a commonly asserted objection to State as distinct from individual responsibility resides in the argument that, in both retributive and utilitarian terms, the State is not the most appropriate target. In broad terms, the State comprises a political community within a specified area and as such may be composed of a very large and diverse population of individuals and various subsidiary organisations and structures of governance. Is the State *as a whole* therefore the most appropriate subject of legal norms and sanctions which are concerned with conduct in governance rather than the behaviour of the total population? Thus it may be asked whether post-World War I reparations were fairly and appropriately applied to the German State and people as a whole,[50] or whether the same would be true of United Nations sanctions directed against South Africa in the period of apartheid or Iraq under the regime of Saddam Hussein.[51] Such State responsibility may lead to a sense of legal and ethical irony in the case of formal responsibility of the State for human rights violations against its own citizens. In such a situation, to associate the people of the State, who are actually the direct victims of the wrong, with the formal responsibility for that wrongdoing appears in some ways quite bizarre. In reality, of course, it is accepted that the citizens are not being blamed for the bad conduct

---

50 See: Yoram Dinstein, *War, Aggression and Self-Defence* (3rd edn, Cambridge University Press, 2001), pp. 100–101; J.M. Keynes, *The Economic Consequences of the Peace* 23 (2 *Collected Writings of J.M. Keynes*, 1971).

51 On the application of *sanctions* against Iraq, see the discussion by Deon Geldenhuys, *Deviant Conduct*, note 17 above, p. 103 *et seq.* Geldenhuys refers to the 'inconclusive' nature of the debate on the impact of these sanctions. But the UN Secretary-General did admit in 2000 that the application of the sanctions had resulted in a 'worsening of a humanitarian crisis – as an unintended consequence' (*Report of the Secretary-General pursuant to paragraph 5 of Resolution 1302 (2000)*, at p. 21).

directed at themselves. But then it seems that the legal process is not honest or accurate (or, in contemporary parlance, 'smart') in its formal targets. Certainly there is a risk that the process of formal censure against the State may be compromised by a counterproductive sense of distributive injustice and political alienation on the part of some of the population of the State.

Secondly, there is a theoretical objection that goes to the heart of State identity and personality. As a legal or moral person the State, after all, is an abstraction which employs certain types of institution for purposes of its physical manifestation. As Roth argues, in the context of international law:

> the state ... exists only as an abstraction, a unit of an equally abstract system. Its legal personality must be represented by a concrete institution. That institution is an apparatus of rule over a territory and population, an apparatus often referred to as 'the state' in another sense of that term ... in international law parlance, this institution is properly known as 'the government', as distinct from the abstraction that is 'the state'.[52]

Roth goes on to argue, importantly for present purposes, that if international law had remained content to deal with issues 'peripheral to the vital interests of states' (such as the treatment of diplomats or recognition of passports), then the distinction between State and government would not have raised many problems. But the increasing concern of twentieth-century international law with issues such as peace and security and the protection of human rights (at the core of States' interests) has brought the distinction between State and government (or, more exactly, between State and *bad* government) to the forefront.[53] For moral and legal purposes, it appears increasingly relevant to enquire whether the abstract State should bear accountability for the delinquent conduct of its material representation in the form of a government.

Such misgivings prompt argument in favour of some disaggregation of the State and its organisations and personnel of governance. This argument may be related to what has already been said above regarding a more legally refined and accurate allocation of

---

52 Brad R. Roth, *Governmental Illegitimacy in International Law* (Oxford University Press, 2000), pp. 8–9. This study by Roth is concerned generally with the difficult legal distinction between State and government.

53 Roth, *Governmental Illegitimacy,* note 52 above, at p. 10.

responsibility to both individuals and organisations. In other words, in the case for example of a large-scale crime against humanity, a morally convincing and practically feasible allocation of responsibility might encompass a range of actors: the head of state, governmental bodies and departments, individuals in official positions, and individuals and groups without official status. But in such a legal sweep, the State would not appear as a relevant actor.

To some extent, legal practice has already moved in this direction. This is evident in particular in three kinds of situation.

(a) Individual responsibility of former heads of state

As noted already, there has been an increasingly expansive approach to individual responsibility in relation to different forms of governmental delinquency, which to that extent has disaggregated conduct which might earlier have been ring-fenced by the protective 'act of state' doctrine. Most notably, as a matter of international law, earlier practice allowing pleas of immunity based on official status as a state agent to be pleaded by former heads of state has been superseded by the principle that, in relation to international crimes, such as genocide, war crimes, crimes against humanity and torture, there should be no immunity once the agent has left office.[54] This precedent, established by the prosecution of political and military leaders in the Nuremberg and Tokyo trials in the aftermath of the Second World War, has been reinforced by the more recent prosecution of former heads of state, such as Pinochet,[55] Milosevic[56] and Saddam

---

54 See for instance the pleadings of both parties (Congo and Belgium) before the International Court of Justice in the *Case Concerning the Arrest Warrant of 11 April 2000.*

55 Augusto Pinochet was the President of Chile between 1973 and 1990 and the head of a very repressive government, under which over 100,000 people were arrested, and many tortured and never seen again. He was in the late 1990s the subject of a famous attempt at extradition from the UK (*R v Bow Street Stipendiary Magistrate and others*, ex parte *Pinochet Ugarte* (UK house of Lords), (1999) 2 All ER 97). Legal proceedings in Chile have subsequently proven protracted, interrupted and uncertain. Cassese has commented: 'for all its theoretical and principled significance, this case has not led to a proper trial, not even in Chile' (*International Criminal Law* (Oxford University Press, 2003), at p. 298.)

56 Slobodan Milosevic, the former president of Yugoslavia, was implicated in the destructive warfare and ethnic cleansing in Bosnia-Herzegovina and Kosovo. He was arrested and indicted in 2001 before the ICTY:

Hussein.[57] While in one sense this most obviously represents a widening of the net of individual responsibility, such arraignment of political leaders may also be seen as a way of specifying *governmental* as distinct from State responsibility. The prosecution and conviction of such individuals acts *symbolically* to hold a regime and system of governance accountable for the delinquency in question.

(b) Responsibility for human rights and humanitarian violations against own citizens

Such disaggregation of responsibility may also be seen as implicit in international proceedings brought against States in respect of the violation of their citizens' rights. For example, when Denmark, the Netherlands, Norway and Sweden brought a claim against Greece in 1968 before the European Commission of Human Rights, alleging violations of the European Convention on Human Rights,[58] this was effectively a proceeding on behalf of the victim Greek citizens against the authoritarian 'Regime of the Greek Colonels' which had seized power in 1967. In such legal process, it is generally understood that it is the government which is in the dock. In much the same way, the subsequent criminal proceedings resulting in the conviction of two leading individuals within that regime (Papadopoulos and Pattakos) in 1974 also served as a legal indictment of the regime and government of which they were part. Taken together these two sets of legal proceedings, which formally involved the State and individuals as conventional legal actors, in substance were both concerned with the conduct of a government, but resulted in two types of sanction, one applying to the regime as a whole, the second applying to individual members of that regime for their part in its activities. The

---

Milosevic Case, IT-02-S4. Milosevic died suddenly while on trial in March 2006.

57 Saddam Hussein, President of Iraq between 1979 and 2003, implicated in the Iraq–Iran War, the invasion of Kuwait and repressive government within Iraq itself. He was captured by American forces late in 2003 and arraigned for trial in July 2004 before an Iraqi court by the Iraqi Interim Government. He was subsequently convicted and executed late in 2006.

58 See the decision of the European Human Rights Commission, 24 January 1968, (1968) *International Legal Materials*, 7: 818. In an intriguing twist of argument – an attempt at innovative legal description and identity – Greece (or, more precisely, the Greek Government) attempted unsuccessfully to defend itself as performing the role of a 'revolutionary government' (*ibid.*, at p. 834).

justification for applying two sets of sanction in this way may be judged on the basis of the criteria for individual and organisational responsibility discussed above. Another example of separation of State and government or regime, again also leading to individual criminal responsibility, may be found in the Nuremberg proceedings. The 'leadership corps of the Nazi Party' (in substance the government of Nazi Germany) was indicted as a criminal organisation, membership of which was then a criminal offence on the part of individuals.[59] Again two kinds of sanction may be identified: the proscription of the regime as a criminal (and prohibited) organisation, and the punishment of individuals for their participation in its activities. There is also, more generally in discussion, evidence of a tendency to distinguish delinquent governments from their States in the use of nomenclature such as 'Nazi Germany', 'Francoist Spain', 'Fascist Italy' and 'Apartheid South Africa'.

(c) Failed and politically divided States

Thirdly, the phenomenon of large-scale disintegration of political authority within a State, leading variously to civil disorder, internal armed conflict, or extreme minority government, or fragmentation into warring factions (sometimes now attracting the description 'failed State'), has encouraged a legal practice of separating the abstract entity of the State from particular governments and dominating regimes and factions. This category includes a spectrum of situations: at one extreme, the stable and enduring regime of a minority government widely regarded as illegitimate; through situations entailing domination or a large degree of control by factions lacking popular and international support; to inconclusive periods of struggle between warring factions at the other extreme. In such situations, 'governments' as such may not be conventionally liable in criminal law terms, but may well be subject to legal measures which may broadly be described as enforcement action, taken in respect of 'serious breaches' of obligations arising from peremptory norms. As argued above, this may now be described as a system of proto-criminal liability at the international level.

A significant kind of enforcement action which may be taken against a government or regime is non-recognition, implying illegitimate status and serving as an exclusionary measure. The

---

59 For a fuller account, see Jørgensen, *Responsibility of States,* note 3 above, Chapter 3.

process of relegating an entity which may have both the outward appearance and effective power of government to a *de facto* status has a long and widespread history in international relations (sometimes resulting in legally anomalous and classification-defying situations, especially for individuals caught in such situations[60]). A significant example of demotion from 'government' to 'illegal regime' arose from the unilateral declaration of independence by the Rhodesian entity, resulting in government by white minority rule of the territory of Rhodesia (now Zimbabwe) between 1965 and 1980. The Rhodesian regime was a clearly specified subject of enforcement action (and to that extent a legal person). Security Council Resolution 216 of 1965[61] called upon all States to refrain from recognition and assistance to the 'illegal racist minority regime', and Resolution 277 in 1970[62] required UN Member States to sever diplomatic, consular, trade, military and other relations with the illegal regime.

The established process of non-recognition, refusal to have dealings with, and use of *de facto* status has evolved over time into a more explicit international practice of dealing with some entities asserting formal governmental status as 'regimes' or 'factions' rather than 'governments'. Again, this is usually for purposes of enforcement measures and a common source of such practice is to be found in Security Council resolutions. The Security Council differentiated, for example, between the State of Afghanistan and the Taliban 'faction'. Resolution 1267 of 1999[63] identified the Taliban as 'the Afghan faction known as the Taliban, which also calls itself the Islamic Emirate of Afghanistan' and required its compliance with earlier anti-terrorist resolutions, while calling on UN Member States to freeze the funds and financial resources of the Taliban. In this way, an apparent governmental and State actor has been legally reclassified as another type of actor, but accorded personality and responsibility as such.

Security Council resolutions have also employed the nomenclature of 'factions' in relation to situations in which there has been a chronic breakdown of State authority and severe internal fighting, notably for instance in relation to organisations such as Unita in Angola,

---

60 See generally the discussion in Roth, *Governmental Illegitimacy*, note 52 above. Resulting practical and legal difficulties of non-recognition are well illustrated by the example of Rhodesia: see, for instance, the case of *Adams v. Adams* (1970) 3 All ER 572 in the UK courts.

61 12 November 1965, 5 (1966) *ILM* 167.

62 6 March 1970, 9 (1970) *ILM* 641.

63 15 October 1999, 38 (2000) *ILM* 235.

the RUF in Sierra Leone and the Khmer Rouge in Cambodia.[64] In such cases it has not been any sense of rebel status, but rather the policies and practices of these factions that has led to their delinquent branding. These cases demonstrate the possible slide from insurgency into terrorism and organised crime and that there is no hard and fast dividing line between governmental agency and organised criminality.

7 Conclusion: delinquent roles and identities

It is evident that both national and international law are striving for a more refined system of accountability for delinquency arising from conduct in governance. The allocation of criminal responsibility as between individual and organisational actors remains a subject of some controversy, especially in so far as it has become part of the international law debate regarding the possible criminal liability of States at that level. At present some Western governments prefer an expansive approach to individual criminal liability in this context, although this has in turn revealed more specific problems in attributing criminal liability to certain categories of individual actor, especially at higher ranks. But, despite the resistance to formally allocating criminal liability to States, the latter have become increasingly accountable for the violation of peremptory international norms, particularly via the regimes set up to ensure the protection of fundamental human rights. The overall picture, therefore, is one of growing accountability for delinquency in governance, on the part of both individual and organisational actors. But it is a complex legal landscape.

The legal ordering of this subject requires a clearer sense of both individual and organisational responsibility in this context and of the

---

64 For further discussion of the history and role of these factions, see Geldenhuys, *Deviant Conduct*, note 17 above, at p. 334 *et seq*. Unita was originally an anti-colonial liberation movement of the 1960s, and became a powerful rebel faction in post-independence Angola and was partly responsible for the devastation ensuing from the protracted civil war over three decades. The RUF (Revolutionary United Front) was operating as a rebel movement in Sierra Leone from 1991 and was notorious for its vicious terrorist methods. The Khmer Rouge, formerly the genocidal government of 'Democratic Kampuchea', evolved into a faction within Cambodia after being ousted from power through the Vietnamese intervention in 1979.

mutual interplay of individual and organisational action. On the one hand, a cogent system of individual responsibility would appear to require further and clearer definition of offending conduct, so as to take account of the different kinds of participation in activity arising within complex organisational structures. The way in which the ICTY has formulated concepts of 'criminal enterprise' and developed ideas of complicity in criminal conduct provides a pointer to the kind of legal development which may be necessary for purposes of forging a convincing theory of individual responsibility. On the other hand, discussion of organisational responsibility appears to be bedevilled by the idea of the State in itself. Separating the State and its institutions of governance may clarify in legal terms the intuitive sense of where organisational responsibility should reside in this context. The State is an abstraction in a way that governments, official institutions and corporate actors are not. There is evidence already of some disaggregation of governments and proto-governmental bodies in legal practice. Whereas the separation of individual actors in governance naturally leads to the use of conventional criminal proceedings and sanctions, that of organisational actors may result in legal process and sanctions which are less obviously 'criminal law' in their form. But, whatever the formal appearance and description of such enforcement procedures, in substance there is no doubt that they represent the legal identification and control of organisational delinquency which matches the use of conventional criminal law in relation to individual subjects.

Chapter 8

The legal control of criminal organisations

Discussion of criminal and terrorist organisations is rendered difficult by an uncertain knowledge of their scope and activities, something which naturally arises from their furtive mode of operation and lack of formal basis. On the other hand, there is a reliable perception that they constitute significant organisational actors in contemporary society. Definitions of both organised criminality and criminal organisations are therefore important but difficult to work out. It is possible, however, to identify different levels of organisation in this context (informal partnerships, networks, cartel-like associations, and corporate-form organisations) and these may provide a helpful basis for argument concerning the allocation of responsibility. Thus networks and cartel-like structures may provide the basis for 'joint criminal enterprise' individual responsibility and there is evidence of some national systems of criminal law developing offences of participation on such a legal basis. On the other hand, some criminal and terrorist organisations possess a structure and role of a kind to suggest a compelling analogy with the corporation in the 'legitimate' world. On that basis they may be seen as appropriate actors for the allocation of some kind of responsibility, and again there is evidence for that in contemporary legal ordering – for example, legal enforcement action at both the international and national level.

I Penetrating and theorising about an obscure subject

Moving the focus of discussion from the more familiar types of organisational actor such as the business firm or corporation and the State and various organisations of governance to organised criminal and terrorist organisations takes us into a more controversial and contested domain of debate. Two methodological and theoretical problems present themselves straight away. First, such delinquent organisations are by their very nature much less easily identifiable and definable. Their delinquent character means that they are naturally shady and furtive actors in the material world, so that any 'outside' understanding of their form and operation is achieved with greater difficulty than is the case with companies or State institutions. There is a greater element of speculation and surmise in relation to criminal groups, whether in the context of public perception, official policy or even academic research. In that sense the subject-matter has a slipperiness which should sound a note of caution at the beginning of this part of the discussion. Secondly, the delinquent character of this kind of organisation may raise ethical objection to the argument that they be treated alongside 'legitimate' companies or public bodies of governance, in that such a process in some way may approve or even serve to legitimise the existence of activities which are from most points of view objectionable. For instance, to present an argument that crime organisations or terrorist groups have some form of legal personality may encounter the objection that legal orders are thereby accommodating the existence of entities which should simply be the subject of legal control and repression. Both these points are serious issues of contention and need to be borne in mind in the discussion here.

In a more specifically academic sense the subject also possesses a related slipperiness. The transparency of both business organisations and governmental bodies renders them relatively easy subjects for research and discussion. Their forms are evident and well categorised and often subject to detailed legal definition and description. In relative terms, their mode of operation is not a hugely impenetrable matter. But what and how much do we (outsiders) know about crime and terrorist organisations in terms of reliable and complete knowledge? Moreover, it is a subject which also lends itself to sensationalist presentation, especially via media-generated excitement, and probably also a fair degree of political manipulation and even exaggeration.[1] All of this may cast some doubt over the validity of

---

1 As Michael Levi comments: ' … it is as well to take into account the huge sensationalist element in modern media treatment of these issues and, above all, that our images of organized crime are socially constructed, often relying on police images that themselves depend on the way in which intelligence and enforcement are organized and

the exercise, in so far as that exercise is to compare rigorously the position and legal regulation of crime organisations alongside entities such as companies and the State.

On the other hand, despite the difficulties of the subject and its discussion, there are some important points of argument in favour of the kind of comparison which is being suggested here. In the first place, even though understanding and knowledge of the working and forms of delinquent organisations may be limited and uncertain, it would be unwise to dismiss the idea of such organised criminality as a myth or pure social construction. Criminal gangs and terrorist organisations undoubtedly exist, have a social significance and generate a high level of concern. They may not possess a regularity and consistency of form and mode of operation (or a high degree of such), but that does not detract from the impact of their activities. Moreover, we should take care not be too easily seduced by the *formal* qualifications and claims to legitimacy of companies and States, which despite their neat and regular legal presentation may sometimes in practice not conform to official description. Enough has been said already about the scope for delinquency within both business and governmental organisations, or the practical collapse of formal structures (for example, in the case of the 'failed State') to make it clear that formal identification and definition are no guarantee of a neat and respectable actuality. Levi for instance provides the following telling comparison between the delinquency of 'legitimate' and 'unlawful' actors:

> Given the $40 billion dollar or so collapse ... of the once seventh largest American corporation, Enron, accompanied by revelations of serious financial misstatements and shredding of documents by auditors Arthur Anderson, which plunged the unfortunate company pensionholders into penury while some directors offloaded their shares at a huge profit, it is tempting to ask which organized crime groups are doing more harm than Enron did.[2]

on more pervasive social mythologies about what sort of persons and what sort of behaviour constitute a "threat to society".' Michael Levi, 'The Organization of Serious Crimes', Chapter 24 in Mike Maguire, Rod Morgan and Robert Reiner, *The Oxford Handbook of Criminology* (3rd edn, Oxford University Press, 2002), 878, at p. 879.

2 Michael Levi, note 1 above, at p. 879.

The point will be developed below that criminal organisations may indeed bear comparison with States and companies, both in terms of structure and the rigour of their activities. Indeed, such delinquent actors may at the same time both imitate and improve upon legitimate forms with an outcome that is both ironic and subversive.

This last observation leads to the second point of argument. Delinquent organisations are valuable objects of study simply because they represent what are often effective and socially significant instances of organisation, and much may be learnt from their role within this parallel universe of delinquent purpose and illegitimate forms. On political, ethical and practical grounds we may regret the admission that an organisation such as al-Qaeda is both effective and significant. But if it is politically and culturally more effective and significant than a number of formally constituted sovereign States, then we should surely make an effort to understand this situation and draw lessons from it. To dismiss it from study and argument on the grounds that it is illegitimate, criminal and morally beyond the pale would be to ignore perilously an important social reality of contemporary society. It would also disregard the value judgments which necessarily underlie any formal ascriptions and labels. Thus, the theoretical ranking of criminal organisations may not be a wholly comfortable exercise, but it may prove to be instructive.

Having made those general points about the subject-matter, it is necessary to address more specifically two central aspects of the idea of criminal organisation: first, what is known or not known of the nature of organised criminality and, following from that, how the phenomenon may be defined; and secondly, the kind of structure implied in such organisation, and how that may compare with more familiar formal organisational structures, such as those of the corporation and the State.

2 Organised criminality

We return first to the point made above: bearing in mind their lack of transparency and formal constitution, how much is known and understood about crime organisations and how does this affect their definition?

It is now a commonplace observation of criminology that this subject is beset by an uncertain and incomplete knowledge and prone to sensationalist and politically motivated manipulation.[3] The same point is equally true of organised 'traditional' crime and terrorist activity. Thus estimates of the extent of such delinquency and claims regarding the nature of the threat posed to 'legitimate' society remain to some extent (and perhaps a large extent) a matter of speculation and political rhetoric. Whereas we are able to estimate quite precisely the number of companies and business organisations, and institutions of governance in the contemporary world, and build upon that some assessment of their operational impact, such calculations in relation to organised criminality are necessarily more in the nature of imprecise guesswork, and are likely to remain so. It is improbable that the 'dark figure' will ever be cleared up.

Yet while we will continue to debate, for instance, the relative economic value of organised crime in relation to legitimate business, we do know for sure that gangs, groups and networks of purposeful delinquent activity do exist and possess some degree of organisation. The relevant question here is more one of identifying structures and modes of operation than working out the extent of activity and of its threat. Nonetheless it is still useful, and doubtless also necessary, to proceed from some basic working definition of what in broad terms should be understood as comprising *organised* as distinct from *individualised* criminality and delinquency.

Sociologists tend to provide descriptions, while lawyers like to work out definitions. Preferably such definitions, if used for practical legal purposes, should be based upon what data sociological research might provide through empirical observation. However, as already pointed out in the above chapters, legal concepts and definition might be driven by strategic enforcement considerations rather than match social data and this appears to be the case also in relation to legal definitions of organised crime. But, in any case, criminological research contains as yet little clear agreement regarding the more precise nature and structure of the phenomenon which is being referred to as organised crime. It might be argued for instance that the American literature has emphasised elements of violence and corruption more than European descriptions. For instance, Maltz's (American) concept of organised crime[4] embodied four essential

---

3 See for instance, P. Van Duyne (1996) 'The Phantom and Threat of Organized Crime', *Crime, Law and Social Change*, 24: 341.
4 M.D. Maltz (1976) 'On Defining Organised Crime: The Development of a Definition and a Typology', *Crime and Delinquency*, 22: 338.

features: violence, corruption, continuity and engagement in various kinds of predicate criminality. On the other hand, Italian analyses of Mafia activities placed more stress on a well-embedded patron/client relationship and process of extortion, rather than management of a range of serious crimes.[5] Within American research there is then some divergence as to how far the Italian-American Mafia model of a vertically integrated and horizontally coordinated organisation ('Boss-Underboss-Soldier', as described in particular by Cressey on the basis of his interviews with Valachi)[6] might be seen as applicable to organised crime generally in North America rather than in urban centres such as New York.[7] As Levi has commented: 'Why, after all, should an organizational model that applies to parts of Italy in some historical periods apply either to the north-eastern US or to the entire US; and even if it accurately depicts crime there, why should it apply throughout, or indeed in any part of the UK, Germany, or Canada?'[8] Perhaps one explanation for this definitional diversity is that there has been a tendency to focus on methods and scope of criminal activity, rather than the fact of organisation in itself, how that differs from other instances of criminality, and why it is important to draw that distinction.

Admittedly, some of the contemporary legal definitions have emphasised more the elements of structure and organisation, but unfortunately in such a broad and general fashion as to reveal hardly anything of an understanding of the concept underlying the rules. This is particularly (and perhaps not surprisingly) true of legal definitions at the international level. Thus the 1998 EU Joint Action aimed at the criminalisation of participation in criminal organisation[9] defines a 'criminal organisation' in the following terms:

---

5 See, for instance, L. Paoli (2002) 'The Paradoxes of Organized Crime', *Crime, Law and Social Change*, 37: 51.

6 D.R. Cressey, *The Theft of the Nation: The structure and operation of organized crime in America* (Harper and Row, 1969).

7 See, for instance, P. Reuter, *Disorganized Crime: Illegal Markets and the Mafia* (MIT Press, 1983).

8 Levi, note 1 above, at p. 881.

9 For a critical discussion, see: Valsamis Mitsilegas (2001) 'Defining Organised Crime in the European Union: The Limits of European Criminal Law in and Area of Freedom, Security and Justice', *European Law Review*, 565.

a structured association, established over a period of time, of more than two persons, acting in concert with a view to committing offences which are punishable by deprivation of liberty or a detention order of a maximum of at least four years or a more serious penalty; whether such offences are an end in themselves or a means of obtaining material benefits and, where appropriate, of improperly influencing the operation of public authorities.[10]

Although the elements of structure and continuity lead this definition, they are simple and unelaborated and quickly give way to detail concerning the nature and purpose of the predicate criminality. Article 2 of the UN Transnational Organized Crime Convention[11] is similar in its approach, defining an 'organized criminal group' as 'a structured group of three or more persons, existing for a period of time and acting in concert with the aim of committing one or more serious crimes ... in order to obtain, directly or indirectly, a financial or other material benefit'. Article 2 (c) does provide further definition of a 'structured group', but in a very wide and inclusive manner: 'a group that is not randomly formed for the immediate commission of an offence and that does not need to have formally defined roles for its members, continuity of membership, or a developed structure'.

Two illustrative comments may be made on such definitions and how they may be used. First, the EU Joint Action definition would seem to cover a business cartel as regulated by Article 81 of the EC Treaty and also that legislation in a number of the Member States which now renders participation in such a cartel a serious criminal offence. This indicates some convergence between the idea of organised criminality and delinquency within the context of legitimate business activity. But secondly, and rather differently, the UN Convention definition of a 'structured group' is so wide and inclusive as to lose any real sense of organisation. It certainly does not fit with the concept and definition of organisation explored and put forward in Chapters 2 and 3 above, where emphasis was laid on elements of worked out structure, role, decision-making and continuing purpose. The intention of the definition is of course to embrace the

---

10 Joint Action, on making it a criminal offence to participate in a criminal organisation in the Member States of the European Union, 21 December 1998, OJ 1998, L 351/1, Article 1.
11 Palermo, 2000.

more dispersed form of 'network' arrangement that may be deftly employed by some criminal and terrorist groups. But in doing so, the provision pushes the idea of organisation perhaps beyond its natural limit and raises questions about the point of defining matters in terms of collective structure in the first place.

Thus, neither criminological observation nor legal definition have as yet provided a very workable concept and definition of an organised crime group. It may be necessary then to pose further questions about the underlying purpose of using a concept of organised crime.

3 Criminal organisation

Rather than struggle for the moment with an agreed description and definition of organised crime or criminality, and the associated idea of an organised crime group, it may be more fruitful to return to the anterior question of why individual criminal or delinquent actors should organise in the first place. The simple question may be posed: instead of acting individually, why should two or more criminal actors work together? And then there is the second conceptual question: when does acting in concert transform the nature of the criminal activity, so that we should re-categorise it as an organisational activity, and how should such re-categorisation affect legal responses to the activity? More specifically, how many individuals working together would form an organisation – would just two be sufficient? Does it make sense to attempt to quantify the matter in this way? Should there not be rather a particular infrastructural threshold which should be satisfied for purposes of designating the concertation as an 'organisation'? It may be seen that these questions relate to structure, and so shift the emphasis in the discussion away from substantive areas of criminality which have sometimes dominated discussion of what has been referred to as organised crime.

At one level, the explanation for acting together with other individual criminals may seem obvious, if the answer is simply that concertation is necessary for the efficient performance of the act (for instance, sheer force of numbers or a necessary supporting role, such as a getaway driver). But this simple truism does supply a clue to the necessity for an organisational framework, in terms of the scale and complexity of the activity. The criminal act is no longer just a single physical assault by one person on another, or theft of a single item from one person by another. It is something more ambitious and complex in its realisation and practically requires the participation of a number of persons. This provides us with a fairly clean distinction between individual and organised criminal activity, but does not yet supply the conceptual grounding for a different ethical and legal reaction, so as to normatively treat the multi-person activity differently from the single-person activity. At what point *normatively* do we consider that the fact of organisation transforms the nature of the criminal act and invites a different response to that which we have for a purely individual act? A convincing answer to this last question would need to identify *something about the process of organisation and the resort to that process* that makes it qualitatively different from the predicate criminality. And one possible and persuasive answer would be to indicate how both the *delinquent ambition* and consequent *scale of activity* are over and above what is comprised in individual offending, so as to justify a higher degree of censure (and hence transform the responsibility for the activity in question). Putting the matter in those terms, it may be sensed that we are now tracing some established legal ground, particularly in relation to the idea of a distinct criminal offence of conspiracy, in which the element of organisation has been seen as adding value to the nature and seriousness of the offence. In short, it is a question of uncovering the purpose of organisation and thereby identifying a distinctive delinquency in that organising activity, over and above the predicate offence.

In practice, it is not difficult to uncover some common purposes of organisation in criminality which enable this exercise to be carried out. As criminal activities become more ambitious and increase in scale, a number of ancillary activities may prove necessary. Most obviously such a list would comprise: financing the criminal activity; organising a range of personnel, equipment and transport; financial and practical disposition and realisation of criminal gains; and the neutralisation of law enforcement. The scale of such activities may vary, ranging from a relatively unsophisticated distribution of roles within a gang, to complex infrastructures of finance and official corruption. But the listing of such infrastructural and facilitative activities serves to make the point that a threshold has been passed, from simple, individualised predicate criminality to something which is systematic, longer-term and dependent on multiple roles and skills.

The forms of such criminal organisation are also likely to be historically and socially contingent and it is possible to trace the emergence of increasingly complex and sophisticated forms, following the opportunities which present themselves in the wake of economic, social and technological development. McIntosh[12] for instance has traced the historical evolution of modes of criminal organisation through the categories of *picaresque banditry*, *craft crime* (e.g. nineteenth-century pickpocketing), *project crime* (major twentieth-century robberies), and *business organisation* (the continuous supply of illegal goods and services). This evolution of forms also makes legal definition by reference to criminal method unsatisfactory, since such an approach (to be found for instance to some extent in the American RICO legislation, discussed below) may prove selective and become historically outmoded. While it is important to recognise (especially for enforcement purposes) that the forms and methods may differ, either across space or through time, the essential focus of legal control should be the function and scale of organisation. But the central question remains: at what point more precisely does organisation in itself become qualitatively different so as to justify a distinctive legal response?

In this respect some of the legal definitions quoted above – for instance that contained in Article 2 of the UN Transnational Organized Crime Convention – set a low threshold, if three persons would suffice and there is no requirement of formally defined roles, continuity of membership or developed structure. A simple partnerhip of three, enduring for a certain period and comprising a number of repeat offences would suffice. The degree of organisation in such an example would be minimal and therefore a dubious ground for treating the offending conduct differently from a number of individual offences.[13] The justification for any distinctive ethical or legal response would require a higher threshold of collective enterprise, evidenced by some system and policy which has objectives over and above each individual predicate criminal act.

In general terms it may be possible to identify four main levels of organisation in this context:

- A spontaneous collaboration spanning a series of offences but with no firm or continuing commitment to that collaboration (*informal partnership*)

---

12 M. McIntosh, *The Organisation of Crime* (Macmillan, 1975).
13 Which is why some critics have attacked the inclusiveness of the definition. See for instance: Valsamis Mitsilegas, Jörg Monar and Wynn Rees, *The European Union and Internal Security* (Palgrave Macmillan, 2003), pp. 95–98.

- A network of collaboration, with an enduring and planned character, but implemented in a decentralised manner which allows for an easy and tolerated turnover of participation (*network*)

- A 'confederal' association of equal participants, acting within a coordinated system, but in tandem, in a relationship that is horizontal and not subject to strong central authority (*cartel*)

- A hierarchical and vertically integrated system of collaboration, with carefully allocated roles for the participants, a strong sense of continuing commitment and an authoritative internal constitutional structure (*corporation*).

Of these four types, the first, described as an informal partnership, would seem to be opportunistic rather than systematic, comprising little real sense of organisation and therefore better described as 'serial' rather than 'organised' criminal activity. Any responsibility attaching to the actors involved would be very much based on their individualised repeat offending. At the other extreme, the fourth hierarchical and highly integrated instance of sustained purposeful collaboration involves an enduring and sophisticated structure that renders the organisation (despite its lack of formal constitution) comparable to a corporate person in the legitimate world. In such a case there may be a strong argument for organisational agency, and this idea will be explored further below.

The two intermediate categories comprise looser but still significant structures, and an element of organisation which arguably should be taken into account in some way in a legal response. Applying the models used in earlier chapters, these may qualify as socially significant collectivities (or 'social groups' according to the categorisation in Chapter 2), and corresponding in some ways to that middle or 'collective' route to individual responsibility outlined in Chapter 4, and to the idea of 'criminal enterprise' explored in Chapters 6 and 7, but not amounting to an autonomous organisation for purposes of agency, as in the case of the fourth category above. These two intermediate categories of criminal organisation will also be discussed further below, in relation to the idea of criminal enterprise, but also in relation to the legal process of attributing legal responsibility through membership of a group or organisation.

4 The criminal organisation as a distinct organisational agent

The premise for this part of the discussion is the perception that a number of delinquent organisations in contemporary society – ranging through criminal gangs and syndicates, paramilitary or military insurgent movements and terrorist groups – have a sufficiently durable and consistent form, clarity of purpose and solid internal constitution as to merit serious consideration as moral and legal agents, and hence subjects of responsibility, distinct from their individual membership. Such organisations may be colloquially thought of as 'dark' or sinister versions of legitimate organisational actors, such as companies, other corporate actors and institutions of governance. This may also be their own subjective perception, in so far, for example, that Mafia groups self-consciously imitate the structures and methods of Roman military organisation or business corporations, or terrorist and insurgent movements aspire to some form of political representation or alternative model of governance. The line of argument here naturally faces a major obstacle in the absence – in virtually all of these cases of delinquent organisation – of a transparent, clearly defined constitutional basis and structure. Rarely will there be an equivalent of a formal incorporating process or founding constitution,[14] so that the identity, shape and working methods of such entities will remain less well defined than those of States and companies. Moreover, as noted already, by the very nature of the subject our information about these matters as outside observers is likely to remain less sure and accurate than would usually be the case regarding corporations and bodies formally constituted for purposes of governance. On the other hand, such difficulties should not invalidate a theoretical model which is based on the fact that such delinquent entities actually behave as though they were business corporations or aspire to take over the role of government, albeit with illegitimate purposes.

For purposes of the present discussion, the terrorist organisation and military insurgent movement will be taken as examples of delinquent organisations which may be presented as candidates for distinct agency and responsibility. Similar arguments may be applied to other delinquent organisations such as crime organisations of the Mafia type, but terrorist and insurgent organisations present a ready

---

14 The main exception is probably the situation involving a governmental organisation subsequently declared to be illegal or criminal, e.g. Nazi organisations.

contemporary example of entities possessing a definite self-identity and willingness to exploit that identity in their engagement with other actors. The model of agency and responsibility put forward here may equally be applied to other entities, depending on factual circumstances.

Entities such as al-Qaeda, Hizbullah and the Taliban[15] possess considerable contemporary political significance, yet have a shadowy legal identity. For many formal legal purposes their legal personality may be seen as no more than that of a collection of individuals, dispersed across a number of territorial (State) jurisdictions. Frequently, legal action directed against the activity of a terrorist organisation will be taken against constituent individual members of such groupings, for instance as individuals involved in the commission or planning of illegal acts. Terrorist organisations are usually not subject directly to measures of legal control, but rather are the target of legal action indirectly, for instance through measures taken against individual members, or more exceptionally against supporting governments. There may however be some ethical and practical argument in favour of holding in some ways the organisation rather than its individual members accountable for some aspects of terrorist activity. In such a case, are there any overriding objections to some measure of organisational responsibility in this context?

It might be objected that a body such as a terrorist organisation is so elusive in its material manifestation (and its effectiveness may depend upon maintaining such a character) that any allocation of legal personality and responsibility may prove practically difficult and therefore pointless. But on the other hand, in practice such bodies often possess an infrastructure, sense of mission and effectiveness of action which compares favourably with actors such as corporations

---

15 Al-Qaeda is an Islamic network of groups and organisations spread around Muslim countries and elsewhere, promoting and implementing radical Islamic policies through activities which range from a humanitarian to terrorist character. The Taliban are an Afghan faction, which emerged in the early 1990s and from 1996 until 2001 exercised political control over Kabul and other parts of the country. The Taliban enforced a strict interpretation of Islamic law and sheltered terrorists such as Osama bin Laden, and were the target of UN sanctions from 1999 and are now a significant insurgency movement within Afghanistan. Hizbullah is a Lebanese Muslim political and military organisation (in Arabic, the 'Party of God'), established in 1982, with some 5,000 members; its activities include military and terrorist operations, but also social welfare programmes.

and States. Indeed, they may be more effective and more powerful than many corporations and States, and so more politically significant. Moreover, a converse argument may also apply: corporations and States may possess a clear legal identity on paper, but their activities may be so open to question and diffuse that the imposition of legal responsibility becomes a problematical issue. Despite an absence of conventional formal foundation, the reality of the existence and operation of terrorist groups may be found in other forms of evidence. Usually such organisations are willing to proclaim their identity and objectives (so that there may be informal 'articles of association') and accept political responsibility for their actions – some of their political effectiveness may spring from having a known and proven role and identity. Moreover, while the allocation of responsibility to delinquent organisations might give rise to a number of technical problems, the latter may be no more difficult to resolve than existing problems relating to the precise attribution of capacity and responsibility to both corporate entities and States.

In fact, measures taken in recent years by both the UN and other organisations and by certain States suggests that there is an existing practice of attribution of legal identity at the international level to a range of entities comprising the like of terrorist organisations and other political groupings. Security Council Resolution 1267 of October 1999[16] is a notable example which distinguished clearly between the identity of Afghanistan *as a State* and that of the Taliban (referred to in the wording of the resolution as 'the Afghan faction known as the Taliban'). Having reaffirmed 'strong commitment' to the sovereignty, independence and territorial integrity of Afghanistan, the Resolution went on to condemn the continuing *use of* Afghan territory, expecially areas controlled by the Taliban, for the sheltering and training of terrorists and the planning of terrorist acts, and to cast the failure of the Taliban to respond to the demands of the earlier Resolution 1214 as a threat to international peace and security. Later Security Council Resolutions of 2001 identify both the Taliban and al-Qaeda as associated targets of international enforcement action: Resolution 1368[17] reiterated the right of self-defence against 'terrorist attack', and Resolution 1373[18] specifically authorised measures under Article 39 of the UN Charter against al-Qaeda.

---

16 UN SC Res. 1267 (1999), 15 October 1999, 38 (2000) *ILM* 235.
17 12 September 2001, 40 (2001) *ILM* 1277.
18 28 September 2001, 40 (2001) *ILM* 1278.

There are further instances of such practice. The US had also invoked the right of self-defence against al-Qaeda and the Taliban in a letter from the US Permanent Representative to the UN to the President of the Security Council.[19] A number of instruments have identified terrorist organisations as the subject of legal measures for the purpose of dealing with their financial assets: for instance EC Regulation 2580 of 2001[20] authorised the freezing of assets of both listed terrorists and terrorist organisations, and other EU measures contain such listing for enforcement purposes.[21] In a somewhat different context, Security Council Resolution 1343 of 2001,[22] relating to Liberia, referred to the Revolutionary United Front (RUF), stating that active support by the Government of Liberia for armed rebel groups, especially the RUF, constituted a threat to international peace and security. In effect this measure treats the relations between a government and an 'armed rebel group' as a matter of international concern and thus regulated by the UN Charter. So, it may be argued: if the activities of terrorist organisations and other armed groups are viewed as constituting threats to international peace and security under the UN Charter, or trigger an exercise of the right to self-defence under international law, or provoke measures of supranational financial control, this surely implies on the part of such entities a legal presence and responsibility of some kind and significance at the international legal level.

The practical political and legal advantages of the development of such legal personality and accountability may be most obvious at the international level. There are some aspects of terrorist activity for instance which have an organisational and collective rather than individual character. For example, by analogy with some recent arguments in favour of the concept of corporate homicide, it may be possible to identify a form of collective action, comprising the development of ideology, provision of an infrastructure of material support, and psychologically fostering the necessary mindset to enable individuals to carry out acts of terrorism. Attribution of a kind of corporate personality and responsibility to terrorist (and other political and military) organisations may then fulfil an appropriate retributive role of moral censure. At the same time it may also

---

19 40 (2001) *ILM* 1281.

20 OJ 2001, L 344.

21 For instance, a Common Position of 21 December 2001 (OJ 2001, L 344), originally compromising 13 organisations and 29 individuals, but subsequently extended.

22 7 March 2001, 40 (2001) *ILM* 1024.

supply a basis for practical measures of legal control focussed on the terrorist organisation rather than its individual members. We have already noted in other contexts the way in which there may be a meaningful distribution of legal responsibility between collective entities and their individual members: for instance as between States and governments held responsible for human rights violations and individuals indicted for crimes against humanity (as discussed in Chapter 7), or the bifurcation of the legal control of business cartels in some jurisdictions (as discussed in Chapter 6). Such developments recognise something of the complexity of human activity in organisational contexts, involving interlocking individual and collective action which may not easily be disentangled yet which merits some separate identification for both moral and practical legal purposes.

A particular advantage may derive from recognition of a more definite legal identity for terrorist organisations, insurgent movements and political factions in the context of the enforcement of anti-terrorist and other international norms. This would be especially true in relation to forcible enforcement action of the kind most appropriately directed at the organisation as a whole. For example, a legal approach at the international level which is willing to translate actual political limitations on State sovereignty (such as the situation of 'failed' States or 'requisitioned' territories) into legal principles of intervention would accommodate a more purposeful, consistent and systematic process of legal control, enabling for instance a justified enforcement action on what is technically the territory of another State against a major terrorist or insurgent presence on that territory. This could provide for a cleaner response to the problem of organisations which effectively occupy and control the territory of vulnerable of sympathetic States and then hide behind the legal shield of State sovereignty. The outcome would then be a more clearly and effectively targeted legal enforcement of international norms. A similar argument might be made in relation to the situation of small 'failed' States, where a political vacuum threatens to provide a convenient site for the operation of organised crime, a fear that motivated the Australian-led intervention in the Solomon Islands.[23]

---

23 The Regime Assistance Mission for the Solomon Islands (RAMSI), established in July 2003, in response to 'insidious levels of crime, corruption and poor governance'.

The contemporary problem of international terrorism is simply a graphic part of the jigsaw of this argument. What has become apparent in recent years is that an organisation such as al-Qaeda is a more significant but less accountable political actor than a number of sovereign States. Some terrorist and other political organisations have *de facto* acquired a quasi-territorial political presence which ought to be acknowledged in any meaningful system of political and legal accountability. If legal textbook writers can accept that insurgent groups or national liberation organisations may be awarded some kind of legal identity and capacity, logically the same could be said of terrorist organisations. Indeed, the latter may easily overlap with the former, just as the formerly legally recognised government of 'Nazi Germany' became in 1945 a group of outlawed criminal organisations, subject as such to legal proscription and the basis for a form of individual criminal responsibility (as discussed further below).

5 Crime through membership

We return now to a consideration of the looser type of criminal organisation discussed above, in relation to which a distinct organisational agency and responsibility may not appear appropriate, yet participation or membership may have some bearing on matters of individual agency and responsibility. Two possible arguments may be examined. First, that evidence of *membership* of the organisation (especially if it has some formal character) could lead to certain presumptions relating to responsibility for individual members for activities carried out within the framework of the organisation. Secondly, that, depending on the role and circumstances of individuals participating in the activities of the organisation, conclusions regarding individual responsibility may be drawn from that *participation*. These two arguments will be considered in turn.

Criminal responsibility attaching to individuals and based on the fact of membership of a 'criminal organisation' is an idea which has been suggested rather than implemented in modern Western criminal law. The presumptive character of such legal liability has usually fallen foul of individualist objection to collective liability of the kinship kind (such as Frankpledge), as discussed in Chapter 4 above. The essence of this objection is that membership is simply a connecting factor which does not in itself reveal anything about the degree or kind of participation in a criminal organisation, and it is the latter which provide an ethically convincing basis for any allocation of individual responsibility. As Cassese explains:

> ... A member of any such group is not criminally liable for acts contrary to law performed by leaders or other members of the group and to which he is extraneous. The principle of individual autonomy whereby the individual is normally endowed with free will and the independent capacity to choose his conduct is firmly rooted in modern criminal law ...[24]

Although the British Government has recently proposed a 'membership offence of belonging to an organised crime group'[25] it is doubtful whether what was precisely intended in this phrase was the creation of a criminal offence based on membership pure and simple.[26] An earlier instructive example of the drafting of a membership offence and its interpretation in practice is provided by the Statute of the International Military Tribunal at Nuremberg[27] in relation to prosecution of war crimes in 1945. Article 9 of the Statute enabled the Tribunal to declare a particular group or organisation to be a 'criminal organization'.[28] Article 10 then provided that:

> In cases in which a group or organization is declared criminal by the Tribunal, the competent national authority of any Signatory shall have the right to bring individuals to trial for membership

24 Antonio Cassese, *International Criminal Law* (Oxford University Press, 2003), at pp. 136–7.
25 UK Government White Paper, *One Step Ahead: A 21st Century Strategy to Defeat Organised Crime*, Cm 6167, presented to Parliament in March 2004, p. 41.
26 See the discussion in: Christopher Harding (2005) 'The Offence of Belonging: Capturing Participation in Organised Crime', *Criminal Law Review*, 690.
27 See more generally for an account of this provision: Nina H.B. Jørgensen, *The Responsibility of States for International Crimes* (Oxford University Press, 2000), Chapter 3; H. Leventhal (1947) 'The Nuernberg Verdict', *Harvard Law Review*, 60: 857. See also the discussion in Chapter 1 above and Chapter 10 below.
28 The Nuremberg Tribunal (IMT) declared three organisations to be criminal under this provision: the Leadership Corps of the Nazi Party, the Gestapo and the SS (*Schutzstaffeln*). Other organisations were declared criminal at the national level, for instance in Poland the administration of the Lodz Ghetto and of the Auschwitz concentration camp.

therein before national, military or occupation courts. In any case the criminal nature of the group or organization is considered proved and shall not be questioned.

The original reasoning behind this idea, as evidenced in American memoranda of 1944, was that difficulties of proof would allow a large number of Axis war criminals to escape conviction and punishment.[29] The burden of proof would be on defendants to show that they did not voluntarily join any such organisation and what was therefore envisaged was a system of summary justice in relation to thousands of individuals – in fact some two million people were within the ambit of the charges against the organisations which were ultimately indicted under Article 9. However, the Tribunal itself modified this policy[30] by announcing that membership in itself was insufficient to bring an individual 'within the scope' of a declaration of criminal organisation, and that persons who 'had no knowledge of the criminal purposes or acts of the organization and those who were drafted by the State for membership' should be excluded from this concept of membership. The Tribunal also decided that the burden of proving the fact of such membership would lie with the prosecution. In the event, therefore, the 'Nuremberg' offence of membership was based upon both a willing membership and proven knowledge of the criminal character of the organisation. So, for example, in the subsequent case of Alstötter et al. (the so-called 'Justice Case'),[31] the defendant Alstötter was convicted of the membership offence on the basis of his knowledge of the criminal purposes of the SS and voluntarily remaining a member of that organisation. A closer examination of the Tribunal's practice thus suggests that membership in this context was understood to mean a purposeful and participating membership. As Danner and Martinez comment:

---

29 See the memo of Colonel Murray C. Bernays (a lawyer in the US War Department), of 15 September 1944, quoted in B.F. Smith, *The American Road to Nuremberg – The Documentary Record – 1944–45* (Hoover Institution Press, 1982), at pp. 35–6. The policy was affirmed by the Secretary for War, Stimson.

30 See the discussion in: Allison Marston Danner and Jenny S. Martinez (2005) 'Guilty Associations: Joint Criminal Enterprise, Command Responsibility, and the Development of International Criminal Law', *California Law Review*, 75: 112 *et seq*.

31 Trials of the War Criminals before the Nuremberg Military Tribunals under Control Council Law No. 10, Nuremberg, October 1946–April 1949 (1950–1953), vols. I and II, 3, 180.

Ultimately, Bernays' vision of thousands of summary trials was replaced by the administrative denazification program instituted by the Allies and subsequent trials for membership in criminal organizations largely did not materialize.[32]

In a modern and contemporary context, therefore, membership as such as a basis of some criminal responsibility would appear to be a theoretical possibility, but not one likely to be given practical application. Some degree of participation would appear to be the accepted threshold for such responsibility.

6 Criminal participation: a contemporary survey

A natural problem in the legal control of criminal organisation as distinct from individual criminality arises from some of the practical difficulties in investigating, proving and allocating responsibility in relation to conduct which is submerged within complex and diffuse organisational structures and networks. In particular, more sophisticated criminal organisations may actually be designed and operated in such a way as to minimise the risk of detection and liability for its participants. For instance, whether the context is conventional 'private' organised crime or large-scale war crimes, it is commonly bemoaned that ringleaders and masterminds deftly evade legal control and the latter typically extends only to catch some of the smaller players. This point was made explicitly in the statement by the UK Government in 2004 that:

It is commonly believed that the existing conspiracy legislation may not always catch the real 'Godfather' figures, does not provide a practical means for addressing more peripheral involvement in serious crime and does not always allow sentencing courts to assess the real seriousness of individual offences by taking into account the wider pattern of the accused's criminal activities.[33]

---

32 Danner and Martinez, 'Guilty Associations', note 30 above, at p. 114. The IMT judges also eventually acquitted four of the seven indicted organisations (the SA (*Sturmabteilungen*), the Reich Cabinet, the German General Staff, and the High Command).
33 White Paper, note 25 above, Cm 6167, para. 6.1 (p. 40).

This perception informs the proposal for developing criminal liability in terms of participation in criminal organisation as distinct from liability based upon more specific action, or predicate offences, perpetrated within the framework of that criminal organisation. The 1998 EU Joint Action on the criminalisation of participation in criminal organisation, mentioned above, has a similar purpose and there are other national legal models of this approach to dealing with organised criminality. As part of this project, the UK Home Office commissioned a comparative survey of organised crime conspiracy legislation, taking as a starting point the so-called RICO (racketeer influenced and corrupt organisations) legislation in the US. This survey by Levi and Smith[34] collected evidence from investigators and prosecutors in a number of jurisdictions, and their report summarised the main elements of special organised crime offences in a range of legal orders: the US, Canada, New Zealand, Italy and the Netherlands.

The survey uncovers on the one hand a range of new or recent legislation dedicated to the legal control of certain aspects of organised criminality and on the other hand well-established and broadly drafted code provisions which are able to accommodate the kind of offending conduct under discussion here. There are some differences in detail, but some common generic elements may be identified. What is broadly required generally in the framing of such participatory offences is first, an agreed sense of the crime organisation which provides the essential framework for criminal liability. Thus, US law[35] refers to engagement in 'a pattern of racketeering activity' or 'collection of unlawful debt' in relation to an 'enterprise'; Canadian legislation[36] uses the term 'criminal organisation'; New Zealand law[37] refers to 'gangs'; Italian law[38] defines a Mafia-type conspiracy as one which uses intimidation, and the system of subordination and *omertà* to commit crimes or obtain economic control; and Dutch

---

34 Michael Levi and Alaster Smith, *A comparative analysis of organised crime conspiracy legislation and practice and their relevance to England and Wales,* Home Office Online Report 17/02, December 2002.

35 Federal RICO (Racketeer Influenced and Corrupt Organisations) Statute: Title IX, Organised Crime Control Act 1970.

36 Amendments in 1997 and 2001 of the Federal Criminal Code (Bill C-24 in 2001).

37 Section 98A of the Harassment and Criminal Associates Act 1997.

38 Article 416 (*bis,* added in 1982) of the Criminal Code.

law[39] refers to an organisation whose object is the commission of crimes. The second necessary element involves an identification of the kinds of participation which go beyond commission of the various predicate offences. Thus we find in US law a list of four RICO offences (in Section 1962(a)–(d) of the legislation): investment of proceeds; acquiring or maintaining an interest in the enterprise; conducting the affairs of the enterprise; and conspiring to do any of the foregoing. The Canadian law requires a knowing involvement in activities which further the organisation's criminal objectives. New Zealand law refers to the intentional promotion or furthering of the activities of a gang. Italian law in a much more general fashion simply requires participation, while the Dutch law refers to either taking part or supporting acts which lead to or are directly connected with the realisation of criminal purposes.

The element of organisation may be described by differing terminology but there appears to be a common broad sense of the concept across the jurisdictions surveyed: an enduring structure established for the systematic achievement of criminal objectives. The American legislation, for instance, requires an ongoing association, comprising a decision-making structure, and mechanisms of control and direction. Dutch law requires evidence of a lasting and structured form of association, acting as a unit. These examples suggest a widely accepted generic sense of 'criminal enterprise', and it may be that problems reside not so much in the concept as in proving its existence. Again, the examples of legislation suggest that the element of participation is conceptually clear enough, despite differences in vocabulary. In each case, the activity being referred to is distinctively supportive of the organisation as a whole and in that way clearly differentiated from the predicate offending which may be regarded as the organisation's 'core' business. The main task for prosecutors is probably once more of an evidential nature – establishing the crucial link between such supportive activities (management of the affairs of the organisation, investing money, acts of planning and advice, using power and influence to protect the organisation) and the organisation itself.

There are therefore a number of established models in some national jurisdictions for this kind of criminal responsibility based upon participation in the activity of delinquent organisations. This is an individual liability, but one which arises not from predicate individual offences but from a contribution to an involvement in

---

39   Article 140 of the Penal Code.

an organisational framework. As such it is a form of responsibility which is based upon both elements of individual contribution and organisational interest and purpose, and thus brings together a sense of both individual and organisational action. The conceptual and theoretical significance of this model will be discussed further below (in Chapter 10). For the present, however, it is worth noting some of the evidential difficulties associated with this approach, particularly in so far as they have been revealed in the context of attempts to regulate organised crime groups.

Evidential issues are prominent in Levi and Smith's research findings. The experience of prosecuting this kind of offence in the US and Italy suggests that particular investigation and prosecution strategies are crucial for purposes of supplying sufficient evidence of knowledge of and connection with criminal organisations – for instance, electronic surveillance and witness testimony collected through offers of immunity and witness protection. The availability of such methods, in terms either of their constitutionality or the willingness or ability to commit resources, may not translate easily from one jurisdiction to another. Levi and Smith explain the matter in the following terms:

> Once criminals have moved beyond the front-line operational stage and have acquired substantial business interests through which they can front activities, infiltration and other undercover tactics may prove too difficult. Some interviewees referred to the inhibitions on potential informants (and victims) arising from fear of the principals. However, it is not clear that RICO legislation would provide a solution to this, for the prosecution must prove a connection between the accused and the set of people performing the predicate acts, and this requires either live witnesses or surveillance from which plausible inferences can be made (or both).[40]

And they go on to indicate the way in which evidential and procedural rules under English law may inhibit some investigation strategies: that the content of telephone tapping could not be used in evidence; and the present disclosure rules, applicable to information about police tactics.

This kind of difficulty may be further exacerbated by the way in which criminal organisation itself is developing, and perhaps

---

40 Levi and Smith, note 34 above, at p. 16.

214

consciously responding to attempts at legal control. Observers of organised crime and terrorist activity report on the way in which crime groups appear to be evolving into looser and 'flatter' networks, as a way of securing their own position.[41] The adoption of less hierarchical and more disconnected structures makes it more difficult for prosecutors to trace lines of authority and command, and the latter are important elements in both the definition of the offence and its proof. A 1998 report from Europol,[42] for example, noted a transition from traditional 'Mafia-type' associations to more decentralised forms, typified by the 'cellular' structure of some terrorist groups. This is a natural and in some respects predictable defensive strategy on the part of organised crime groupings. But it sounds a warning note for law enforcement – the enactment of new offences may sound the appropriate rhetoric of law enforcement, but the legal outcomes may eventually prove disappointing if the possibility of taking cases to trial and securing conviction is compromised by this kind of difficulty. It is also worth noting comparatively that, in the rather different context of EC cartel control, most appeals against a finding of infringement or the amount of a fine which succeed to any extent do so on grounds of insufficient evidence of a company's specific involvement in certain aspects of an undoubted network of cartel activity.[43] Again, the difficulty resides not so much in demonstrating the existence of a particular delinquent organisation but in finding proof, to the requisite standard, of specific individual participation. And that again may be an issue, at least in strategic terms, of choosing between individual and organisational responsibility.

7 Criminal organisation as a site for theoretical modelling

The purpose of devoting part of the discussion in this work to the situation of 'delinquent' or criminal organisations, alongside that of

41 See, for instance, Jessica Stern, *The Ultimate Terrorists* (Harvard University Press, 1999); John Lea (2004) 'Hitting Criminals Where It Hurts: Organised Crime and the Erosion of Due Process', *Cambrian Law Review*, 35(79): 87, referring to the problem of 'newer looser criminal networks with shifting memberships and temporary alliances'.

42 Europol, *1998 EU Situation Report on Organised Crime* (The Hague, 1 January 2000).

43 See Christopher Harding and Alun Gibbs (2005) 'Why Go to Court in Europe? An Analysis of Cartel Appeals, 1995–2004', *European Law Review*, 30: 349.

'legitimate' organisations in the context of business and governance, was to add to the analysis of individual and organisational responsibility, and seek any further illuminating lessons on that issue. To an extent it may be seen that some of the earlier lessons and conclusions may be confirmed, and that is perhaps unsurprising in so far as delinquent organisations sometimes imitate or even compete with legitimate organisational actors in both the economic and political spheres. But the enquiry into efforts of legal control of delinquent groups and bodies also appears to have been valuable in itself, in that, in a number of legal orders, these moves towards regulation have involved some significant forging of legal concepts and testing of strategies which contribute to the wider exercise of unravelling the relation between the individual and the organisational and determining agency and allocating responsibility as between different types of actor. In fact, the domain of delinquent organisations provides a rich site for this kind of legal fashioning. It has been shown that the overarching category of delinquent organisation embraces a wide diversity of groups and bodies, ranging through political factions, military insurgency movements, terrorist groups, sophisticated networks of organised criminality and smaller-scale criminal gangs. As such organisations appear in the contemporary world as increasingly significant and powerful actors possessing a developed identity of their own, efforts at legal control have increased and developed greater focus, at both national and international levels. This developing process of regulation has in this way provided a kind of laboratory for testing ideas and strategies regarding legal and criminal responsibility as a crucial feature of any regime of legal control.

One lesson to be drawn from this particular discussion is that any conclusions on the question of responsibility may depend on the organisational type in question and the context of its operation. Thus some different models appear to be emerging in relation to political factions and terrorist organisations on the one hand, and 'conventional' criminal organisations and gangs on the other hand. The former tend to possess more well-defined and more formal structures and a more openly claimed identity as compared to the latter. In that context, a model of autonomous organisational agency may appear more compelling and indeed has already been adopted to some extent in legal practice, especially at the international level. In particular, in relation to the need for international legal enforcement action, the legal targeting of delinquent factions and terrorist groups has already established a kind of regime of accountability, although (as in the case of some governmental actors discussed in the previous Chapter) this may not resemble very closely the model of classical criminal law. Nonetheless, the kind of measure that may be used in relation to such actors may be seen to imply a level of responsibility and employ repressive sanctions in a manner analogous to that of criminal law. On the other hand, in relation to 'private' criminal organisations, the means of legal control appears still to favour a system of individual responsibility, but one that is dependent upon organisational context, so that it may perhaps be more accurately described as one based on the individual *acting within* an organisation.

This conclusion may also help to clarify what we are actually seeking in a process of allocating responsibility and the concept of responsibility in itself. We should remind ourselves that responsibility entails both utilitarian and retributive elements. In the context of *criminal* responsibility a primary purpose is not just the regulation but the prohibition of certain conduct, and that entails both a process to ensure that the conduct in question is terminated and not repeated and also a means of restoring normative value by recovering the damage brought about by the violation of significant norms. Taking the fairly straightforward example of significant delinquent organisations such as the Nazi party or al-Qaeda, the process of legal responsibility is both a matter of utilitarian removal and retributive accountability for the injury that they inflict. Thus measures of proscription and military enforcement action are as much a part of the picture as court judgments and the imposition of individualised sanctions. But the former may, for both practical and moral reasons, more appropriately attach to the organisational actor, while the latter may often be meaningfully linked to individual members of the organisation. And in order to accomplish the latter, it may be necessary to develop ideas of individual responsibility further in the direction of participatory as distinct from predicate offending.

In this way the concept of the delinquent organisation and a study of its legal control brings into sharp relief the issue of relating individual and organisational action, by providing a good testing ground for emergent contemporary models of legal regulation. It remains then, in the last section of the book, to draw together more fully these conclusions on both organisational agency and the participation of individuals in organisations into an overall theoretical structure of criminal responsibility.

Part III

Criminal organisation and criminal enterprise

.

Introductory note

The preceding discussion has been largely concerned with the exploration of different models of criminal responsibility. The starting point has inevitably been the 'classic' individualist model, which takes the individual human actor as a natural unit of agency and candidate for any allocation of moral or legal responsibility. It has been seen how this classic model predominantly informs the content and process of contemporary Western criminal law. Criminal responsibility has therefore to a large extent followed the biological human being and thus also found its expression in the psychological and physical characteristics of the individual human actor. However, in a society increasingly characterised by the presence and impact of organisations and organisational structures, the dominant role of the classic individualist model may be validly questioned. Two possible lines of enquiry have emerged from the earlier theoretical and contextual discussion. The first of these considers the possibility that organisations may be regarded as possessing their own distinctive and autonomous identity, so that a convincing case may be made for saying that some organisations in some circumstances may be seen as autonomous agents and appropriate subjects for the allocation of responsibility in relation to certain activities and events. The second line of enquiry relates to the role of individuals within organisational structures and considers the identification of different forms of individual agency and responsibility within such a context. Here the principal outcome would be a distinction between more specific actions (or 'predicate' offending) carried out within an organisation and that kind of action which in a wider sense designs, promotes and facilitates such predicate offences. The latter in effect combines a model of individual responsibility with one of organisational context, leading to a form of individual responsibility arising from involvement in an essentially collective enterprise. In one sense this third model may be located at a point between that of classic individual human responsibility and that of an autonomous organisational responsibility, since it combines elements of both the individual and the collective.

The emergence of the latter two alternative models may be seen as a response to perceived inadequacies and problems relating to a sole deployment of the classic individualist model. There are both ethical and practical limitations which have become evident in relation to the individualist approach, arising from its application in complex organisational environments. Most obviously, for example, there may be difficulties regarding the ethical basis for the allocation of responsibility to an individual whose conduct may have been significantly affected by an organisational environment, or practical problems of evidence in relation to an individual's role within a complex organisational structure. Such doubts regarding the continued allocation of responsibility to individuals as predicate offenders have therefore prompted the exploration of alternatives sites of responsibility: the organisation itself, or the individual as a kind of organisational actor. The construction of such alternative models of responsibility may be seen then as a response to the individual–organisation dilemma as an issue in contemporary society.

The discussion in Part II above has explored the problem of allocating responsibility as between individuals and organisations in three particular contexts, chosen for their contemporary significance as sites of legal discourse and practice. The cases of business delinquency, delinquency in governance and organised criminality provide instructive material for purposes of bringing together theory and practice in relation to the subject of criminal responsibility. As a report on legal development, what emerges is a patchy and incomplete picture, with some gaps and inconsistencies, but also some converging tendencies. Sometimes organisational actors have been accepted as moral and legal agents and have been treated as legally responsible actors, notably for example in the case of companies and States and governments. But the precise allocation and nature of legal responsibility may vary according to context, and may be determined in particular by more specific enforcement objectives. Certainly there is an argument then for a more consistent and surer theoretical basis for such decisions about responsibility. Nonetheless, it must still be recognised that a certain amount has happened in a number of legal orders: companies are sometimes convicted of criminal offences, States are held legally responsible for serious violations of international law which are tantamount to an international criminality, and the International Criminal Tribunal for the former Yugoslavia has used the concept of criminal enterprise to extend the scope of individual criminal liability. It is important to see the theoretical relationship between these various developments and to be able to construct a coherent overall picture of what is happening across the board.

The purpose of the final two chapters in this section is to examine in turn and more theoretically the two alternative models of criminal responsibility. The salient features of these two models of responsibility will be identified and some critical arguments considered relating to their application and the limits to which such approaches may be taken.

Chapter 9

The organisation as an autonomous criminal actor

To what extent, then, is it sensible or meaningful to talk about the 'criminal organisation': as an organisational actor (such as a company, government or criminal gang) which may in itself be held criminally responsible for conduct which is distinct from that of its individual constituent members? The criteria of organisational agency worked out in Chapter 3 may be used to justify such organisational responsibility, but in any such allocation of responsibility it is important to have a clear idea and definition of the nature and scope of the offending conduct to which such responsibility relates. Organisations commit different offences from individuals and an important reason for saying that is to recognise the limits of individual responsibility. Organisations and individuals should not be viewed as each other's alter ego, and organisational responsibility should begin where individual responsibility ends. The outcome is therefore something distinctive in terms of role, offending conduct, identity of the responsible actor and perhaps also the resulting sanctions which are used to convey judgments of responsibility.

In this chapter we return to the basic question: does it make sense, ethically and practically, to say that an organisation, such as a company, or a State, or a criminal grouping, should be held responsible for certain actions rather than individuals working within such organisations? In some contexts, as already seen, companies and States have indeed been held legally responsible in a number of legal orders, and in some instances, criminally responsible. However, when this has happened, the theoretical and legal basis for such responsibility has not always been entirely clear or easily agreed.

Thus, while the broader legal responsibility of corporate bodies such as commercial companies is both necessarily and comfortably accepted, the more specific issue of their criminal responsibility is more controversial, both as to its basis and extent. Again, the responsibility of States and governmental actors is taken for granted as a matter of international law and public law. But international lawyers continue to argue the point whether it is possible to talk about the 'criminal State', and more generally the dividing line between individual and governmental responsibility remains a matter of argument and legal development. In short, across a range of legal orders, we do not yet have a clear verdict on the question of how far criminal responsibility may be allocated to organisational actors, and this continues to be a challenging matter for both legal theory and practice. There is at the very least some need for a coherent and agreed basis for allocating responsibility, of whatever kind, between individual and organisational actors.

The reasons for allocating criminal responsibility to organisational actors in certain circumstances will be considered more fully below. But in the first place it would be helpful to reprise the theoretical basis for organisational agency, as the basic justification for allocating criminal responsibility to such entities.

I The criteria of organisational agency

It will be recalled that the principal objection to organisational criminal responsibility arises from the individualist argument that it is not meaningful to ascribe responsibility to abstract constructions which are in any case reducible to a number of individual human members, and that the latter remain the determining actors for purposes of evaluating either ethically or practically any activities under the organisational aegis. It is therefore necessary to show convincingly that there is a distinct organisational agency which may in certain situations be a more sensible site for allocating responsibility, and in particular criminal responsibility.

The discussion in Chapter 3 above suggested a number of criteria of distinct organisational identity and agency. These are the conditions, it is argued, that are necessary to demonstrate the existence of a separate and independent entity, capable of its own moral action distinct from its component human members, both as a matter of sociological fact and normative capacity. These criteria may be listed as: (a) an organisational or group rationality; (b) an irrelevance of persons; (c) a structure and capacity for autonomous action; and (d) a representative role.

Organisational rationality is a necessary indicator of distinct identity and capacity for independent action. In short, this is an ability to reflect on conduct and engage in decision-making in a way that is not simply the sum of a number of individual human mentalities but a capacity for rational process which is something over and above the specific contribution of any particular human members of the organisation. To overcome the individualist objection that an alleged organisational rationality is no more than what may be decided by one or more of its human members, it may be conceded that organisational rationality has its origin in human activity, but is essentially the product of *a process of human interaction* which transforms the character of the rationality.[1] Human interaction is a different matter from individual human contributions and interaction itself has a transformative dynamic. Put another way, the interaction of a number of human individuals produces a collective culture which then becomes the commanding determinant of organisational action. In French's language, the conglomerate replaces the aggregate.[2]

The issue of organisational rationality is related to the second criterion listed above, that of *the irrelevance of persons*. This is the concept employed by Coleman[3] to indicate more exactly the irrelevance or non-essential character of specific human individuals. In more sociological terms, this refers to the idea that the *role* of an individual actor replaces the personal identity of such an actor. What is important is that there is a defined role of chief executive officer or head of government, irrespective of the personal identity of the individual occupying that position at any given time. In theoretical and normative terms the existence and survival of the organisation depends not on the availability of X or Y to lead the organisation or conduct its affairs, but on an enduring structure comprising defined roles for any qualified individual to occupy. To see the matter in this light is to appreciate the nature of the distinct organisational

1 See Larry May and Stacey Hoffman, *Collective Responsibility: Five Decades of Debate in Theoretical and Applied Ethics* (Rowman and Littlefield, 1991), at p. 3; and see further the discussion of this idea in Chapter 3 above.

2 Peter A. French (1979) 'The Corporation as a Moral Person', *American Philosophical Quarterly*, 16; *Collective and Corporate Responsibility* (Columbia University Press, 1984).

3 James S. Coleman, *The Asymmetric Society: Organizational Actors, Corporate Power and the Irrelevance of Persons* (Syracuse University Press, 1982).

rationality and the way in which it transcends specific individual contribution.

The third criterion is also related to the first two. A *structure and capacity for autonomous action* is the practical realisation of a distinct rationality and decision-making process, enabling the latter to be implemented and take material shape. It comprises both necessary physical infrastructure and some recognition of the identity and role of the organisation on the part of other actors. In short, then, this is the ability to have dealings, as an organisation and not as a collection of individuals, with other relevant actors.

The final criterion of *role* supplies meaning to the existence and activities of the organisation, thus providing specific identity. The organisation must exist for a purpose, since (as a matter of sociological definition, discussed in Chapter 2) it is not a random collective but a purposeful grouping. Its *raison d'être* – carrying out particular tasks and fulfilling certain objectives – will be linked to the pursuit and maintenance of particular interests, and in that sense the role of the organisation is representative of those interests. Furthermore, this supplies a clue as to the need for organisational as distinct from individual action. Such interests are better served through organisational action, as would be evident for example in the reasons for incorporation as a company, or the political formation of a State or international organisation. The role criterion acts as a justification for the existence of an organisation, while also supplying its character and identity, but is equally important as a justification for organisational as distinct from individual agency.

At this point it is perhaps worth adding and emphasising that this concept of organisational agency avoids any reliance on an attribution of an *alter ego* for purposes of constituting an organisational personality. One of the reasons for seeking a genuinely autonomous organisational identity is to escape the anthropomorphic tendency to equate the human components of the organisation with the organisation as such and simply see the latter as an alternative form of human actor. This has been the approach for instance in English criminal law in so far as it has attributed corporate criminal responsibility to companies by treating corporations as an alternative manifestation of the personalities of the directing human beings within that corporate structure.[4] The outcome has been a transfer of

---

4 For a general account of this line of case law, see A.P. Simester and G.R. Sullivan, *Criminal Law: Theory and Doctrine* (2nd edn, Hart Publishing, 2003), at pp. 254–5.

responsibility from human to corporate actors, but on the theoretical basis that the company is no more than an expression of the will and decision-making of certain leading human members within the company. This idea of 'identification', which merges the personalities of the company and its controlling individuals by an anthropomorphic process of discovering a unity of person, has found particular favour with British judges. A classic statement is that of Viscount Haldane, LC in a judgment of 1915:

> ... A corporation is an abstraction. It has no mind of its own any more than it has a body of its own; its active and directing will must consequently be sought in the person of somebody who for some persons may be called an agent, but who is really the directing mind and will of the corporation, the very ego and centre of the corporation.[5]

The anthropomorphic analysis finds a particularly full expression in the words of Lord Denning:

> A company may in many ways be likened to a human body. It has a brain and a nerve centre which controls what it does. It also has hands which hold the tools and act in accordance with directions from the centre. Some of the people in the company are mere servants and agents who are nothing more than hands to do the work and cannot be said to represent the mind or will. Others are directors and mangers who represent the directing mind and will of the company and control what it does. The state of mind of these managers is the state of mind of the company and is treated by the law as such.[6]

A major problem arising from this fiction of corporate existence resides in its simplistic assumption that the corporate actor is similar to a human body in its workings. Such an approach underestimates the complexity and subtlety of much corporate action and imposes an already simplified biological model upon an equally simplified appreciation of corporate management and internal behaviour. As a result there is then limited opportunity for allocation of criminal

---

5 *Leonards Carrying Co. Ltd v. Asiatic Petroleum Co. Ltd* (1915) AC, at p. 713.

6 *H.L. Bolton (Engineering) Co. Ltd v. T.J. Graham & Sons Ltd* (1957) 1 QB 159, at p. 172.

responsibility to corporate persons as a matter of English law. As Simester and Sullivan have pointed out:

> The company's culpability is a derivative of human culpability. Within the doctrine's own terms, a finding that the company possessed the mens rea for an offence may only be made if some individual of sufficient seniority possessed the mens rea for the offence. This narrowness is the doctrine's major limitation in terms of obtaining corporate convictions. If we confine our attention to charges of corporate manslaughter, to date four such charges have been brought. Successful prosecutions have been confined to small companies where the top management ran the company in a 'hands on' manner. In a company of any complexity and size, it is exceedingly unlikely that an official of sufficient stature to count as an *alter ego* would be found grossly negligent in respect of particular safety matters …[7]

The 'identification' doctrine is thus open to the criticism of being sociologically misleading, philosophically flawed, and legally restrictive.[8] A sounder basis for organisational responsibility would lie in the idea of autonomous organisational action, untied to any individualist insistence on an identity of human and organisational activity.

2 Paradigms of organisational agency

It may be useful at this point briefly to note the main forms likely to be taken by such an autonomous organisational actor, as an agent which may be allocated criminal responsibility. There are, on the one hand, some organisations which have been held criminally responsible in relation to certain activity, although the basis for doing so may have been unclear and the reasons for doing so open to argument or opposition (for instance, to satisfy enforcement interests, while courting double jeopardy objections). On the other hand, there are other examples of organisations which have not yet

---

7 Simester and Sullivan, *Criminal Law,* note 4 above, at p. 255.

8 For further criticism, see, e.g. Andrew Ashworth, *Principles of Criminal Law* (4th edn, Oxford University Press, 2003), at p. 118; Michael Jefferson, *Criminal Law* (6th edn, Longman, 2003), p. 243 *et seq.*

become established as criminal actors, while theoretically there may
be persuasive grounds for regarding them as such. A number of
examples in both the above categories have been discussed in Part
II above. Also, following the organisation of discussion in Part II,
we may refer to three main paradigms of organisational agency in
contemporary society: the corporation, the governmental institution,
and the delinquent organisation.

For many practical purposes, reference here to the corporation is to
the company as a business firm. In contemporary society the company
is an actor of considerable quantitative and qualitative significance,
appearing frequently and playing a crucial role in economic life, and
even to some extent in non-economic realms such as the social and the
cultural. Companies, through the process of incorporation (although
this is not essential) are accorded legal personality in a large number
of legal orders, and are designed as subjects of legal responsibility. In
a number of situations, as seen in Chapter 6, companies have been
held responsible under criminal law and are technically capable of
committing a range of offences, although this range of offending,
and its legal basis, may vary from one legal order to another. Thus,
there is little controversy in any reference to companies as corporate
criminal actors. But, as we have seen in the earlier discussion, the
nature of the offences committed by companies, the relation of
this offending to the associated action of individuals, and the legal
basis for corporate criminal responsibility may all be open to
argument.

Governmental institutions – whether cast in the form of States,
governments, departments of State or intergovernmental organisations
– are also uncontroversial in terms of their possession of legal
personality and consequent legal responsibility. However, differently
from the case of companies, organisations of governance are in the
practice of legal systems less comfortably accepted as criminal actors.
In other words, their legal responsibility is usually characterised as
being non-criminal. States and governments may be held responsible
for serious human rights violations, or may be defendants in civil
proceedings, but rarely appear in the dock of a criminal court.[9] As

---

9 Exceptionally, there have been some interesting examples of State bodies
being prosecuted and convicted under criminal procedure: for instance
in the Netherlands during the 1990s – see the summary in Nina H.B.
Jørgensen, *The Responsibility of States for International Crimes* (Oxford
University Press, 2003), pp. 78–9. One example concerned a district
authority being prosecuted and convicted of an environmental offence,

seen in Chapter 7, attempts within the International Law Commission to fashion international rules relating to State criminal responsibility foundered in recent years. Yet arguments may be made in principle to support the imposition of criminal responsibility on a range of governmental organisations. The problem does not lie in the theory, but arises from political and enforcement interests.

The third paradigm of organisational agency put forward here is more controversial in both theory and legal practice. Unlike corporations and State or public institutions, delinquent organisations such as criminal gangs and terrorist groups by their very nature are not formally constituted within legal orders. They are therefore less easily identifiable in formal terms. But two points may be made in this respect. First, it should be noted that formal processes of incorporation and constitution, although no doubt desirable for evidential purposes, are not crucial for purposes of legal personality and hence legal responsibility (as discussed in Chapter 4 above). For instance, trade unions are not incorporated persons under English law, yet have legal personality. Secondly, formal processes of creation cannot always guarantee a straightforward identity in reality, as for instance in the contemporary example of the 'failed' State. On the other hand (as seen in Chapter 8), some delinquent organisations possess for practical purposes a clear structure and role, combined with an enduring character, and are really no more elusive as subjects of law than some corporate and State actors. Moreover, there may be a fine dividing line in practice between 'illegitimate' organised crime and political organisations and 'legitimate' business and government: as seen already, yesterday's terrorist may become today's head of government, and yesterday's head of government may become today's war criminal. The objections to legal personality and responsibility in the case of delinquent organisations are political and ethical rather than theoretical or even practical: that bequeathing legal status on such entities would in some sense enhance their standing and legitimise their existence. But such misgiving may not outweigh some of the ethical and practical advantages of organisational agency and responsibility as discussed above.

In order to make clear the relation between this list of paradigms and the preceding discussion relating to the criteria of organisational agency, it may be worth indicating more precisely how each paradigm

---

but no penalty was applied (the 'Limburg' case, HR 9 June 1992, NJ 1992, 784).

would satisfy these criteria. This may be seen from the grid in Table 9.1 below.

3 The importance of offence definition

It is argued here, then, that in so far as legal responsibility has been or may be imposed upon an organisational actor, that allocation of responsibility is most convincingly justified on the basis of the actor's agency in the way explained above – that is, as a genuinely autonomous actor, distinct from its human components. Viewed in that way (and not, for instance, as an *alter ego* of a particular human individual within the organisation), an entity such as a company or a government may be seen as a morally appropriate subject of responsibility. The underlying reason and justification for this allocation of responsibility to an organisation is that certain types of action cannot meaningfully be seen as a matter of individual agency but may be assigned to the decision-making processes and policies of an organisation. It is not therefore a matter of alternatives – that, for instance, *either* the company *or* its CEO may be held responsible for the same act. In either direction, such an alternative form of responsibility would have a vicarious character, and be open in that way to well-known ethical objection.[10] From this, it may be seen that there is an important link between agency and allocation of responsibility on the one hand, and definition of the offending conduct on the other hand. This last point should be used to inform any critique of the allocation of responsibility between different types of actor.

Thus, while both individuals within an organisation and the organisation itself may be viewed as being involved in the same web or network of activity, their respective acts may be distinguished as *contributing differently* to the overall enterprise of the organisation. Typically, for example, an organisational act may be defined as the formulation of a policy (for instance, genocide), while an individual act may be defined as a specific act of implementation of that policy (for instance, a specific instance of genocidal killing). This kind of categorisation of activity and conduct for purposes of offence definition is a crucial exercise within the process of distinguishing individual and organisational responsibility. If such offence definition

---

10 See Jefferson, *Criminal Law*, note 8 above, at pp. 240–2, who refers to the possible incompatibility of the doctrine of vicarious liability with provisions of the Human Rights Act 1998.

Table 9.1

Paradigm	Criteria of agency	Evidence
Corporation (e.g. company set up for business purposes)	Organisational rationality	Defined decision-making process in articles of incorporation and internal regulations
	Irrelevance of persons	Office (e.g. CEO) is crucial, not individual identity of office-holder
	Structure and capacity for autonomous action	Material infrastructure (offices, personnel) and recognised status (dealings with similar actors)
	Role	Defined in incorporating document and policy statements
Governmental organisation (e.g. State)	Organisational rationality	Defined decision-making process in constitution and formal rules
	Irrelevance of persons	Office (e.g. President) is crucial, not individual identity of office-holder
	Structure and capacity for autonomous action	Material infrastructure (territory, population, governmental structure) and recognised status (through international processes of recognition)
	Role	Defined in constitution and political statements
Delinquent organisation (e.g. terrorist organisation)	Organisational rationality	Defined decision-making process in internal operational rules and command structure
	Irrelevance of persons	Enduring organisational roles, despite loss of individual members
	Structure and capacity for autonomous action	Material infrastructure (physical and economic resources, personnel) and formal identification as a delinquent actor (e.g. in Security Council resolutions)
	Role	Enunciated in internal and public policy statements

is carried out carefully and convincingly it will for instance avoid double-counting and overlapping classification which may obfuscate the allocation of responsibility and raise questions about its ethical basis. What is required therefore is an analysis of webs of interrelated activities in order to locate distinct agencies (and thus sites of responsibility) within what are often complex organisational contexts. In view of such complexity, it may be a challenging matter to unravel evidence of activity, causal relations between actions and the assignment of roles in both a social and psychological sense. It will be recalled that these are some of the essential components of responsibility identified in Chapter 5 above.

We have seen already in relation to cartel offending, for example, how an activity such as price fixing may become rather too casually the site of offence-weaving by attributing the same offence to different actors (the human individual and the company).[11] Does it make sense under the US Sherman Act to say that a company and one of its executives conspire together to commit the same act if the identity and role of the respective actors are not clearly differentiated? If the executive is simply the *alter ego* of the company then the rationale for alleging a conspiracy, which is necessarily the joint action of two separate and autonomous agents, simply disappears. Moreover, if the company and executive are distinguished separately as autonomous agents then it is also, in factual terms, difficult to see how they may conspire to commit the same act (such as price fixing) since their distinct agencies depends upon their fulfilling distinct roles. In other words, they cannot, as distinct and independent agents, commit price fixing in precisely the same way (although they could of course as the *alter ego* of each other). Thus the present policy under the Sherman Act of charging both with a conspiracy to do the same cannot have its cake and eat it. On the one hand, either the company or its executive could commit, as the *alter ego* of each other, the same act but cannot conspire with each other. On the other hand, the company and its executive could, as *independent agents*, conspire together, but would have distinct roles in that venture – they could not conspire each to carry out exactly the same act of price fixing, since that would be a conspiracy simply to replicate each other's behaviour, or, we might say, a conspiracy to be the same person doing the same thing. A convincing allegation of conspiracy under the Sherman Act would require the company and the executive to perform in relation to each other distinct but equally essential roles within the overall

---

11 See, p. 131 et seq. Chapter 7 above.

operation of price fixing. Thus it would be necessary to distinguish two offences of price fixing, such as an agreement to enter into a price fixing arrangement (which might be attributed to the company) and participation in a specific price fixing deal, working out the details and overseeing its implementation (which might be attributed to particular individuals). A conspiracy between company and executives would then be a meaningful concept, since they would be agreeing as distinct actors to carry out different roles within a network of related actions directed towards a common purpose.

This kind of analysis can be used in other contexts. For instance, as noted in Chapter 8, it would seem more appropriate to allocate responsibility for a policy and programme of apartheid to an organisational actor such as a government than attribute such systemic conduct to an individual.[12] On the other hand, there may be more specific actions involving implementation of such a policy which may be meaningfully attributed to individuals, but in relation to which responsibility would be of a different order. Similarly, in the context of organised crime, as discussed in Chapter 8, a 'godfather' role may be usefully distinguished from a 'foot soldier' role for purposes of attributing different levels of responsibility.[13] On the other hand, there may also be situations in which the role of an organisational agent might be distinguished, not so much for purposes of allocating different responsibility to organisational and individual actors, but rather to reserve responsibility for the former without attributing any individual responsibility. Thus, for example, any responsibility for a long-term policy resulting in serious environmental risk and damage may be a matter so far beyond the role of any one individual actor that any consideration of individual responsibility would simply not make sense, whereas the long-term and enduring participation of a governmental actor in such a policy could justify the allocation of organisational responsibility.[14] In the latter kind of case, the 'offence' would need to be defined in terms of systemic and blatant disregard of significant values, a form of conduct meaningfully attributable to

---

12 See the argument by Jørgensen, *The Responsibility of States,* note 9 above, at p. 245.

13 See pp. 211 et seq.

14 See Toni Erskine, 'Assigning Responsibilities to Institutional Moral Agents', Chapter 1 in Toni Erskine (ed.), *Can Institutions Have Responsibilities?* (Palgrave Macmillan, 2003), at p. 35: 'The United States can respond to acute environmental crises by upholding the conditions of the Kyoto Convention ... while the individual citizen cannot.'

an organisational culture rather than individual actions. The same could be (and indeed has been) argued in relation to corporate criminal responsibility for transport and industrial 'disasters'.[15]

But in any of these situations care must be taken not to slip into the process of offence-weaving and offender-multiplication. There must be persuasive grounds for asserting that, for instance, beyond specific predicate offences there lies another body of conduct which enables such predicate offending to occur and in that way comprises a distinct agency, form of offending and responsibility. While recognising that the 'mastermind' and the 'hit-man' are necessary partners, it is also appropriate to recognise the causal complexity underlying certain outcomes. Issues of agency and responsibility represent a response to this complexity of outcome in seeking to distinguish ethically separate contributions. In a context of organisational sophistication and complexity, it is relevant to consider the possibilities of distinct organisational agency alongside that of or in place of individual agency. Some of the advantages of this approach may be considered next.

4 The case for the criminal organisation

The argument for recognising some distinct organisational agency and possible legal and criminal responsibility is not only a matter of clearer understanding and appreciation of action, both in terms of conduct and outcomes, as just explained. It is also, and in ethical terms in a very important way, a matter of ensuring fair and appropriate treatment of individuals.

A significant objective of organisational responsibility is the limitation of individual responsibility. A driving force in this argument is the sense that while human actors may be the manifest perpetrators of certain action, an organisational context or the possibility of organisational agency might be a reason for reducing or eliminating the individual responsibility which might at first sight flow from such individual involvement. Thus the sleepy train driver might be seen as the responsible actor in relation to a train crash, or the frenzied soldier as the responsible actor in relation to killing not justified by military necessity. But behind a first reading of such events there may lie less obvious processes such as organisational cultures

---

15 See in particular Celia Wells, *Corporations and Criminal Responsibility* (2nd edn, Oxford University Press, 2001).

which encourage risk-taking to maximise profit[16] or the induction of human beings as killing machines.[17] It is the recognition of this kind of organisational force which has given rise to argument that seeks to transfer or reduce the responsibility of the ostensible human culprit. But for purposes of achieving accountability, responsibility removed in this way should be located somewhere, and in some situations a corporate or organisational actor such as a company or government may provide an appropriate site for that responsibility. Establishing the agency of such 'non-human' actors, and relating that agency to relevantly defined offending conduct, provides the ethical and legal basis for this kind of transfer of responsibility, while at the same time not losing the attribution of responsibility.

This is not to say that such a process of relocating responsibility in the direction of organisational actors will be easy or uncontentious, since (as noted already) it may involve some difficult reading of complex facts and circumstances. To return to the two examples given immediately above: how should we read and understand the way in which a corporate working culture might inculcate bad working habits on the part of employees, or the way in which military training might indoctrinate military personnel and affect behaviour in a battleground situation? Such basic questions give rise to more particular questions which would draw upon issues of ethics, sociology and psychology. But the difficulty of the task should not dissuade us from the project; recognising the existence of organisational complexity is not a reason for then avoiding the issue.

5 Processes of enforcement and sanctions

One of the doubts frequently expressed in relation to the agency and responsibility of organisational actors such as corporations and governments relates to the difficulty of accommodating such actors within conventional legal processes of rule enforcement and sanctioning. The well-known anthropocentric axiom may be quoted: 'no soul to damn, no body to kick' – or, to put the matter more

---

16 See generally: Gary Slapper and Steve Tombs, *Corporate Crime* (Longman, 1999).

17 See for instance, Jessica Wolfendale (2006) 'Training Torturers: A Critique of the "Ticking Bomb" Argument', *Social Theory and Practice*, 32, and (2006) 'Stoic Warriors and Stoic Torturers: The Moral Psychology of Military Torture', *South African Journal of Psychology*, 25: 62.

practically, is it possible to arrest, put in the dock of a court, or punish an abstract entity, or non-human actor? The answer to the question is that it arises itself from an anthropocentric perspective on legal process, and draws its inspiration from a failure of imagination. More specifically, it may be responded: if it is possible to imagine the legal personality of a company or a State, why is it then so difficult to imagine the trial or punishment of such entities? As Celia Wells has commented, part of the problem may lie in traditional linguistic usage: '... words such as "person" are assumed to be metaphysically limited ... *the language* of rationality and autonomy reflects our understanding of the individual.'[18] And Wells goes on to argue that decisions concerning responsibility should be based on normative rather than linguistic arguments.[19]

Admittedly, if we are proceeding from an idea of criminal law process and responsibility which is for the most part rooted in an individualistic conception of dealing with the actions of human beings, then subjecting organisations to such a process does require some adjustment and probably the development of new procedures.[20] But, once anthropocentric assumptions have been shaken off, it is a far from impossible task and the legal forms which need to be used may be readily available or worked out. A company may have to defend itself in court through representative human actors, but it already does so in exercising well-accepted aspects of its legal personality, for instance when entering into contracts (or, States when 'signing' treaties). Certain types of sanction may be imposed on organisations with no need to transfer their form or function – typically, for example, financial penalties or prohibitory orders. In reality organisations do possess souls to damn and bodies to kick, although their souls and bodies may not take the same material form as those of human beings. There are the functional equivalents of capital punishment: the legal and physical existence of a company or State may be terminated. In a very real sense this happened, for instance, to 'Nazi Germany' in 1945. There are functional equivalents of imprisonment, when the freedom and activities of corporations

---

18 Celia Wells, *Corporations and Criminal Responsibilit,y* note 15 above, at pp. 65–66.

19 *Ibid.*, p. 66.

20 Again, as Wells has observed: 'Traditional notions of criminal responsibility might be ill-suited for application to organizations, but from this it should not be assumed that they are immune from critical analysis in general', *ibid.*, p. 64.

and States are legally and materially constrained. There are functional equivalents of probation ordering when the future activities of organisations are subject to externally imposed conditions or subject to a compulsory process of monitoring. In other words, the analogies exist and may be further developed; it is simply that they need to be recognised for what they are.

This last point of argument may be applied in particular to procedures of enforcement. Certain processes are clearly not described as criminal proceedings but may represent their functional equivalent. This is particularly so at the international legal level at which, as already discussed, there may be a reluctance to apply the language of criminal liability to actors such as States and governments. But procedures which lead to the establishing of human rights violations, or the imposition of sanctions, or the use of UN-authorised enforcement action, embody a substantive element of censure and have an undoubted repressive character. Whatever formal labels are applied, such processes involve findings of significant norm violations and objectives of penalty and legal control.

However, the issue of sanctions which may be appropriately applied to organisational actors may give rise to practical questions in addition to that of formal description. Indeed, the choice and effectiveness of such sanctions may be seen as a significant sub-field of penology in its own right. In relation to both corporate and governmental actors there exists a rich choice of measures, beyond the range of conventional penalties applied to human actors within the more individualistic penal models. For example, much might be learnt from other legal fields from which different kinds of remedy and measure might usefully be translated to deal with the organisational offender. As Coffee remarked in relation to the adoption of disciplinary measures directed at corporations:

> It is a curious paradox that the civil law is better equipped at present than the criminal law to authorise [disciplinary or structural] intervention. Corporate probation could fill this gap and at last, offer a punishment that fits the corporation.[21]

In other words, measures worked out originally in the context of civil process could be incorporated into the criminal law framework of

---

21 J.C. Coffee Jnr (1981) '"No Soul to Damn No Body to Kick": An Unscandalized Inquiry into the Problem of Corporate Punishment', *Michigan Law Review*, 79(386): 459.

probation, which could then be imaginatively applied to organisational actors. Fisse and Braithwaite indicate how a range of strategies, such as stock dilution, probation, punitive injunctions, adverse publicity and community service might be used in response to corporate offending.[22] In relation to the idea of the punitive injunction, for example, they argue that, as a penal variant of the civil mandatory injunction, such a measure:

> could be used not only to require a corporate defendant to revamp its internal controls but also to do so in some punitively demanding way. Instead of requiring a defendant merely to remedy the situation by introducing state-of-the-art preventive equipment or procedures, it would be possible to insist on the development of innovative techniques. The punitive injunction could thus serve as both punishment and super-remedy.[23]

In another context and in an analogous way, Pella[24] has argued that States and governments might be subject to a raft of sanctions, ranging through the severance of diplomatic relations, economic boycotts and embargoes, censure, deprivation of representation or membership of organisations, occupation of territory or even loss of political independence (and examples of all of these may be found in the past 50 years of international relations).

The problem with such sanctions, whether applied to corporations or governmental entities, is not so much whether they can meaningfully exist, but rather how they actually take effect. More particularly, concerns are often expressed concerning the risk of collateral damage and 'spill over' arising from the blunt targeting of corporations and States as a whole. It may be argued for instance that for financial penalties imposed on corporations to be either retributively appropriate or deterrent in effect they must be so large as to court the risk of driving companies out of business, with consequent damage to innocent parties such as employees and investors, or even the structure of the market.[25] Or it may be

---

22 Brent Fisse and John Braithwaite, *Corporations, Crime and Accountability* (Cambridge University Press, 1993), p. 42.

23 *Ibid.*, at p. 43.

24 V.V. Pella, *Memorandum Concerning a Draft Code of Offences Against the Peace and Security of Mankind* (1950) A/CN.4/39.

25 For a very revealing recent study of the risk of bankruptcy arising from large fines imposed on companies participating in cartels, and the

predicted that sanctions imposed upon delinquent governments may cause more harm to innocent or even victim populations of the State in question so as to become politically and legally counter-productive.[26] Fisse and Braithwaite again provide a telling metaphor for this important argument by referring to the need to:

> replace corporate sanctions which 'pound like bludgeons at the periphery of large corporations' [Coffee's phrase] with more refined sanctions which strike like an épée at the vital sensitivities of responsible actors. To bring the analogy into the domain of late twentieth-century warfare, the sanctions now deployed against corporations resemble Scud missiles. Usually they land harmlessly in the wilderness; when they get close to the target, they are usually shot down by defensive systems; and when they do strike the target area, they often inflict unconscionable damage on the innocent. What we need instead are smart bombs, which, by bouncing beams of light back and forth between bomb and target, are able to make surgical strikes.[27]

Fisse and Braithwaite therefore advocate the deployment of measures which penetrate more finely the organisational structure, and in particular those strategies which are likely to contain the penal effect within key parts of that structure so as to encourage a spontaneous reform of bad parts and internal bad practice, such as required and monitored internal restructuring and disciplinary action, reform of standard operating procedures and internal compliance systems. In some senses, this is to employ the general model of probationary requirements, shifting the responsibility for reform to the defending organisation, but subjecting the latter to continuing surveillance to ensure that the measures in question are implemented.

---

way in which such risks may be used in legal argument, see: Andreas Stephan, 'The Bankruptcy Wild Card in Cartel Cases', University of East Anglia Centre for Competition Policy, CCP Working Paper 06-5 (2006). More generally see the discussion by Fisse and Braithwaite, *Corporations, Crime and Accountability*, note 22 above, under the heading 'Escaping the deterrence trap', pp. 189–90.

26 The classic example is provided by the reparations imposed on Germany following the end of the First World War.

27 Fisse and Braithwaite, note 22 above, at pp. 187–88.

An important lesson from this discussion is therefore that, if organisational responsibility is imposed, the sanctions need to be 'smart'. There is clearly the risk that large and undiscriminating penalties and control measures (massive fines and reparations, or military intervention, for example) may prove not only ineffective but also counter-productive. Rather, the sources of organisational malaise and delinquency need to be specifically located and finer aspects of organisational identity be used as sites of responsibility.

Chapter 10

The criminal enterprise as a facilitating framework

The problem of individual–organisational interactions and of allocating responsibility for such activities most obviously presents the choice between 'classic' individual responsibility (human individuals acting qua *human individuals) and organisational responsibility based upon the organisation as a single autonomous actor. Less obvious is the resolution of individual–organisational interactions by working out a form of individual responsibility which derives essentially from involvement in a collective enterprise. Here we have the idea of the joint delinquent enterprise (such as the joint criminal enterprise in war crimes trials, or the business cartel in European competition proceedings) which provides the legal basis for a participatory individual responsibility. For this purpose, it is important to distinguish both 'predicate' individual offending and any organisational offending from such a third category of participatory conduct. This form of individual responsibility, which appears increasingly significant in contemporary legal ordering, brings together elements of the individual and the collective in such a way as to resolve some of the dilemma of how to respond to individual–organisational interactions.*

This final chapter explores a model of criminal responsibility which occupies some space between the more obvious pillars of individual and organisational responsibility. As explained already, this third model combines an element of individual responsibility, in that ultimately an individual is held responsible, with an element of organisation and organisational context, in that the route to individual responsibility lies through some significant participation in the activities of the organisation. This is a model, therefore, in which the existence of the organisation and the performance of a certain role within the structure of the organisation are paramount for purposes of allocating responsibility to the individual in question. As such, this model thus addresses something of the significance and complexity of organisations in contemporary life and responds to the perception that a number of activities comprise elements of both the individual and the organisational, both of which need to be accommodated within a satisfactory model of moral and legal responsibility.

I 'Enterprise' and 'predicate' criminal responsibility

The essential background to the argument just presented above is the complexity of organisational activity, which may involve a number of human individuals performing different roles. In some cases, an individual role within this kind of context may in itself straightforwardly comprise a discrete act for purposes of moral evaluation and the assignment of legal responsibility. For instance, a specific act of homicide, rape or damage to property, perpetrated as part of a State-organised programme of ethnic cleansing will easily qualify as a criminal offence in its own right, clearly implicating the individual human perpetrator of the offence. Such predicate offending is and will remain an important site for the allocation of individualised criminal responsibility. The doubts that are likely to arise in such cases will relate mainly to the possible relevance of organisational structures and culture on the attribution of responsibility to individuals, in the form for example, of superior orders, coercion and the inculcation of attitudes and values. On the other hand, there may be other aspects of the life and work of an organisation which are both distinct from such predicate offending, but are also distinct from a purely organisational agency. These activities are carried out by individuals, yet occur only within the framework of the organisation and serve the organisation's needs. Such actions derive their meaning from the organisation's purpose and operation and thus are defined with reference to that collective activity of 'joint enterprise'.

Different labels have been applied to this concept of individual involvement in some organised structure; for instance, 'common purpose' or 'common design' or 'common criminal action', or 'joint enterprise'. But its essential character and rationale is well explained by Cassese in the following terms:

... in the case of deportation of civilians or prisoners of war to an extermination camp, a commander may issue the order, several officers may organize the transport, others may take care of food and drinking water, others may carry out surveillance over the inmates so as to prevent their escape, others may search the detainees for valuables or other things before deportation, and so on ... All participants in [such] a common criminal action are equally responsible, if they (i) participate in the action, *whatever their position and the extent of their contribution,* and in addition (ii) *intend to engage in the common criminal action.* Therefore they are all to be treated as *principals,* although of course the varying degree of culpability may be taken into account at the sentencing stage .... The rationale behind this legal regulation is clear ... (i) each of them is indispensable for the achievement of the final result, and on the other hand, (ii) it would be difficult to distinguish between the degree of criminal liability, except for sentencing purposes.[1]

This analysis provides a useful starting point for an exploration of the concept of the joint criminal enterprise, in providing a typical example and then supplying the conditions for responsibility and the underlying justification for this category of responsibility. From this we can begin to see the essential legal components of 'joint enterprise liability' as an intended contribution to that enterprise and actual (though varying) participation, and the basis for responsibility in terms of that participation being in each case indispensable but of uncertain specific causal significance to the final outcome of the enterprise. It is also important at the outset to distinguish this kind of joint enterprise responsibility from both predicate offending, as described above, and the concept of a criminal conspiracy.

The distinction between what may be conveniently referred to as predicate offending and what falls within the scope of 'joint criminal enterprise liability' is important to grasp for purposes of clear discussion. At the very least, this distinction is of importance to the argument in this work, since it is based on different models of individual responsibility as outlined above. Predicate offending is based on the 'classic' model of personal individual responsibility. 'Joint enterprise' offending is based on the third, 'individual within an organisational context' model.

---

1 Antonio Cassese, *International Criminal Law* (Oxford University Press, 2003), pp. 181–83.

Predicate acts or offences are those which are the ultimate subject[2] or objective of an enterprise, organised programme of activity or conspiracy: for instance, acts of extortion in a racketeering activity, the homicide in a conspiracy to kill, or the 'substantive' or 'ultimate' offence such as theft or rape in an act of burglary. As such, predicates constitute specific delinquent objectives within a wider framework of organised delinquent activity, and as criminal offences they are self-contained criminal acts in their own right. In that way, predicate offences may be and frequently are prosecuted independently, since they are often relatively easily proven, and both the moral responsibility and legal liability of the perpetrator are not in doubt. The problem, however, is that prosecution of such predicate offences and no more may miss a wider picture of significant delinquency comprising the planning, encouragement, and facilitation of such 'end' offences. Indeed, the predicate offending usually will not have taken place without such anterior organisation, and there is therefore a strong moral argument that those responsible for such acts of organisation should also bear criminal liability in connection with the achievement of the predicate criminality. In one example, that of burglary, within which the perpetrator of the predicate act is also the perpetrator of the organisational act (trespass on property), this provides the rationale for the distinct offence of burglary, as something additional to the theft or other listed criminal objective. In another example, that of conspiracy, the underlying planning or agreement to carry out unlawful or criminal acts, is itself then cast as offending conduct in its own right.[3] But perhaps an increasingly important context for distinction is that of organised criminality, where it is sought to incriminate significant and crucial directing and organising activities, which then need to be distinguished from the predicate or end offending. There was some discussion in Chapter 8 above of actual and proposed means of criminalising such 'peripheral' activities in organised crime at the national level (for instance the American RICO legislation). It is this objective of capturing the organisers of organised criminality which explains the recent significant emergence of 'joint criminal enterprise' liability in other contexts.

An important distinguishing feature between predicate offending and conspiracy on the one hand, and behaviour encompassed within

---

2 The term 'predicate' derives from the Latin *praedicare*. In a grammatical context, it is 'what is said of the subject', and more generally connotes assertion or affirmation as a quality, property or attribute of something.
3 But see below on the different definitions of conspiracy.

the concept of the joint criminal enterprise on the other hand, is that the latter might not in itself appear to be criminal or unlawful conduct. This is clear from Cassese's example: organisational acts of planning, administration, guarding and the like smack more of bureaucracy than crime. As such, they are therefore inherently difficult to prosecute, since such persons do not have obviously dirty hands. Indeed, this is the classic dilemma regarding the criminal mastermind and godfather kind of role, within which a key motivator of criminal activity is careful to keep a personal distance from the criminal outcomes by means of a chain of command and direction for which there is very little evidence of the kind required by legal process. A classic example is provided by the notorious Nazi defendant Adolf Eichmann,[4] who presented himself as a bureaucratic administrator[5] and archetypically non-criminal personality.[6] In terms of criminal organisation, it is in some sense part of the role of the 'hit-man' or 'foot soldier' to run a higher risk of detection and legal accountability than the 'boss' who presents him (more rarely, her) self as a legitimate businessman, public servant or politician. The purpose

---

4   Adolf Eichmann (1906–1962) was, under Nazi Germany, the Head of Gestapo Department IV B4 for Jewish Affairs. He was a senior government official who masterminded the implementation of the 'Final Solution'. At the Wannsee Conference in 1942 Eichmann, Heydrich and 15 other Nazi bureaucrats produced a general plan for administrative and financial measures for the extermination of an estimated 11 million persons, and Eichmann subsequently oversaw the implementation of these plans. In 1960 he was abducted by Israeli agents from Argentina and taken to Israel, where he was tried and convicted of crimes against humanity, and executed in 1962.

5   See the judgments of the District Court of Jerusalem and Israeli Supreme Court, 36 (1961) *International Law Reports*, 5, 277. Eichmann pleaded a defence of superior orders: 'Why me? Why not the local policemen, thousands of them ... Everybody killed the Jews.'

6   See the poem by Leonard Cohen on Eichmann: 'All There Is To Know About Adolf Eichmann', first published in the collection *Flowers for Hitler*. Cohen emphasises the man's apparent normality and average appearance:
    What did you expect?
    Talons?
    Oversize incisors?
    Green saliva?
    Madness?
    (Leonard Cohen, *Stranger Music: Selected Poems and Songs* (Jonathan Cape, 1993)

of joint criminal enterprise liability (and some of its analogues and related concepts such as conspiracy and prohibited membership) is to capture such crucial organisational actors as serious offenders, and lift their veil of legitimacy by establishing an overarching criminal motivation and dedication.

In summary, therefore, predicate offending is the staple diet of criminal law, comprising recognisable criminal conduct within well-established offence definitions and representing the material realisation of criminal organisation and enterprise. Typically therefore such offending comprises a range of acts of personal violence, property offending and intimidation. Joint criminal enterprise offences on the other hand comprise directing and facilitating activities which contribute significantly to the eventual commission of the predicate offences.

It can be seen already that the idea of conspiracy is also related to this kind of criminal structure or organisation. As a concept, conspiracy sometimes gives rise to difficulty, partly because the concept is used variably in different contexts and legal orders.[7] In broad terms, conspiracy is usually employed to denote a joint plan to commit an unlawful or criminal act. As such, and because it is a *joint* design, it may be seen in itself as an anterior form of offending behaviour. The coming together of a number of people to plan something unlawful is seen as action which is distinctly threatening to social order.[8] But legal systems differ in their definition of criminal conspiracy and the extent to which the concept is used to criminalise behaviour. The least extensive version of conspiracy (and this is perhaps the preferable version, since it is also the neatest and least confusing) is to confine its scope to the matter of agreement, plan or design between two or more persons, so that any liability is based simply on that act of agreement. However, sometimes the idea of conspiracy has been extended to embrace further acts of implementation, so that the liability for conspiracy also extends to those predicate acts. This version of conspiracy liability has been on

---

7 For further critical discussion of the offence of conspiracy, see A.P. Simester and G.R. Sullivan, *Criminal Law: Theory and Doctrine* (2nd edn, 2003, Hart Publishing), at pp. 294–5. Although published some time ago, a still useful and incisive discussion of the legal basis for the offence of conspiracy can be found in I.H. Dennis (1977) 'The Rationale of Criminal Conspiracy', *Law Quarterly Review*, 93: 39.

8 On the justification for conspiracy as an offence in itself, see the judgment of the US Supreme Court in *US v. Rabinowich*, 238 US 78.

occasion described as 'imputed liability', or in an American context *Pinkerton* liability, after a Supreme Court judgment in 1946[9] which confirmed this version of liability. It was also the kind of conspiracy liability which was proposed for the Nuremberg Tribunal in the earlier 'Bernays memorandum':

> ... should be charged ... with conspiracy to commit murder, terrorism, and the destruction of peaceful populations in violation of the laws of war ... once the conspiracy is established, each act of every member thereof during its continuance and in furtherance of its purposes would be imputable to all other members thereof.[10]

This idea of conspiracy eventually found its way into Count One of the Nuremberg Indictment.[11] The effect of this expansive concept of conspiracy is thus to collect together most of what is done within the overall criminal organisation and impute liability for all of that to the original planners. This 'wide-ranging and aggressive use of conspiracy'[12] has encountered objection, both subsequently in the Nuremberg process and under US law, and indeed is open to the theoretical objection that it confuses acts of planning and implementation and the responsibility for these respective roles (or, as Danner and Martinez express the matter, 'intertwines conspiracy

---

9 *Pinkerton v. US* (Supreme Court judgment) (1946) 328 US 460.

10 The memorandum was prepared by Murray C. Bernays (a lawyer in the US War Department); quoted in B.F. Smith, *The American Road to Nuremberg – The Documentary Record – 1944–45* (Hoover Institution Press, 1982), at pp. 33, 36–7.

11 Count One alleged that all of the defendants 'during a period of years preceding 8 May 1945, participated as leaders, organizers, instigators, or accomplices in the formulation or execution of a common plan or conspiracy to commit ... Crimes against Peace, War Crimes, and Crimes against Humanity ... and, in accordance with the provisions of the Charter, are individually responsible for their own acts and for all acts committed by any persons in the execution of such plan or conspiracy.'

12 Allison Marston Danner and Jenny S. Martinez (2005) 'Guilty Associations: Joint Criminal Enterprise, Command Responsibility, and the Development of International Criminal Law', *California Law Review*, 75: 116.

as a substantive crime with conspiracy as a theory of liability'[13]). It is suggested therefore that in working out a coherent ordering of criminal responsibility within an organisational context, the idea of conspiracy should be confined to its more limited role, which distinguishes it clearly from predicate offending, and locates it as a kind of offending which initiates the programme of activities of the joint criminal enterprise.

It would also be useful to say something about 'offences of membership' at this stage. As seen in the discussion in Chapter 8, membership of prohibited organisations has sometimes been put forward as a basis for criminal liability in itself. This is another stratagem designed to widen the net of criminal law control and capture a range of supporting actors in relation to a criminal enterprise. From the prosecutor's point of view this approach has the advantage of rendering evidence for purposes of liability very easy to establish. But, as has been seen,[14] the fact of membership has generally been viewed as over-presumptive for evidential purposes and on ethical grounds has not gained very much support. But, for purposes of this theoretical sketch, membership is another form of involvement with criminal organisation and for that reason does fit into the landscape of the joint criminal enterprise. It will be recalled, however, that the conclusion in Chapter 8 was that *participation* of some kind rather than membership is likely to be seen as the most convincing basis for establishing an 'enterprise liability'.

Finally, it may be helpful to distinguish two senses in which the term 'joint criminal enterprise' may be used in this kind of discussion. One sense is purely descriptive: the term is used factually to refer to the organisational structure within which a range of offending activities (from the planning and design of the enterprise (as a conspiracy) to the ultimate predicate offences) take place. This use of the term may be illustrated by the scheme laid out in Figure 10.1 below.

The second sense is normative, in that the idea of such a joint enterprise is used as a basis for legal liability. It is in this second sense that the term has been increasingly employed in relation to offences of direction and participation, in that the enterprise and its objectives become essential components of both the *actus reus* and *mens rea* of those offences (see the discussion below under section 3 of this chapter). In this sense, the enterprise is not simply a descriptive umbrella but something which requires careful definition and

---

13 *Ibid.*, at p. 116.
14 See above, Chapter 8, p. 210.

CONSPIRACY (agreement, plan or design)
MEMBERSHIP AS AN OFFENCE (rarely used)
JOINT CRIMINAL ENTERPRISE OFFENCES (offences of participation)
PREDICATE OFFENDING (e.g. offences of violence, property offences, intimidation)

Figure 10.1 Joint enterprise as an organisational structure and site for offending

evidence for legal purposes, and acquires a normative significance as something which is itself the subject of legal prescription. Just as conspiracy may be both a substantive offence and a basis for liability, it is worth bearing in mind these two senses in which joint enterprise may be used in the discussion here.

2 Paradigms of participation in joint delinquent enterprise

One of the most striking points to emerge from this study concerns the emergence of some paradigms of the joint enterprise model in a number of distinct contexts of legal regulation. Each of the three main contexts studied in Part II of this work (business, public governance and organised delinquency) may be seen as sites for the use of this model, enabling in each case the imposition of legal and criminal responsibility on actors participating in an organised activity precisely on account their participation. In short, this comprises the evidence for the development of this particular model of individual responsibility across a range of situations calling for legal regulation. It would be appropriate now to recall and summarise these paradigms of 'organisational individual responsibility'.

Firstly, it is interesting to note the coincident appearance of the generic idea of criminal or delinquent enterprise in different contexts: the anti-competitive business cartel under European Community law; the 'joint criminal enterprise' or 'common purpose' or 'plan' as part of the jurisprudence of the International Criminal Tribunal for the Former Yugoslavia (ICTY); the 'criminal organisation' as defined in the 1998 EU Joint Action on criminalising participation in a criminal organisation, and the concept of an organised crime 'commission' under US law. These are all examples of organisations or structured associations, formed to carry out illegal activities, and providing significantly for the facilitation of such activities. Descriptively they have much in common and may be conveniently placed together under a single generic heading such as 'joint criminal enterprise'. In each case, they provide an essential legal framework for establishing what have been described above as offences of participation (direction and facilitation) as well as in some cases also offences of conspiracy and predicate offending. There is some conceptual fuzziness in these developments, of the kind noted above, especially the tendency to fail to distinguish substantive offending from a basis of liability, as already noted in the case of conspiracy. Thus, terminology and argument may not always clearly differentiate the facilitating structure from the offending conduct, or the kinds of offence committed within the organisational framework (for instance, conspiracy, supportive participation or predicate offences). Nonetheless, the coincident development along broadly similar lines is striking and merits some closer analysis. The examples may be taken in turn.

(a) The 'European cartel offence

Strictly speaking, the working out of liability for cartel infringements, under Article 81 of the EC Treaty,[15] is not a matter of criminal law. But the procedures of investigation, enforcement and sanctioning are analogous to criminal law proceedings and in a number of national legal systems participation in business cartels now ranks as a criminal offence. At the very least, therefore, the 'cartel offence', as developed in the case law of the European Court of Justice (ECJ) and Court of First Instance (CFI), is part of a repressive and penal system of law enforcement, and the kind of responsibility assigned to companies in relation to their involvement in cartels which infringe the EC competition rules bears comparison with criminal responsibility.[16] What might now be described as the 'European cartel offence', in respect of which sanctions are imposed, is not so much a matter of conspiracy in itself or predicate activities such as price fixing or market sharing, but rather a number of forms of participation in an organisational structure, that is the cartel. To be sure, the cartel is

---

15 See generally the discussion in Chapter 7, above.
16 See generally the argument in Christopher Harding and Julian Joshua, *Regulating Cartels in Europe* (Oxford University Press, 2003).

based upon an agreement or concerted practice (to use the wording of Article 81), which might approach the general idea of conspiracy, especially since a plan or unimplemented intention to engage in prohibited practices would suffice for some degree of liability (Article 81 prohibits either an 'object' or 'effect'). Predicate prohibited activities as defined in Article 81 also have to be the subject of the cartel's activities. But what is more specifically condemned in the case law *as a kind of offence which justifies the imposition of fines*, rather than activity which is simply prohibited, is the engagement in the 'cartel as a whole'. This may be seen from the following statement of the Court of First Instance:

> In view of their identical purpose, the various concerted practices followed and agreements concluded formed part of schemes of regular meetings, target price-fixing and quota fixing. Those schemes were part of a series of efforts made by the undertakings in question in pursuit of a single economic aim, namely to distort the normal movement of prices on the market in polypropylene. It would be thus artificial to split up such continuous conduct, characterized by a single purpose, by treating it as consisting of a number of separate infringements. The fact is that the applicant took part – over a period of years – in an integrated set of schemes constituting a single infringement, which progressively manifested itself in both unlawful agreements and unlawful concerted practices.[17]

If this description of the 'cartel offence' (what the CFI refers to here as a 'single infringement') is analysed more closely, we can detect elements of a common plan, predicate outcomes (the manifested unlawful practices), and also the knowing participation in an 'integrated set of schemes' – a kind of long-term participation in a series of planning and implementation activities. Liability for the 'offence' and imposition of sanctions is therefore legally based on such participation in the cartel, rather than specific acts of fixing prices or quotas. This was further clarified in a statement by the European Commission, when it explained that:

> The infringement consisted of a complex of agreements and concerted practices in which each undertaking played its part. It

---

17 Cases 1/89 etc., *Rhône-Poulenc v. Commission* (1991) ECR II-867, at pp. 1074–5.

is not alleged that each ... participated in each and every aspect of the anti-competitive arrangements set out or did so for the whole duration of the infringement.[18]

Another way of expressing this approach[19] is to say that the main or 'cardinal' liability is based on evidence of some kind of knowing involvement in the work of the cartel and the precise extent of that involvement does not need to be proven. The latter is relevant, however, to any decisions about penalties, since the quantum of penalty should reflect the seriousness of the offending conduct, which necessarily depends on such matters as the role of individual members of the cartel, the duration of their involvement and the impact of their involvement. This then may be regarded as an 'ordinal' liability, which locates individual offenders on a penal tariff for purposes of deciding on sanctions. Such a process of course reflects common criminal justice practice, whereby a decision on liability for purposes of conviction is followed by a decision on liability for purposes of any penalty, the latter 'sentencing' process taking into account specific and individual features and circumstances of the offence.

The 'European cartel offence' therefore fits within the third model of responsibility, entailing individual responsibility following from involvement in a collective activity. The European Courts have affirmed the individual character of this responsibility, in response to some arguments on the part of cartelists that this was in fact a species of collective responsibility, which infringed the principle of personal responsibility.[20] The CFI for example has stressed that a party's liability for participating in a cartel as a whole was based upon an *individual* awareness that the collusion in which it was involved was

---

18 *Pre-Insulated Pipes,* OJ 1999, L24/1, at p. 55. In the same decision, we can read a list of typical participatory activities within the cartel infrastructure: meetings to discuss and set prices, quotas and model price-lists; agreements to exchange certain categories of information; enforcement measures, which might go so far as to include threats of reprisal, and perhaps involving 'diplomacy' and a 'shifting constellation of alliances' (*ibid.,* at p. 51).

19 See also the analysis in Christopher Harding (2004) 'Forging the European Cartel Offence: The Supranational Regulation of Business Conspiracy', *European Journal of Crime, Criminal Law and Criminal Justice,* 12: 275.

20 On the compelling nature of this principle, see Cassese, *International Criminal Law,* note 1 above, at pp. 136–9.

part of an overall plan and that the overall plan included all the constituent elements of a cartel.[21] This clarifies the nature of the *mens rea* as an awareness of the objectives and scope of the cartel and a willingness to engage in some, if not all, of its activities.

(b) The ICTY 'joint criminal enterprise'

Interestingly, the idea of joint criminal enterprise,[22] as developed in particular in the jurisprudence of the ICTY, is like the concept of the cartel offence in being very much a product of judicial decisions. There is no specific provision for this category of liability in the Statute of the ICTY, although the judges have found its formal basis in Article 7(1) of the Statute, but the idea appeared very early in the *Tadić* case,[23] the first full trial heard by the Tribunal. The concept was introduced by the Trial Chamber in that case and affirmed by the Appeals Chamber. The latter held that, although the language of Article 7(1) referred to 'first and foremost the physical perpetration of the crime by the offender himself', crimes within the Tribunal's jurisdiction 'might also occur through participation in the realisation of a common design or purpose'.[24] The Appeals Chamber then analysed such 'common purpose liability' in three main categories.[25] The first category involved acting in pursuance of a common design with the same intention: for instance in relation to a killing, acting on a common plan to kill and intending to kill, then assisting in some aspect of the common design even if not perpetrating the killing itself. The second category comprises systems of ill-treatment, typically for instance a concentration camp. Here liability is based upon active and knowing participation in a system of repression with the intention of furthering the latter. The final, and more controversial category, involves participation in a common design and then being held responsible for acts which are a natural and foreseeable consequence of giving effect to that common purpose. This last formulation covered the case of Tadić himself – engaging in an

---

21 Case T-305/94 etc., *LVM and others v. Commission* (1999) II-ECR, at p. 1156.
22 For an informative and important critical overview of the origins and recent development of the concept of joint criminal enterprise, see Danner and Martinez, 'Guilty Associations', note 12 above.
23 *Prosecutor v. Tadić (Appeal)*, ICTY Appeals Chamber, Judgment of 15 July 1999, case no. IT-94-1-A.
24 *Ibid.*, at para. 188.
25 *Ibid.*, at para. 195 *et seq.*

act of ethnic cleansing when the killing of victims was a natural and foreseeable consequence of such action, even though the defendant could not be proven to be the actual killer within the group. The Appeals Chamber found that Tadić had participated in the common criminal purpose to expel the non-Serb population from the Prijedor region, that the killing of non-Serbs was foreseeable in the light of this purpose, that Tadić was aware of the risk, but still participated willingly in the common plan.

From that early beginning 'common purpose' or 'joint criminal enterprise' has become an important part of the prosecution policy at the ICTY and of the Tribunal's decision-making, culminating in the high-profile trial of Slobodan Milosevic (see Chapter 8 above). It has also started to make an appearance in other jurisdictions, such as that of the International Criminal Court (ICC) (in Article 25 of the Court's Statute), the Special Court for Sierra Leone, the Special Panel for Serious Crimes in East Timor, and the US military commissions.[26] It is easy to understand the appearance of this form of responsibility in the context of war crimes or terrorist trials. In a situation such as that involving guerrilla fighting or ethnic cleansing, evidence of the direct perpetration of offences might be difficult to find, while it is at the same time clear that a group of persons was undoubtedly responsible and all the individuals concerned were willing and knowing participants in that group activity and each intended the criminal outcome. The classic model of individual criminal responsibility naturally carries with it difficulties of proof (as do cartel cases in another context), and to deduce liability from evidence of willing and knowing participation in the group activity side-steps some problems of evidence while addressing ethical objections which would arise from a simply imputed or vicarious liability. Just as the cartelist willingly contributes to a known anti-competitive outcome, so Tadić willingly contributed to a predictable illegal outcome in the form of homicide. In both cases, the resulting individual responsibility flows from a crucial involvement in a collective enterprise.

(c) Participation in organised crime: European and American models

In relation to the legal control of organised crime, a well-attested problem is the difficulty of framing a legal case against 'Godfather' figures, legal advisors, corrupt politicians and enforcement agents in

---

26 For an overview of these developments, see the discussion by Danner and Martinez, note 12 above, at p. 154 *et seq.*

the pay of criminal groups, bankers who facilitate money-laundering and the like. A number of legal initiatives aimed at the crucial periphery of organised criminality have also drawn upon the model of individual responsibility through participation in a collective activity or enterprise. This can be seen for instance in the application of the American Racketeer Influenced and Corrupt Organisations (RICO) legislation.[27] Referring to 'enterprises' involving a pattern of racketeering activity or collection of unlawful debts, the legislation criminalises investing the proceeds of such an enterprise, acquiring or maintaining an interest in the enterprise, or conducting its affairs. Such participatory offending has been the basis for some successful prosecutions of major figures in organised crime, one celebrated instance being *United States v. Salerno*,[28] or the 'Commission' case, resulting in the conviction of a number of Mafia heads of families. The prosecution was framed around the allegation that the Cosa Nostra families together constituted a 'Commission', which was a criminal enterprise for purposes of the legislation, and that the senior figures within the families had acted within this commission to authorise, aid and abet predicate activities such as bid-rigging, extortion and homicide. Long prison sentences were imposed.

The EU Joint Action of 1998[29] employs a similar approach, referring first to a form of criminal enterprise (a 'structured association', defined in Article 1 of the Joint Action), and then specifying various categories of participation which should be criminalised by the EU Member States. Alongside the conventional conspiracy and predicate offending, Article 2(a) lists engaging in another activity of the organisation, knowing that it will contribute to the achievement of a criminal activity. The generic *mens rea* for all forms of participation listed in Article 2 is the intent and knowledge 'of either the aim and general criminal activity of the organisation or the intention of the organisation to commit the offences in question'. As discussed in Chapter 8 above, the purpose of the Joint Action is to ensure that all Member States have legislation on this model to criminalise such participation in the work of criminal enterprises.

---

27 Title IX of the Organized Crime Control Act 1970, Pub.L.91-452, 84, Stat. 922. See generally, Michael Levi and Alaster Smith, *A comparative analysis of organised crime conspiracy legislation and practice and their relevance to England and Wales* (Home Office Online Report 17/02, 2002).

28 *US v. Salerno et al*. (1992) 505 US 317.

29 See the discussion in Chapter 8 above.

Both the RICO legislation and the Joint Action therefore encompass a range of directing or facilitating activities, but again the outcome is an individual responsibility in relation to activities which, without their intended contribution to the illegal collective cause, might well appear as legitimate business or other activities in themselves.

3 Defining offences of participation

We are able to see therefore some significant evidence of the coincident development of offences of participation in prohibited collective activities within a range of different legal contexts. The core of legal development in these examples is similar but there is some flakiness around the edges, in relation to the more precise definition of the legal components of such offences and how they relate to other forms of offending conduct, such as conspiracy and predicate criminality. It may be useful then to consider what might be put forward as a desirable uniform definition for this species of participatory offence.

The essential components appear clear enough. In terms of *actus reus* there should first be some prohibited organisation or enterprise, and then some supportive participation in the activities of that organisation. The prohibited nature of the organisation would be established by reference to its established purposes or objectives, which may very well comprise further predicate offending behaviour. Participation may take various forms and it is naturally difficult to supply an exhaustive list. Some of the existing legislation does list certain forms of participation, but this approach may prove unduly limiting. In terms of the *mens rea* there should again be two principal elements. First, there should be a knowledge or awareness of the nature of the organisation and its prohibited or criminal purposes. Secondly, there should be an element of 'specific intention', comprising an intention to carry out some directing or supporting role in relation to the activities of the organisation. A more controversial point concerns the extent to which liability should cover not only an intention but also a reckless or negligent participation – as, for example, in the case of *Tadić*, joint criminal enterprise liability, based upon a natural and foreseeable consequence of participation.

Thus a model definition might read:

It is an offence to participate in a directing or supporting role in the activities of a prohibited/illegal/criminal organisation/ enterprise, knowing the prohibited nature of the organisation and with the intention of directing or supporting its activities (or aware that achievement of the organisation's prohibited purposes would be a natural and foreseeable result of such participation).

As already argued, an important point regarding this definitional exercise is the desirability of clearly demarcating the line between such 'participatory' offending and both conspiracy-type offences and predicate offending. What have been referred to in this discussion as predicate offences fit into the classic individualist model of responsibility associated with the principle of personal responsibility. Similarly any offence based on the act of conspiracy or agreement is (despite the joint nature of the act) similarly based upon a personally and directly perpetrated illegal act. The participatory offences are different in that they are not in themselves necessarily unacceptable or delinquent acts, but only take on that character when placed in the context of being in support of illegal organisational goals. So we return to the argument that this entails a different route to legal responsibility, as a form of individual responsibility which results from involvement in a collective action. This is an important distinguishing feature to bear in mind, since it affects issues of substantive liability and evidence, as seen from discussion of some of the examples above. In such cases, what is objectionable in principle is the organisation – the anti-competitive cartel, the genocidal paramilitary force, the criminal or terrorist gang, for instance. Supportive participation in such organisations, *as a predicate act*, is not in itself likely to be a crime and therefore has to be defined as a crime by reference to some involvement with the organisation. The basis for responsibility is different in this respect, and this should be recognised in any critical discussion of this area of criminal responsibility. In both legislation and the practice of criminal justice it is therefore helpful if a clear distinction is drawn between different categories of offending, in particular between (a) the agreement or conspiracy which sets matters in train; (b) supportive participation in the enterprise; and (c) predicate acts representing the prohibited outcome of the enterprise. These three categories may well require different substantive, procedural and evidential rules.

Returning more specifically to the above definition, it should be noted that some components of the definition may naturally give rise to difficulty, in particular the concept of the organisation or enterprise and how the participating role may be understood. Neither 'organisation' nor 'enterprise' are terms which are susceptible to closer definition, and other terms may also be used to connote this kind of entity (such as 'structured association' in Article One of the EU Joint Action). The precise parameters of an organisation and enterprise may be clearer in some kinds of case than in others. A business cartel, as a concept and in practice, is likely to be clearly identifiable in most cases, regarding its membership, scope of activities and purposes. Similarly, many criminal gangs may prove to have clear boundaries and goals. On the other hand, the joint criminal enterprise, as used by the ICTY to deal with situations occurring in the aftermath of the break-up of the former Yugoslavia, has appeared much less easy to pin down in matters of scope and purpose. Since the language of joint enterprise has been in that context used interchangeably with the vocabulary of 'common plan' or 'design', in practice the joint enterprise has been used to cover a range of factual situations: for instance, an organised system of repression, such as a concentration camp; a plan to rid the Prijedor region of its non-Serb population (the *Tadić* enterprise); or a general programme of ethnic cleansing in a large region of Bosnia. Thus, the ICTY joint enterprise is a much more variable concept, in terms of its scale of activity and its range of purposes, and it may be easily appreciated that managing a particular camp or removing people from a particular village at a particular time are much more bounded and precisely defined compared to the large-scale and complex joint enterprise with which Milosevic was associated. This may be very important for purposes of liability. To accuse Tadić of being involved in the plan to cleanse Prijedor would seem reasonable from the facts, but less so to hold him responsible for a wider range of acts comprised in the larger enterprise of ethnic cleansing designed by Bosnian Serb military and political leaders. As Danner and Martinez comment:

> Some individuals, particularly senior political or military figures, may justly be charged with wrongdoing that encompasses atrocities committed over several years and throughout a particular region ... holding Tadić liable, however, for all the crimes visited on Bosnian Muslims in the early 1990s would seem patently unjust.[30]

What is important, therefore, is to identify clearly and precisely in individual cases the enterprise in question, as something factually relevant to the role of the particular defendant. The problem, however,

---

30 Danner and Martinez, 'Guilty Associations', note 12 above, at p. 150.

is that in a context of ongoing strife and fighting it is possible to identify a myriad of structures as organisations and enterprise, varying greatly in scope and function, and to a large extent the choice of enterprise for purposes of framing a charge may be very much in the discretion of the prosecutor. As Danner and Martinez argue, the practical solution may be to restrict the defendant's role within the enterprise to something which is significant. This would answer something of the objection that small fishes in the big pond may be caught in the net. In other words, there should be some proportionality in the charges as between the enterprise and the kind of participation. The test of 'significant contribution to the enterprise' has been used in some of the cases dealt with by the ICTY Trial Chambers. For instance, in the case of *Kvoćka*, the Trial Chamber listed the kind of factor which should be taken into account in deciding whether an individual's participation in an enterprise was significant in this sense:

> ... the size of the criminal enterprise, the functions performed, the position of the accused ... the seriousness and scope of the crimes committed and the efficiency, zealousness or gratuitous cruelty exhibited in performing the actor's function ... Perhaps the most important factor to examine is the role the accused played vis-à-vis the seriousness and scope of the crimes committed.[31]

It would be difficult at a legislative level to be more specific in the definition of the organisation or enterprise and a judicial specification of a significant participation relevant to the activities of the enterprise therefore appears to be a more effective way of ensuring that the net of liability is not cast too widely.

Finally, in relation to matters of definition, it has already been noted that some existing legal provision specifies the nature of the participating activity – for instance, the American RICO legislation lists activity in the form of 'investing proceeds', 'acquiring or maintaining an interest', or 'conducting the affairs'. Such categories are themselves more or less specific, but there may be a risk in this approach of omitting some significant forms of involvement. While illustrative listing is unobjectionable, it may be that a formulation

---

31 *Prosecutor v. Kvoćka*, ICTY Trial Chamber, Case No. IT-98-30/1-T (2 November 2001), at para. 373.

which is both clear and inclusive, such as 'activities which support the organisation's objectives'[32] would provide the best approach.

4 The case for the criminal enterprise

From what has already been said, the justification for this kind of responsibility should now be clear enough. In the context of criminal organisation, there is a potentially large but shadowy area of activity, separate from the final predicate offending and from the initial concept of the organisation which might be captured in the concept of a criminal conspiracy. This infrastructure of often complex supportive activity may be difficult to penetrate legally since it may be on its face inoffensive or it may be unprovable in the normal way: advising or administering, looking after supplies or driving a vehicle, commanding through coded language, belonging to a group which carried out homicide when there is no evidence which member of the group actually perpetrated the killing, and the like. In short, this is a body of activity for which morally there should be some accountability, yet which cannot fit easily into the structure of predicate or conspiratorial offending. The allocation of responsibility thus requires an amalgam of individual accountability and organisational role – the latter is essential to achieve the former.

This form of responsibility may capture the involvement of both the highest and the lowest ranks within an organisation, as may be seen from the following examples.

> I authorised a number of military and political actions while in my presidential office in Belgrade, but I was not physically present in Srebenicia while any fighting or loss of life occurred there.[33]

---

32 For some existing examples, see, for instance, the amended Canadian Federal Criminal Code ('activities which further the organisation's criminal objectives', or Section 98A of the 1997 New Zealand Harassment and Criminal Associates Act ('to promote or further the activities of the gang'). See also the discussion in Christopher Harding (2005) 'The Offence of Belonging: Capturing Participation in Organised Crime', *Criminal Law Review*, 690.

33 The position of Slobodan Milosevic. The initial indictment against Milosevic (Case No. IT-01-51-1 (22 November 2001)) alleged participation in a joint criminal enterprise, the purpose of which was the 'forcible and permanent removal of the majority of non-Serbs, principally Bosnian

We approved a programme of agreed pricing between ourselves and a number of other companies, but we did not attend the meeting of 1 January when a list of co-ordinated prices were agreed in relation to product x.

I was present in the room and guarded the exit while X was confined, but I was not the person who used a knife to cut his throat.[34]

I prepared the chemicals which were to be used in the gas chamber in the concentration camp, but I was never physically present in the gas chamber when the chemicals were used.[35]

In each example, there is clear evidence of awareness of the criminal objectives of an organisation, and of a willingness to support and facilitate their achievement, which, despite the distance of the actor concerned from the final criminal outcome, justifies some allocation of responsibility for that outcome. It is important to note that this process does not entail an imposition of collective or vicarious liability for the acts of other persons. These actors are being held individually and personally responsible, in a way distinct from the predicate offenders, but nonetheless for that outcome as facilitated by their own particular participation in the enterprise set up to achieve that end. In that sense, such responsibility does not violate the principle of individual responsibility which is widely considered to underpin modern systems of criminal justice. The ICTY has strongly affirmed

---

Muslims and Bosnian Croats, from large areas of the Republic of Bosnia and Herzegovina' (para. 6). The indictment also made it clear that by 'using the word "committed" in this indictment, the Prosecutor does not intend to suggest that the accused physically committed any of the crimes charged personally. "Committed" in this indictment refers to participation in a joint criminal enterprise as a co-perpetrator' (para. 5).

34 Similar to Tadić's case.
35 See for instance *Wolfgang Zeuss and others* (the *Natzweiler* trial), British Military Court sitting at Wuppertal, verdict of 29 May 1946, discussed by Cassese, *International Criminal Law*, note 1 above, at p. 185. The defendants in that case (concerning the murder of four members of the French Resistance) included the commandant of the concentration camp, the head of its political department, the camp doctor, a prisoner employed in the crematorium, a camp medical orderly, a clerk in the political department, the camp dentist, and some military personnel.

this point. Recognising the peremptory character of that principle, the Appeals Chamber stated in the *Tadić* appeal that:

> the basic assumption must be that in international law as much as in national systems, the foundation of criminal responsibility is the principle of personal culpability: nobody may be held criminally responsible for acts or transactions in which he has not personally engaged or in some other way participated (*nulla poena sine culpa*). In national legal systems this principle is laid down in Constitutions, in laws, or in judicial decisions. In international criminal law the principle is laid down, *inter alia*, in Article 7(1) of the Statute of the International Tribunal ...[36]

This principle was subsequently applied by the Supreme Court of Bosnia and Herzegovina in a joint enterprise context in the case of *Tepeź*, demonstrating how the defendant's participation and complicity satisfied the requirements of personal culpability. The Court explained the liability of the defendant in this way:

> The appeal fails to note that the contested judgment states that the accused carried out these actions with three other named individuals (as well as others), which means that he perpetrated the crime for which he has been pronounced guilty in complicity with others. It further means that in cases of this kind where it is not possible to isolate individual actions and their consequences or distinguish the degree to which each person was involved in their execution, it suffices that these actions complement each other and together form a single entity, which the accused wishes to achieve by being involved. Therefore it was neither possible nor necessary for the court of first instance to separate only the actions of the accused. It suffices that the accused participated in executing these actions, even if it had only been one or two actions of personal involvement in the beating of civilians.[37]

---

36 *Tadić Appeal*, note 23 above, at para 186.
37 *Tepeź Milomir*, Supreme Court of Bosnia and Herzegovina, decision no. K-122/99, 1 October 1999, English translation of transcript supplied by Antonio Cassess (See Cassese, *International Criminal Law*, note 1 above, at p. 182.) Note the similarity of the reasoning in this extract with that of the European Court of First Instance regarding the concept of the 'cartel as a whole', discussed above.

The underlying justification for joint criminal enterprise liability and its analogous forms is thus a matter of individual personal responsibility but in respect of an act of complicity, and it is this complicity in the enterprise which provides the basis for both liability and the evidence.

5 The boundary of enterprise responsibility: issues of specificity

Finally, we might reflect on how far this model of criminal responsibility might be taken and developed. Examination of its application in the above contexts demonstrates clearly its utility for purposes of both moral accountability and effective law enforcement, whether the subject matter be corporate members of business cartels, godfather figures in organised crime, former heads of State, concentration camp orderlies, or members of paramilitary groups acting in shadowy and confused situations. But it is also important to identify the boundaries of such 'enterprise responsibility', in terms of an ethically justifiable basis for allocating responsibility of this kind. Two issues in particular come to mind: the boundaries and nature of the criminal enterprise; and the question of foreseeable rather than intended consequences of the enterprise.

Definition of criminal or prohibited enterprises or organisations has already been discussed. The point of concern here is to ensure that in a factual sense the scope and scale of such an enterprise is kept within meaningful limits for legal purposes. Indeed, this may be seen as a requirement of the principle of specificity, the purpose of which is, in Cassese's words:

> to clearly indicate ... the conduct prohibited ... the principle is aimed at ensuring that all those who may fall under the prohibitions of the law know in advance which specific behaviour is allowed and which conduct is instead prohibited.[38]

In short, a criminal enterprise should not be so loose in its definition that potential members cannot be sure whether they are involved or not. On the one hand, the example of the business cartel is unlikely to raise such problems, since in practice such an arrangement will involve a limited number of corporate actors and be closely defined

---

38 Antonio Cassese, *International Criminal Law*, note 1 above, at p. 145.

in relation to an economic market.[39] But at the other end of the spectrum, a meta-level programme of genocide such as the Nazi 'final solution' may be less easy to handle legally. As an enterprise, the 'final solution' was on such a huge scale, involving so many people carrying out various roles, that it cannot in itself help to indicate the nature of responsibility in individual cases. It is, simply speaking, too all-encompassing and runs the risk of the same fate as an idea such as the war guilt of a whole nation, which (with hindsight) provided an unsatisfactory moral and practical basis for post-World War I reparations. As a structure for conduct, an enterprise or organisation needs to be sufficiently specific for purposes of identifying the role of individuals working within that structure. Most would probably agree that being a citizen of Nazi Germany was insufficient as a role for purposes of allocating responsibility for the 'final solution'. On the other hand, participating knowingly and willingly in the work of an extermination camp, even at low-ranking level, would suffice: but then we have redefined both the enterprise and the actor's role. Similarly, as noted above, Milosevic's role can be accommodated with the 'grand' enterprise of ethnic cleansing in large parts of Bosnia, but not Tadić's role. In the context of war crimes, crimes against humanity and terrorism, care needs to be taken in identifying and defining the scope of particular criminal enterprises and it is a critical point that at present this task is often left to the discretion of prosecutors.

The potential problems arising from an expansive and loose definition of criminal enterprise are examined by Danner and Martinez[40] in relation to the apparent adoption of the concept for purposes of the US military commissions set up recently to deal with alleged terrorist and 'enemy combatants'.[41] Danner and Martinez refer to the US Government's efforts:

---

39 For instance, in the 'prosecuting' practice of the European Commission, alleged cartels are carefully defined in relation to the relevant product or services market, the identity of the companies involved, the unlawful anti-competitive objectives, and the arrangements undertaken to achieve the aims of the cartel. The cartel enterprise is highly specified.

40 Danner and Martinez, note 12 above, at p. 160 *et seq*.

41 The US military commission is a form of military tribunal, the legal basis for which is provided by Article I, section 8, clause 10 of the US Constitution, which provides authority for national trials of persons committing criminal offences against 'the law of Nations'. Article II of the Constitution confers on the President the title of 'Commander in Chief', so authorising the President to establish military commissions.

to characterize terrorist groups as participants in an armed conflict and to attach legal significance to membership or other affiliation with such terrorist groups. For example the military commission regulations define the term 'enemy' to include 'any organization of terrorists with international reach'. Similarly in the case of Jose Padilla, the alleged 'dirty bomber' arrested and detained by the United States as an 'enemy combatant', the government contends that Padilla can be treated as an 'enemy combatant' under the laws of war because he is 'associated' with al Qaeda, the 'organization' with which the United States is engaged in an armed conflict.[42]

Thus, in this example, something like the concept of criminal enterprise is being used in relation to persons *associated* with an *enemy organisation with international reach* with whom a State is *engaged in armed conflict.* Here the net is cast very wide, conveniently for prosecutors and law enforcement interests, but doubtfully in relation to the principle of specificity.

Similarly, the question of foreseeable as distinct from intended consequences of participation in a criminal enterprise raise issues of specificity, as well as culpability. Foreseeable consequences was famously introduced into the jurisprudence of the ICTY in the *Tadić* ruling, and significantly extends responsibility beyond the clearly specified goals of the 'common plan' to outcomes which were not necessarily intended as part of the enterprise but were natural and foreseeable consequences. In the classic Tadić scenario, killing may not have been a goal of the ethnic cleansing as such, but was found on the facts to have been a foreseeable outcome for the perpetrators, and as such every member of the group would be liable for such killing, whether they were physically involved in it or not. In other words, awareness of the risk and willingness to go ahead with the plan provides for responsibility on the basis of a reckless state of mind at least. In the words of the Appeals Chamber in *Tadić:*

> While murder may not have been explicitly acknowledged to be part of the common design, it was nevertheless foreseeable that

---

On 13 November 2001, President George W. Bush issued *Military Order: Detention, Treatment and Trial of Certain Non-Citizens in the War Against Terrorism,* in response to the terrorist attacks on 11 September 2001.

42 Danner and Martinez, note 12 above, at pp. 162–3.

the forcible removal of civilians at gunpoint might well result in the deaths of one or more of these civilians.[43]

A criticism of this basis of liability is that it takes responsibility close to either that which might be based on membership of the group in itself, or to that allowed as so-called *Pinkerton* conspiracy under American law, under which acts of some members of the conspiracy are imputed to all the members. On the facts of *Tadić* the defendant appeared sufficiently proximate to the killings to justify some allocation of responsibility. But once again, this would seem to be a matter of the *significance of his participation and contribution to the enterprise*, and it would seem that this last element is crucial as a controlling device for purposes of ensuring that responsibility is kept within appropriate bounds.

---

43 *Prosecutor v. Tadić*, decision of the Appeals Chamber, note 23 above, at para. 204.

Endnote

Briefly then, what lessons are to be drawn from this analysis and survey of criminal responsibility in the context of modern organisational activity? In the wider perspective, ranging across business, public governance, and organised criminal activities, a complex landscape emerges, comprising a patchy pattern of individual and organisational accountability, sometimes overlapping, sometimes alternative. In some contexts companies may be held liable as criminal actors, while in other contexts they are not so held liable. States and governments may incur legal responsibility for some purposes, but there is resistance to the notion of the 'criminal State'. The legal identity of organised criminal and terrorist groups is as yet tentative, but legal orders necessarily have to grapple with strategies of legal control. What is clearly lacking in a global sense is a consistent and coherent legal theory and legal practice on the subject of organisational responsibility. Much depends at present on both context and on more immediate enforcement imperatives.

It will be recalled that in the first chapter three main questions were posed for purposes of probing the issue of individual and organisational responsibility: those of the ontology of organisations, the allocation of responsibility as between individuals and organisations, and how organisational structures and cultures should be taken into account in the assessment of individual responsibility. Is it possible to draw out any answers to those questions from the patchwork of legal principle and practice referred to above?

The first two questions require perhaps an inter-related answer. Any attempt to bring some order into the subject so as to supply a more coherent infrastructure for legal development requires a clear and convincing model of agency upon which to base any allocation of legal and criminal responsibility. Coming to terms with the impact of organisations in contemporary life involves some resolution of the fundamental puzzle of organisational agency: the fact that organisations comprise and derive their existence from human individuals, yet also control and influence individuals. The conclusion of the foregoing discussion, drawing upon the sociology and philosophy of collective action, is that there is genuine scope for an organisational agency, which is distinct from and operates alongside that of the human individual. But the dividing line between the two kinds of agency needs to be carefully considered and drawn consistently across the various fields of human and organisational activity. Care should be taken to avoid an easy replication of individual and organisational personalities in respect of the same acts, and not to slip into unhelpful *alter ego* identification of human and corporate actors. If organisations are to be held responsible for criminal activity, their role and capacity must be clearly and consistently identified as non-human, and in that way the limits of individual human action clearly appreciated. The conclusion therefore is that it is not fanciful or unhelpful to talk about criminal corporations, criminal governments, or criminal gangs as appropriate sites of legal accountability. But we should be clear in our minds about the reasons for allocating responsibility to such entities, rather than to the individuals who may make up such organisations, and how we see and understand the relation between human individuals and organisational actors. The criteria of organisational agency outlined in the discussion above are offered as a workable foundation for the allocation of responsibility as between the two kinds of actor. The corollary of this is that the respective offences (and thus areas of responsibility) of individuals and organisations need to be clearly distinguished and delineated, and such an exercise is necessarily based on these criteria of agency.

The third question is addressed through the idea that another route may be navigated in the tricky waters of individual and organisational activity. The 'third solution', which combines individual responsibility and organisational action, leads to the idea of the criminal enterprise as a governing framework for some decisions of criminal responsibility. The criminal enterprise occupies a position somewhere between the human individual and the autonomous organisation as moral agents, but is not an agent as such but rather a facilitating device for agency of a different kind. In the final analysis there are only individuals or organisations, but there are some 'complicit' individuals who derive their identity from the organisational project, such as a business cartel or a political or criminal conspiracy.

In such a way, therefore, we can visualise for instance the criminal dictator who murders, Caligula-style, with his or her own hands; who is complicit in a systematic massacre as a criminal enterprise; and who lends his or her name, and is legally subsumed within, a regime of governance which carries out its own distinct and criminal activities. Hopefully, in this way we can make some normative sense of the complexity of contemporary organisational life.

References

1 A note on the literature

There is, in the first place, a large literature on the philosophical and jurisprudential debate regarding agency and legal personality, some of it of course extending back over a long time. Interestingly, much of the more substantial theoretical work on the subject has been published outside Britain and many of the leading works have a North American provenance: for instance, to cite just a few, Coleman's *Individual Interest and Collective Action* (1982), French's *Collective and Corporate Responsibility* (1984), Dan-Cohen's *Rights, Persons, and Organisations* (1986), and Pennock and Jackson's collection, *Criminal Justice (Nomos XXVIII)* (1985). Such works are major theoretical texts and have served as key reference points. The same is true of the work of H.L.A. Hart in Britain, more specifically on issues of responsibility (*Punishment and Responsibility,* 1968). But it is notable that all of these works are now almost 20 years old, if not older. More recently, there have been full and accessible summaries of these theoretical debates by Fisse and Braithwaite (1993) and Wells (1993, 2001), but both these works are mainly concerned with particular aspects of corporate criminal liability.

Within the more specific context of criminal law writing, the main focus of attention has been the topic of corporate liability and its application to a particular form: the company (or firm) in the context of business activity. Much of the writing here has also been concerned with more technical legal aspects of attributing criminal liability to such corporate actors. Norrie, as part of his discussion in *Crime, Reason and History* (1993 and 2001) provides an overview of both the theoretical debate and the development of corporate liability in English criminal law. Three works in particular deal squarely and fully with the issue of crime and the corporation: Fisse and Braithwaite's *Corporations, Crime and Accountability* (1993), Wells' *Corporations and Criminal Responsibility* (1993 and 2001), and Gobert and Punch's *Rethinking Corporate Crime* (2003), although to a greater or lesser extent all from an 'internal' criminal law perspective. Fisse and Braithwaite (both based in Australia) address the underlying theoretical aspects of the subject, but for the most part consider a particular thesis: that in the regulation of companies, criminal liability has shifted too much from the individual to the corporate, and so they seek to establish a more appropriate system of legal 'accountability'. Wells again tackles the underlying theory, but is very much concerned with the desirable attribution of criminal liability to firms, and particularly in the context of dangerous corporate behaviour and the issue of corporate manslaughter.

Despite the appearance of the above-mentioned works, the field as a whole remains thin in terms of the publication of wider-perspective research. There are few monographs by legal writers or even criminologists, and within both disciplines those interested in the subject admit to their minority status. One of the leading criminal law texts published in Britain categorically relegates the subject of corporate criminal responsibility by asserting that 'the necessity for corporate liability awaits demonstration' (J.C. Smith and B. Hogan, *Criminal Law* (Butterworths, 10th edn, 2002, at p. 207). Much writing on criminal law appears still to be under the influence of methodological individualism. Similarly, many criminologists, especially outside North America, have seemed reluctant to probe the subject of business and corporate crime (the reasons for this are discussed by Maurice Punch in *Dirty Business: Exploring Corporate Misconduct*, 1996). Therefore, while much theoretical spadework has been completed, the task of applying such argument across a broader spectrum of inter-related individual and organisational activity is still in its infancy.

Moving beyond the context of the business firm, and addressing the position of delinquent polities and crime and terrorist groups, the existing literature tends to have its background in public law and international law, and (leaving aside the recent emergence of 'international criminal law' which is more a product of criminal than international law, with the notable exception of Antonio Cassese) international lawyers tend to fight shy of the 'criminal'. International relations theory has more recently begun to grapple with the issue of ascribing moral responsibility in the international arena, for instance in relation to States and international organisations (see, in particular, Erskine (ed.), *Can Institutions Have Responsibilities?* (2003)). But it is conceded that this is as yet a relatively neglected area of enquiry. In terms of legal, criminological and political science writing, the projection of the idea of crime and criminal law on to much of this subject-matter, and more specifically the application of argument concerning legal identity and criminal responsibility, therefore has a clear novelty.

2 Select references

Argyris, Chris (1999) *On Organizational Learning*. Blackwell Business.

Ashworth, Andrew (2003) *Principles of Criminal Law* (4th edn). Oxford University Press.

Barnard, Chester I. (1938) *The Functions of the Executive*. Harvard University Press.

Berle, Adolf A. and Means, Gardiner C. (1932) *The Modern Corporation and Private Property*. Macmillan.

Bernard, T. (1984) 'The Historical Development of Corporate Criminal Liability', *Criminology*, 22: 3.

Blau, Peter M. (1967) *Exchange and Power in Social Life*. Wiley and Sons.

Blau, Peter M. (1968) entry in *The International Encyclopaedia of the Social Sciences*, vol. XI, at p. 298. Crowell Collier and Macmillan.

Bovens, Mark (1998) *The Quest for Responsibility: Accountability and Citizenship in Complex Organisations*. Cambridge University Press.

Brodbeck, May (1958) 'Methodological Individualisms: Definition and Reduction', *Philosophy of Science*, 25: 1.

Brown, W.J. (1905) 'The Personality of the Corporation and the State', *Law Quarterly Review*, 21: 365.

Bucy, Pamela (1991) 'Corporate Ethos: A Standard for Imposing Corporate Criminal Liability', *Minnesota Law Review*, 75: 1095.

Calkins, Stephen (1997) 'Corporate Compliance and the Antitrust Agencies Bi-Modal Penalties', *Law and Contemporary Problems*, 60: 127.

Cassese, Antonio (2003) *International Criminal Law*. Oxford University Press.

Cassese, Antonio (2005) *International Law* (2nd edn). Oxford University Press.

Clegg, Stewart and Dunkerley, David (1980) *Organization, Class and Control*. Routledge and Kegan Paul.

Coffee, J.C. Jnr (1981) '"No Soul To Damn, No Body to Kick": An Unscandalized Inquiry into the Problem of Corporate Punishment', *Michigan Law Review*, 79: 386.

Coleman, James S. (1982) *The Asymmetric Society: Organizational Actors, Corporate Power and the Irrelevance of Persons*. Syracuse University Press.

Coleman, James S. (1986) *Individual Interest and Collective Action*. Cambridge University Press.

Coleman, James S. (1990) *The Foundation of Social Theory*. Harvard University Press.

Conley, John M. and Barr, William, M. (1997) 'Crime and Custom in Corporate Society: A Cultural Perspective on Corporate Misconduct', *Law and Contemporary Problems*, 60: 5.

Crawford, James (2002) *The International Law Commission's Draft Articles on State Responsibility: Introduction, Text and Commentaries*. Cambridge University Press.

Cressey, D.R. (1969) *The Theft of the Nation: The structure and operation of organized crime in America*. Harper and Row.

Dan-Cohen, Meir (1986) *Rights, Persons, and Organisations: A Legal Theory for Bureaucratic Society*. University of California Press.

Danner, Allison Marston and Martinez, Jenny S. (2005) 'Guilty Associations: Joint Criminal Enterprise, Command Responsibility and the Development of International Criminal Law', *California Law Review*, 75.

Davidson, Donald (1971) 'Agency', in Robert Binckley, Richard Bronaugh and Ausonio Marras (eds), *Agent, Action, and Reason*. Blackwell.

Dennett, Daniel (1976) 'Conditions of Personhood', Chapter 7 in Amélie Oksenberg Rorty (ed.), *The Identity of Persons*. University of California Press.

Dennis, I.H. (1977) 'The Rationale of Criminal Conspiracy', *Law Quarterly Review*, 93: 39.

Dicey, A.V. (1914) *Law and Opinion in England* (2nd edn). Macmillan.

Dinstein, Yoram (2001) *War, Aggression and Self-Defence* (3rd edn). Cambridge University Press.

Donaldson, Gordon and Lorsch, Jay W. (1983) *Decision-Making at the Top: the shaping of strategic discretion*. Basic Books.

Donaldson, Thomas (1989) *The Ethics of International Business*. Oxford University Press.

Erskine, Toni (2003) 'Assigning Responsibilities to Institutional Moral Agents: The Case of States and Quasi-States', Chapter 1 in Toni Erskine (ed.), *Can Institutions Have Responsibilities? Collective Moral Agency and International Relations*. Palgrave Macmillan.

Etzioni, Amitari (1964) *Modern Organizations*. Pentice Hall.

Feinberg, Joel (1970) *Doing and Deserving*. Princeton University Press.

Ferran, Eilís (1999) *Company Law and Corporate Finance*. Oxford University Press.

Fisse, Brent and Braithwaite, John (1988) 'The Allocation of Responsibility for Corporate Crime: Individualism, Collectivism and Accountability', *Sydney Law Review*, 11: 468.

Fisse, Brent and Braithwaite, John (1993) *Corporations, Crime and Accountability*. Cambridge University Press.

Foxton, David (2002) 'Corporate Personality in the Great War', *Law Quarterly Review*, 118: 428.

French, Peter A. (1979) 'The Corporation as a Moral Person', *American Philosophical Quarterly*, 16: 207. Reprinted as Chapter 9, in Larry May and Stacey Hoffman (eds), *Collective Responsibility: Five Decades of Debate in Theoretical and Applied Ethics*. Rowman and Littlefield.

French, Peter A. (1984) *Collective and Corporate Responsibility*. Columbia University Press.

Gaeta, Paola (1999) 'The Defence of Superior Orders: The Statute of the International Criminal Court v Customary International Law', *European Journal of International Law*, 10: 172.

Galbraith, John Kennedy (1977) *The Age of Uncertainty*. BBC/André Deutsch.

Geldenhuys, Deon (2004) *Deviant Conduct in World Politics*. Palgrave Macmillan.

Gellner, Ernest (1968) 'Holism vs Individualism', in May Brodbeck (ed.), *Readings in the Philosophy of the Social Sciences*. Macmillan.

Gobert, James and Punch, Maurice (2003) *Rethinking Corporate Crime*. Butterworths/Lexis Nexis.

Hall, Richard H. (1972) *Organizations: Structure and Process*. Prentice-Hall.

Hammond, Sir Anthony and Penrose, Roy (2001) *Proposed criminalisation of cartels in the UK* (report prepared for the Office of Fair Trading, November).

Harding, Christopher (2004) 'Forging the European Cartel Offence: The Supranational Regulation of Business Conspiracy', *European Journal of Crime, Criminal Law and Criminal Justice*, 12: 275.

Harding, Christopher (2005) 'The Offence of Belonging: Capturing Participation in Organised Crime', *Criminal Law Review*, 690.

Harding, Christopher (2006) 'Business Collusion as a Criminological Phenomenon: Exploring the Global Criminalisation of Business Cartels', *Critical Criminology*, 14: 18.

Harding, Christopher (2006) 'Vingt Ans Après: Rainbow Warrior, Legal Ordering, and Legal Complexity', *Singapore Yearbook of International Law*, 10.

Harding, Christopher and Joshua, Julian (2002) 'Breaking Up the Hard Core: The Prospects for the Proposed Cartel Offence', *Criminal Law Review*, 933.

Harding, Christopher and Joshua, Julian (2003) *Regulating Cartels in Europe: A Study of Legal Control of Corporate Delinquency*. Oxford University Press.

Hart, H.L.A. (1950) *Definition and Theory in Jurisprudence*. Clarendon Press.

Hart, H.L.A. (1968) *Punishment and Responsibility: Essays in the Philosophy of Law*. Oxford University Press.

Hart, H.L.A and Honoré, Tony (1985) *Causation in the Law* (2nd edn). Oxford University Press.

Held, Virginia (1991) 'Can a Random Collection of Individuals be Morally Responsible?', *The Journal of Philosophy*, 68 (1970) reprinted as Chapter 6 in Larry May and Stacey Hoffman (eds), *Collective Responsibility*. Rowman and Littlefield.

Hindess, Barry (1990) 'Classes, Collectivities, and Corporate Actors', p. 157 in Stewart R. Clegg (ed.), *Organization Theory and Class Analysis: New Approaches and New Issues*. Walter de Gruyter.

Jørgensen, Nina H.B. (2000) *The Responsibility of States for International Crimes*. Oxford University Press.

Katz, Daniel and Kahn, Robert L. (1966) *The Social Psychology of Organizations*. Wiley.

Kelsen, Hans (1945) *General Theory of Law and State*. Russell and Russell.

Lacey, Nicola (2001) 'In Search of the Responsible Subject', *Modern Law Review*, 64: 350.

Lacey, Nicola (2004) *A Life of H.L.A. Hart*. Oxford University Press.

Lamoreaux, Naomi R. (2000) 'Partnerships, Corporations, and the Problem of Legal Personhood'. UCLA and the National Bureau of Economic Research.

Laski, Harold J. (1916) 'The Personality of Associations', *Harvard Law Review*, 29: 404.

Leventhal, H. (1947) 'The Nuernberg Verdict', *Harvard Law Review*, 60: 857.

Levi, Michael (2002) 'The Organization of Serious Crimes', Chapter 24 in Mike Maguire, Rod Morgan and Robert Reiner *The Oxford Handbook of Criminology* (3rd edn). Oxford University Press.

Levi, Michael and Smith, Alaster (2002) *A comparative analysis of organised crime conspiracy legislation and practice and their relevance to England and Wales*. Home Office Online Report 17/02, December 2002.

Machen, Arthur W. (1911) 'Corporate Personality', *Harvard Law Review*, 24: 253, 347.

Maltz, M.D. (1976) 'On Defining Organised Crime: The Development of a Definition and a Typology', *Crime and Delinquency*, 22: 338.

Mark, Gregory A. (1987) 'The Personification of the Business Corporation in American Law', *University of Chicago Law Review*, 54: 1441.

May, Larry (1987) *The Morality of Groups: Collective Responsibility, Group-Based Harm and Corporate Rights*. University of Notre Dame Press.

May, Larry and Hoffman, Stacey (eds) (1991) *Collective Responsibility: Five Decades of Debate in Theoretical and Applied Ethics*. Rowman and Littlefield.

McDonald, Michael (1987) 'The Personless Paradigm', *Toronto Law Journal*, 37: 212.

McIntosh, M. (1975) *The Organisation of Crime*. Macmillan.

Mitsilegas, Valsamis (2001) 'Defining Organised Crime in the European

Union: The Limits of Criminal Law in the Area of Freedom, Security and Justice', *European Law Review*, 565.

Mitsilegas, Valsamis, Monar, Jörg and Rees, Wynn (2003) *The European Union and Internal Security*. Palgrave Macmillan.

Moore, Michael S. (1985) 'The Moral and Metaphysical Sources of the Criminal Law', p. 11 in J.R. Pennock and J.M. Chapman (eds), *Criminal Justice*. New York University Press.

Nolte, Georg (2002) 'From Dionisio Anzilotti to Roberto Ago: The Classical International Law of State Responsibility and the Traditional Primacy of a Bilateral Conception of Inter-State Relations', *European Journal of International Law*, 13: 1083.

Norrie, Alan (2001) *Crime, Reason and History: A Critical Introduction to Criminal Law* (2nd edn). Butterworths.

Norrie, Alan (1991) 'A Critique of Criminal Causation', *Modern Law Review*, 54: 685.

Paoli, L. (2002) 'The Paradoxes of Organized Crime', *Crime, Law and Social Change*, 37: 51.

Parsons, Talcott (1960) *Structure and Process in Modern Societies*. The Free Press.

Pellet, Alain (1999) 'Can a State Commit a Crime? Definitely, Yes!' *European Journal of International Law*, 10: 426.

Pennock, J.R. and Chapman, J.M. (eds) (1985) *Criminal Justice*. New York University Press.

Pollock, Sir Frederick and Maitland, F.W. (1898) *History of English Criminal Law*. Cambridge University Press.

Punch, Maurice (1996) *Dirty Business: Exploring Corporate Misconduct*. Sage.

Reuter, P. (1983) *Disorganized Crime: Illegal Markets and the Mafia*. MIT Press.

Rindova, Violina P. and Starbuck, William H. (1997) 'Distrust in Dependence: The Ancient Challenge of Superior-Subordinate Relations', in T.A.R. Clark (ed.), *Advancements in Organization Behaviour: Essays in Honour of Derek Pugh*. Ashgate.

Rodensky, Lisa (2003) *The Crime in Mind: Criminal Responsibility and the Victorian Novel*. Oxford University Press.

Roth, Brad R. (2000) *Governmental Illegitimacy in International Law*. Oxford University Press.

Selznick, Philip (1948) 'Foundations of the Theory of Organization', *American Sociological Review*, 25.

Silverman, David (1970) *The Theory of Organizations*. Heinemann.

Simester, A.P. and Sullivan, G.R. (2003) *Criminal Law: Theory and Doctrine* (2nd edn). Hart Publishing.

Slapper, Gary and Tombs, Steve (1999) *Corporate Crime*. Longmans.

Smith, B.F. (1982) *The American Road to Nuremberg – The Documentary Record, 1944–45*. Hoover Institution Press.

Starbuck, William H. (2003) 'The Origins of Organization Theory', Chapter 5 in Haridimos Tsoukas and Christian Knudsen, *The Oxford Handbook of Organization Theory*. Oxford University Press.

Stern, Jessica (1999) *The Ultimate Terrorists*. Harvard University Press.

Stoljar, S.J. (1973) *Groups and Entities: An Enquiry into Corporate Theory*. ANU Press.

Stone, C.D. (1975) *Where the Law Ends: The Social Control of Corporate Behaviour*. Harper and Row.

Stone, C.D. (1980) 'The Place of Enterprise Liability in the Control of Corporate Conduct', *Yale Law Journal*, 90: 1.

Thompson, Dennis (1985) 'Criminal Responsibility in Government', p. 200 in J.R. Pennock and J.M. Chapman (eds), *Criminal Justice*. New York University Press.

Tonnies, Ferdinand (1957) *Gemeinschaft und Gesellschaft*, first published 1887, English translation by Charles P. Loomis, *Community and Society*. Michigan State University Press.

Van Duyne, P. (1996) 'The Phantom and Threat of Organized Crime', *Crime, Law and Social Change*, 24: 391.

Vincent, A. (1989) 'Can Groups Be Persons?', *Review of Metaphysics*, 42: 687.

Von Gierke, Otto (1887) *Die Genossenschofstheorie*. Berlin.

Weber, Max (1947) *The Theory of Social and Economic Organization*, transl. A.M. Henderson and Talcott Parsons. The Free Press.

Weber, Max (1978) *Economy and Society*. University of California Press.

Weiler, J.H.H., Cassese, A. and Spinedi, M. (1989) *International Crimes of States*. De Gruyter.

Weitzenboeck, Emily M. (2001) 'Electronic Agents and the Formation of Contracts', *International Journal of Law and Information Technology*, 9: 204.

Wells, Celia (2001) *Corporations and Criminal Responsibility* (2nd edn). Oxford University Press.

Werden, G.J. and Simon, M.J. (1987) 'Why Price Fixers Should Go To Prison', *Antitrust Bulletin*, 917.

Wolf, S. (1985) 'The Legal and Moral Responsibility of Organisations', p. 267 in J.R. Pennock and J.M. Chapman (eds), *Criminal Justice*. New York University Press.

Wolfendale, Jessica (2006) 'Stoic Warriors and Stoic Torturers: The Moral Psychology of Military Torture', *South African Journal of Philosophy*, 25: 62.

Wolfendale, Jessica (2006) 'Training Torturers: A Critique of the "Ticking Bomb" Argument', *Social Theory and Practice*, 32.

Index